Frame Relay
Internetworking

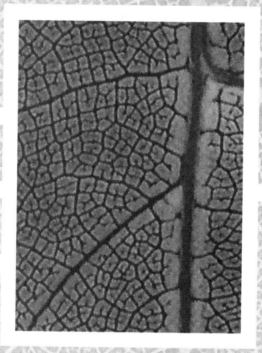

Liza Henderson

Tom Jenkins

San Francisco • Paris • Düsseldorf • Soest • London

Associate Publisher: Guy Hart-Davis
Contracts and Licensing Manager: Kristine O'Callaghan
Acquisitions Editor: Maureen Adams
Developmental Editor: Tracy Brown
Editor: Diane Lowery
Technical Editor: Ariel Silverstone
Book Designer: Bill Gibson
Graphic Illustrator: Tony Jonick
Electronic Publishing Specialist: Franz Baumhackl
Project Team Leader: Lisa Reardon
Proofreader: Richard Ganis
Indexer: Ted Laux
Cover Designer: Archer Design
Cover Photographer: The Image Bank

Library of Congress Card Number: 99-63823
ISBN: 0-7821-2519-0

Manufactured in the United States of America

10 9 8 7 6 5 4 3 2 1

This book is dedicated to my mom, Lourdes, my dad, Ernesto, and my brothers, Ernesto Jr. and Michael. I thank you for your prayers and love that has no boundaries—even distance. I also want to dedicate this book to Murph, Noemi, and Isabella Shelby for your loving support in everything.
—Liza

This book is dedicated to my immediate family: David, Barbara, Christa, Travis, Blake, Andrew, and Summer. Thanks for all the love, support, and home-cooked meals during the writing of this book and throughout my life.
—Tom

Acknowledgments

We would first like to thank all the Sybex people who helped us get this book from concept to reality. We would like to thank Acquisitions Editor Maureen Adams and Development Editor Tracy Brown for getting us started in the right direction and making sure the book was organized correctly. We'd also like to thank the editor, Diane Lowery, for keeping us on schedule, editing, and holding our hands through the publishing process, as well as the tech editor, Ariel Silverstone, for his expert eye and opinion. Other Sybex people who deserve thanks are Electronic Publishing Specialist Franz Baumhackl, Project Team Leader Lisa Reardon, Proofreader Richard Ganis, and Graphic Illustrator Tony Jonick.

We would like to acknowledge Liza Draper of McQuillan Ventures for helping us find and select Sybex as our book publisher.

We would also like to thank some of our coworkers here at TeleChoice, Inc. for their help in reviewing and providing guidance in one or more chapters of the book: Christine Heckart, executive vice president of consulting; Beth Gage, director of consulting; Eric Zines, senior consultant; Jeff Phillips, consultant; Tim Weis, consultant; Eric Rasmussen, associate consultant; Mark Mannell, research analyst; and the entire TeleChoice production department—Sandy Daniels, Melodee Kelly, and Wendy Stokes.

In addition, there were several people who we called on to review chapters and provide expertise in certain areas. We would like to thank the following people for their contributions: Todd Bahner, ADC Kentrox; Dale Frasier, Sprint; Praveen Goli, Ascend Communications; Robert Gourley, MCI WorldCom; Melanie Hanssen, MCI WorldCom; Geoff Matson, Nortel Networks; Tom Noone, AT&T; Ken Rehbehn, Visual Networks; and Jim Stump, Sprint. We would also like to thank our friends for keeping us sane during the writing of the book. The following people made sure we went for walks and runs, played tennis, went to the gym, mountain biked, roller-bladed, and did things to clear our minds and prevent "writer's block": Jayme Burton, Shannan Bushing, Kendra Coffman, Scott Coffman, Rob Eppich, Bill Hadley, Kim Jones, Nicole Lebeda, Igor Marusic, Chris Painter, Kelly Smakal, and Rina Sohn. You guys are the greatest.

Contents at a Glance

Table of Contents

Introduction

Finding a high-performance yet economical transport service is the seemingly impossible goal of nearly every network manager. If you are like most, this goal appears hopeless at times. At other times you may feel as though you have too many options.

Until relatively recently, your network and service options probably amounted to little more than a decision about what speed of private line you wanted to connect between two sites. Frame relay and other public data services—services that use a shared infrastructure to support multiple customers—now represent additional options to solve new and old networking problems.

Public data-service options can include IP-based Virtual Private Networks, X.25, SMDS, Asychronous Transfer Mode (ATM), and frame relay, among others. Any one, or perhaps a combination, of these technologies, as well as the services offered based on these technologies, may provide the optimal solution for your specific network requirements.

Due to increased competition among telecommunications providers, there has been a significant growth in the number of service options. In an effort to attract and retain customers, service providers feel pressure to offer new and enhanced services. Since 1991, one of the most popular services continues to be frame relay. If frame relay services have made your list of possible services or if you have already decided to use frame relay, this book will give you the most important information regarding understanding, implementing, and managing your frame relay network.

Who Should Read This Book

This book is designed for corporate executives and IT professionals responsible for evaluating various networking solutions to meet the company's business and financial goals. Although the book offers some high-level technical information about frame relay technology, how it works, and how to design a network, it primarily focuses on the reasons why and when a company should consider evaluating frame relay. It provides information about the typical problems that frame relay addresses, the applications it supports, the networking environment in which frame relay thrives, how it compares to other technologies (pros and cons), as well as the networking and business benefits frame relay enables.

How This Book Is Organized

Chapter 1 provides the foundation of the book. Here you learn the different ways frame relay can be defined—an interface standard protocol, a switching technology, and a public data service. You will also see how changing business traffic patterns and protocols have led to frame relay's popularity and usefulness.

Chapter 2 takes you through a detailed discussion of the benefits network managers often reap when migrating to a frame relay service. The benefits are grouped into two general categories: tactical and strategic benefits. After reading this chapter you'll know when and why companies deploy frame relay.

Chapter 3 discusses how frame relay works. The chapter begins with the composition of a frame and the typical service components, such as access links, ports, and PVCs. The chapter ends with a description of the role of CPE (Customer Premises Equipment) in handling traffic.

Chapter 4 contains additional information regarding the access link discussed in Chapter 3. There are numerous ways to access a frame relay network, including DS-0 through DS-3/ES-3, xDSL, dial-up, ISDN, switched 56/64, cellular, and others. Different access alternatives allow you to connect different users from telecommuters and mobile workers to users at your headquarters.

Chapter 5 comprises two major sections: frame relay services and pricing. In the first section the characteristics of services offered by U.S. long-distance providers, U.S. local providers, and non-U.S. providers are outlined. In the second section, the most common pricing structures are discussed, along with the advantages and disadvantages of each.

Chapter 6 specifically addresses how frame relay networks are able to handle SNA traffic. With over 50 percent of all frame relay networks carrying SNA traffic, it's necessary to address this in its own chapter. There are many different ways to handle SNA, each with its own advantages and disadvantages.

In Chapter 7, you'll get information on a topic most network managers forget to address until it's too late—disaster recovery. If you are transporting mission-critical traffic across a frame relay network, certain network segments are automatically protected, and others are not. This chapter discusses the different options for further protecting your traffic.

Chapter 8 is where you will learn about how frame relay networks can transport not only data traffic but also your voice traffic. Using your frame relay network for on- and off-net voice transport can provide significant cost and management savings but only if you address key issues during the network design and CPE selection processes. Chapter 8 explains these key issues.

Read Chapter 9 to find out more about frame relay classes of service. Classes of service allow your network to meet the unique performance requirements of mission-critical and less-critical applications. In some cases, you'll have to pay more for better performance, so having a good understanding of how frame relay classes of service work will help you manage your bottom line costs.

Chapter 10 provides an in-depth discussion on Switched Virtual Circuits (SVCs). Unlike PVCs, SVCs provide connections on demand using SVC-capable CPE. In this chapter, you'll learn how SVCs can simplify network design and management while improving performance in certain situations.

Chapter 11 is all about connecting your frame relay sites with sites using ATM services. Frame relay–to-ATM service interworking (FRASI) allows seamless communications between sites using these different technologies. FRASI allows you to choose the most appropriate technology on a location-by-location basis.

In Chapter 12, the topic of network management is discussed. Network management can help you maintain control over your network and track its performance over time. This chapter outlines the primary objectives of network management and provides an outline for possibly outsourcing your network-management responsibilities to your service provider or a third party.

Chapter 13 is where you will learn details about Service Level Agreements (SLAs). You will learn the typical components, measurement calculations, exclusions, and credits. After reading this chapter, you will have a good understanding of the importance of SLAs and how they can help ensure the performance of your frame relay service.

Chapter 14 shows the process and issues to consider when designing your frame relay network. The 6-step process begins with determining your network objectives and ends with installing a pilot network. By following this proven process, you will end up with a valid design to begin your implementation or Request for Proposal (RFP) process.

Chapter 15 builds on the information you learned in Chapter 14. This chapter discusses the process of selecting a service provider and outlines a proven methodology for managing the RFP process. Due to some of the characteristics of frame relay, which are not found in private-line networks, the RFP process and decision criteria can be very different. Be sure to read this chapter if you are considering deploying a frame relay network.

In Chapter 16, you will learn about how frame relay services, which were built originally to address multiprotocol traffic, are faring in an increasingly IP-centric world. This chapter outlines the impact the migration to IP has had on frame relay and what the likely future will be.

We would very much love to hear from you if you have any feedback, have any questions, or just want to drop us a line. You can reach Liza at lhenderson@telechoice.com and Tom at tjenkins@telechoice.com.

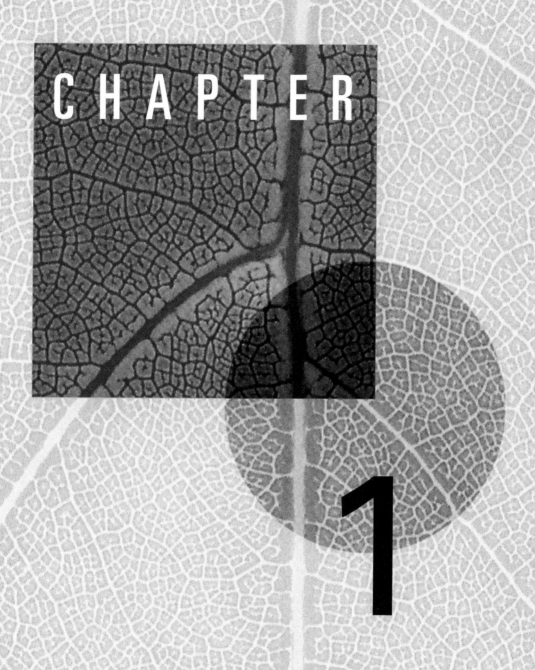

CHAPTER

1

What Is Frame Relay?

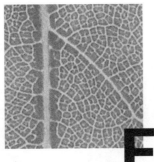

Frame relay is a wide-area networking solution that provides connectivity and communication between multiple locations supporting a variety of applications. Frame relay can help you do the following:

- Improve application and/or network performance.

- Improve network availability and reliability.

- Increase network flexibility to help reconfigure the network quickly.

- Improve network efficiency and use.

- Simplify the network architecture.

- Relegate the maintenance and management of the network to a service provider that has in-depth networking expertise.

- Save on transport, access, and equipment costs.

- Reduce operations costs and overall cost of ownership.

- Provide a migration path to other services, such as ATM (Asynchronous Transfer Mode), IP-based (Internet Protocol-based), and VPN (Virtual Private Networks) services.

- Enable your company to achieve its strategic business and financial goals.

Telecommunications technologies continue to evolve at a rapid pace, and frame relay is no exception. Although frame relay may still be considered the "new kid on the block" in some parts of the world, it is, by far, one of the most mature packet-based technologies. In the early days, many other packet technologies experienced rocky kick-starts and were eventually forgotten, but frame relay weathered the storm and rapidly became implemented worldwide. It created enough momentum not only to propel itself but also to promote the use of complementary technologies, such as ATM, private lines or leased lines, IP-based services, the Internet, and others.

This chapter gives you a historical overview of frame relay, with insights into the main drivers behind the emergence of frame relay.

Defining Frame Relay

You can use the words "frame relay" in many different contexts. Frame relay can refer to an interface standard protocol, a switching technology, and a set of public services. When you use all three definitions of frame relay, a single sentence can be constructed: Frame relay services require a frame relay interface that supports information formatted as frame relay "frames" and transported across frame relay or cell switches.

Frame Relay: An Interface Standard Protocol

As an interface standard protocol, frame relay defines the format of the information sent across the interface. When sending information, the information is encapsulated in a frame format to build the frame. This encapsulation process is similar to sending a letter in the mail: you can think of the information as the letter and the envelope as the frame. The frames also vary in size, which is also similar to letter envelopes.

Frame Relay: A Switching Technology

The OSI (Open Systems Interconnection) model is a framework of standards for understanding communications between different systems. The OSI model organizes the communications process into seven different categories. Communications follow the seven layers as information moves up the seven-layer stack, beginning at the physical transport medium (with fiber optics, coaxial cables, and copper wiring) at layer one and terminating at the application at layer seven.

Frame relay belongs to layer two of the OSI model, which is the Data Link layer. Layer two describes the format of the information and determines how the network handles the data. At this layer, some frame relay networks switch frames to deliver them to desired destinations, although some frame relay services switch *cells* rather than frames. Unlike frames, cells are fixed in length. During cell switching, the network accepts frames from the source and then converts the frames to fixed-length cells before placing them on the logical connection for transmission across the network. The network then converts or reconstructs the cells back to frames before delivery to the final destination.

Frame Relay: A Public Service

You can take advantage of frame relay in a private or public network implementation. A private implementation leaves the design, implementation, maintenance, and management of the frame relay network up to you. In a private network, you own the networking infrastructure, including the frame relay switches and interswitch trunking facilities to support your company's wide-area applications. This means that you need capital to purchase the necessary frame relay equipment to build the network.

Consider a private implementation if you have an internal networking staff that understands frame relay technology and has the expertise to operate the network.

On the other hand, a service provider or carrier owns and operates a public frame relay network. The service provider designs the network to support multiple companies that subscribe to its public frame relay service.

A frame relay service offers more than the underlying network, interfaces, and interconnections. A frame relay service may include the following:

- Network redundancy and automatic rerouting
- Multiple access alternatives
- Application- and/or protocol-specific support
- Priorities or qualities of service
- Network management
- Fault isolation and troubleshooting
- CPE (Customer Premises Equipment) and maintenance options

- Configuration and management options
- Interworking with other networks and other services
- Other enhanced features, value-added services, and complementary options

Although you have a choice of implementing a private frame relay network or subscribing to a public frame relay service, this book primarily concentrates on the needs of end users that may not have the time, money, resources, or expertise required to implement a private network.

The rest of this book helps you better understand public frame relay services and how you can use these services to meet your communications needs effectively.

A Short History of Frame Relay

Frame relay is a unique networking solution that represents a combination of well-established technologies. Frame relay's roots are circuit switches using time-division multiplexing and X.25 packet switches using statistical multiplexing. Frame relay combines the high speed and low-delay features of time-division multiplexing with the bandwidth sharing and packet-interleaving capabilities of statistical multiplexing.

Frame relay was originally defined by the ITU-T (formerly known as CCITT, or Consultative Committee on International Telegraphy and Telephony), the international committee organized to develop telecommunications standards to ensure interoperability. ANSI (American National Standards Institute) followed with its version that defined the signaling and core aspects of frame relay. The Frame Relay Forum, an organization founded in 1991 to promote the understanding, development, and adoption of frame relay products and services, developed additions to the core functions. The Frame Relay Forum membership consists mostly of representatives from various service providers and equipment vendors.

The first frame relay services focused primarily on LAN-to-LAN interconnectivity and did not support traditional terminal-to-host transactions, voice, and fax applications. Today, however, many companies use public frame relay services to integrate multiple applications that were formerly supported over separate and parallel networks.

The first frame relay service became available in early 1991. By the end of that year, several providers launched services. Early frame relay services had basic features and rudimentary capabilities. Additionally, only a few router vendors supported frame relay, and nonrouter equipment options were not available at that time.

Today the story is much different. In the U.S., all the major IXCs (Inter-eXchange Carriers) provide nationwide services; access providers, many regional service providers, and some ISPs (Internet Service Providers) offer frame relay services. The services have comprehensive feature sets, robust capabilities, global connectivity, as well as value-added services. Sales have escalated with many service providers experiencing double- to triple-digit revenue and customer-growth rates. While the rest of the world lags behind the U.S. by about one to three years in launching frame relay services, many service providers around the world, particularly in Europe, Australia, and some parts of Asia and South America, have followed suit and have aggressively marketed and sold their services.

Businesses adopted frame relay relatively quickly and easily because of its similarities to X.25. Frame relay required minimal and inexpensive modifications to existing CPE (Customer Premises Equipment). In most CPE, support for frame relay simply required a software upgrade for which equipment vendors don't typically charge extra. This situation allowed rapid adoption by end users and helped to fuel the growth.

Nearly all WAN-access CPE support frame relay today. Frame relay–capable CPE includes routers, bridges, access concentrators, switches, front-end processors, probes, cards that plug into traditional time-division multiplexers, and FRADs.

In the early days of frame relay, the industry used the term *FRAD* to generically refer to CPE that supports frame relay. In those days, FRAD stood *for Frame Relay Assembler/Disassembler*. The meaning of FRAD evolved to become *Frame Relay Access Device*. Nowadays, FRAD refers to CPE that can aggregate or concentrate different applications and/or protocols for delivery to a frame relay network. FRADs can support LAN, SNA (System Network Architecture), fax, voice, and many other protocols. Some FRADs are more than just concentrators; some can support routing, prioritization, encryption, and other enhanced networking features.

The introduction of more sophisticated CPE with more comprehensive feature sets opened opportunities to support a wide variety of applications over frame relay. For example, IBM made frame relay an integral part of its strategic direction. Its controller family, FEPs (front-end processors), and most of IBM's other networking products now have frame relay interfaces. IBM also has cards that fit directly into your computer that format the information into frame relay frames to allow direct access to a frame relay service.

In early 1994, the Frame Relay Forum adopted specifications closely aligning frame relay with ATM, offering interoperability between technologies and providing a migration path as business and networking requirements change. These specifications enable frame relay transport across ATM infrastructures and seamless interconnectivity of a frame relay location to an ATM location. Refer to Chapter 11 for more information regarding interoperability between frame relay and ATM.

Computing Evolution Driving Frame Relay

Business needs drive applications; applications riding on computing platforms drive networks. This section examines the computing evolution to help you understand the drivers behind the emergence of frame relay and the problems frame relay addresses. This section starts from the mainframe-based infrastructures to the deployment of LANs. It focuses on the challenges with connecting various LANs across the wide-area network that drove the need for a solution that would minimize or alleviate these concerns.

In the 1970s, most businesses operated a computing environment where the processing power, intelligence, and repository for information resided on a mainframe at a central location. The devices on the end-user desktops consisted of a keyboard and a console used for text entry only. These desktop devices did not have processing power and hence are called *dumb terminals*. Businesses typically used this architecture, where dumb terminals communicate with a host mainframe, for transaction-oriented applications.

If we liken the corporate data network to the central nervous system of the company, then mainframes are the brains. Inside the mainframe, the storage facility is an adjunct to the central processing unit, or *CPU*. Files taken from memory travel a very short distance before they reach the central processing unit. The data is processed and then sent back to storage.

Network users interact with the mainframe through desktop terminals, but the terminals themselves do not process or store information. Specific business applications are written that allow users to update information in the central databases or to request information from them.

Remote dumb terminals connect to mainframes over hierarchical networks. In many terminal-to-mainframe applications, the remote site only sends very small requests to the mainframe, and the mainframe simply stores the new information and/or sends back a file or a screen update, as shown in Figure 1.1. The most common terminal-to-host architecture is IBM's System Network Architecture (SNA).

FIGURE 1.1

Remote terminals send small requests, and the mainframe sends a file or a screen update.

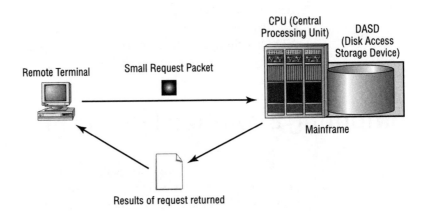

The networks built to support this traditional data-processing hierarchy were themselves hierarchical (Figure 1.2). The traffic flow is fairly orderly and predictable, as well, at least when everything runs smoothly. Speeds across the wide-area network typically operate at 9.6Kbps or less. A strict pecking order and the flow of information goes from top (i.e., mainframe) to bottom (i.e., dumb terminal) and bottom to top but not side to side. Strict division of labor characterizes this environment. Most of the action occurs at the top of the hierarchy.

Although many companies still use this model, other alternative computing architectures coexist in today's environment. The next sections introduce the emergence of alternative computing architectures.

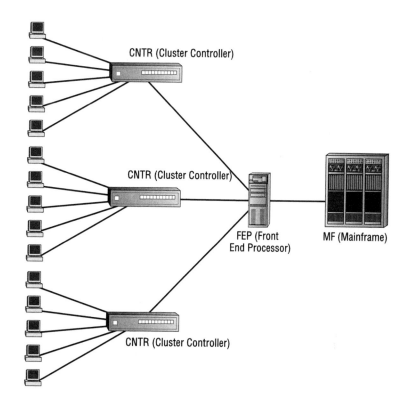

Power to the Desktop

Enter the personal computer (PC)—a network device that distributes processing power, intelligence, and storage capacity to the desktop. The PC lessens or eliminates the reliance on centralized processing. Although this sounds simple and harmless, it has an immense impact on networking topologies.

As PCs began to proliferate in the workplace, application or software companies developed new business applications that use the processing power available in the desktop device. This model allowed users to create files and databases and to store them locally on the desktop. Cost comparisons began to show that many applications could be developed and maintained on PCs in a dramatically less-expensive fashion compared to mainframes.

In addition to the substantial cost savings possible with some applications, this computing model could also reduce the time it took to develop new business applications in a PC environment. Businesses simply could not ignore the cost and speed advantages of the PC; hence, the explosion of PC deployment.

The Advent of LANs

In overcoming the cost and development constraints of mainframe environments for some applications, the PC creates its own unique set of problems.

As software companies began to develop applications for the PC, it became necessary to give many users access to these applications. And because PC storage capacity was less expensive, it made sense to rewrite some previously mainframe-based applications for a more distributed environment. The PC model primarily allowed sharing of information through "sneakernet" initially. End users copied files onto floppy diskettes and walked them over or shipped them to other users needing the information.

As companies' dependence on PCs increased, it became painfully obvious that sneakernet would not offer a long-term solution. Companies needed a way to share information more quickly and more efficiently. Connecting PCs together to allow shared storage and shared access to printers and information became an industry itself. LANs (local area networks) emerged to tie together PCs within close geographical proximity. Initially, operating at speeds of 4Mbps, 10Mbps, and 16Mbps (and now going far beyond this at 100Mbps and above), the LAN offers a fast and elegant method for turning a group of PCs into a cost-effective mainframe alternative for some applications.

The LAN solved the problem of allowing users within the same department to share applications. Groups of LANs, connected by simple bridges or gateways, allowed users on different floors or across the campus to communicate electronically and share information.

At first, linking LANs seemed fairly simple. Congestion was not a big concern because of the relatively high LAN speeds. The problems really began when access to remote locations (e.g., outside the headquarters or main building) became necessary.

The Problems of Connecting LANs

LANs were initially intended for local use, hence the name local area network. Connecting LANs across a WAN (wide area network) poses some interesting challenges. Understanding the nature of the underlying applications will help you better understand these challenges and the elegance of frame relay as a solution.

Comparing SNA and LAN Traffic

Transaction-oriented networks often use polling. Using IBM's System Network Architecture (SNA) as an example, polling is the process by which the front-end processor (FEP) systematically asks each remote cluster controller to determine whether any information is awaiting transmission. The cluster controller only sends information to the FEP when asked to do so. The FEP acts like a traffic officer managing the remote controllers, and traffic flows in a very orderly fashion.

SNA's network operation relies heavily on this aspect of control and traffic predictability. LANs lack these characteristics. In LAN environments, information can pass between any two or more sets of network devices at any time and in any direction. File sizes are not predictable either. There is no polling and no FEP to keep all of the transactions orderly.

Although polling works to keep the traffic orderly, polling introduces a significant amount of network overhead. The request/acknowledgment sequences that take place between FEPs and remote cluster controllers mean that network traffic is continually generated and transmitted across the WAN, even when no actual application information needs to be transferred. Transporting polling information across the WAN results in network bandwidth inefficiencies.

Unpredictability of LAN Traffic

When a user on a terminal-to-mainframe network wants to change or manipulate data in some way, the user sends a request back to the place of central storage, processing happens centrally, and the mainframe sends the output back to the user only. With LANs, the processing is not done centrally, and the processing unit does not reside next to the storage unit.

If a user on one LAN wants to access and manipulate a file on a remote LAN, the entire file can be sent from where it is stored on LAN A to the processor in the requesting user's desktop on LAN B. There is nothing methodical or orderly about this process. There is no predictability to the transmission, like the methodical SNA network. LAN internetworks are chaotic and reactionary. They are also more homogeneous (i.e., peer-oriented) or flatter compared with the hierarchical SNA environment (Figure 1.3).

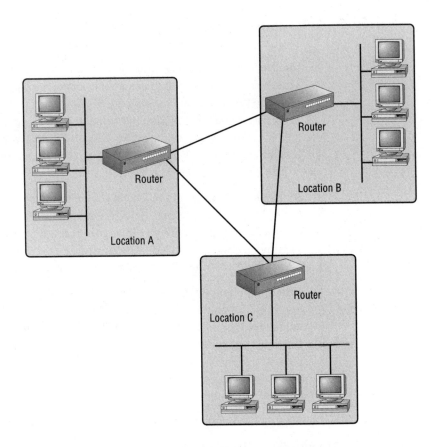

On a LAN where capacity is several megabits or more, sending a 4MB file
between desktops has minimal impact on network congestion. But on a
9.6Kbps WAN connection, the impact can be devastating—particularly if
mission-critical transactions slow down because of the LAN file being transmitted. Remote LANs connected across a WAN comprise an internetwork.

Any-to-Any Transmissions

The term *internetworking* emerged as a descriptor for the process of interconnecting networks.

Do not confuse *internetworking* with the term *interworking,* used and described later in this book.

Any LAN might need to get information from, or send information to, any other LAN, which creates a problem when connecting LANs. The requirement for connectivity among LANs has grown, especially with the emergence of electronic-mail applications as a way to facilitate the exchange of documents and as an alternative to playing phone tag.

Connecting LANs using traditional leased lines is difficult because to maintain a full or even a partial mesh topology requires many physical lines, router ports, and CSU/DSUs (Channel Service Unit/Data Service Units) or NTUs (Network Termination Units). (*Mesh* means any-to-any connectivity in the case of a fully meshed network and a subset of that in a partially meshed network.) In fact, the formula for a fully meshed network is the number of LAN sites (N) times the number of sites minus one (N–1), divided by two.

```
Number of Leased Lines Required = N×(N-1)/2
```

If you have five locations, to create a fully meshed physical network of private lines requires ten private lines. If you have six sites, the number increases to fifteen, an increase of five circuits as a result of one new site. As the number of LANs to interconnect across a WAN grows in a linear fashion, the cost to maintain the mesh grows significantly. Additionally, you have to factor in the high cost of WAN ports on a router (or bridge) and the cost of each CSU/DSU or NTU.

Consequently, companies rarely deploy fully meshed leased-line networks, especially with a large number of locations. In the best of cases, some companies implement partial mesh networks to save money. Although you can achieve some cost savings by deploying private lines in a partial-mesh configuration, it introduces multiple tandem (intermediate) points that create additional hops. This situation can result in increased delays across the network. In a router-based network, routers also need the sophistication to continually calculate the most economical and least congested route over which to send traffic. This problem created the need for a solution that allows high levels of performance by maintaining more direct connectivity between the LANs but does not present a cost structure that escalates dramatically as the number of network sites increases.

Bridges and Routers

Network capacity is expensive, at least on the WAN, and efficient use of this capacity helps to save money and increase network performance. A great deal of this increased performance can result from effective selection of CPE.

In the early days of frame relay, bridges and routers were the most commonly used devices to connect LANs over the WAN.

Bridges Bridges were the first devices to hit the streets for LAN-to-LAN connectivity. Bridges operate at layer two of the OSI model. Bridges filter traffic by determining whether a packet stays on the same LAN from which it received the packet or goes to another LAN on the network. Other than this simple filtering and forwarding function, the bridge does not help to route the traffic to its ultimate destination.

Bridges operate at the lower half of the Data Link layer, called the *MAC* (Media Access Control) layer of the OSI model. The bridge has a fairly simple technology and filtering system, which makes the bridge less expensive than its more intelligent cousin, the router. The bridge offers a good internetworking solution within campus or building environments where capacity is much less expensive compared to connectivity across the WAN.

Routers Routers operate at the Network Protocol layer, or layer three, of the OSI model. Routers have a more sophisticated filtering and routing system than the bridge. Routers usually cost more. With more advanced filtering and routing capabilities, the router makes better use of expensive wide-area network capacity. Routers work best with routable protocols, such as TCP/IP, AppleTalk, and Novell IPX. However, they can also support nonroutable protocols through encapsulation, bridging, or other router, vendor-specific networking schemes.

A bridge introduces high overhead and generates unnecessary traffic when it needs to send a file to a remote destination, and it does not know the most direct path to the destination device. The bridge may send explorer packets or broadcasts and assume that the first acknowledgment received represents the most direct route, or it may broadcast the first packet to all interfaces to determine how to forward the information. It then uses this same route for sending the file. These explorer packets create overhead on the network and can sometimes increase network congestion. The router addresses the bridge's inefficiencies by preselecting the route without having to send explorer or broadcast packets.

Routers grew out of a need for a more intelligent bridge device. The router has a more sophisticated filtering and forwarding system than a bridge. It "routes" traffic to its end destination by sending the packets over the most efficient path. Therefore, the router reduces the overall level of unnecessary network overhead traffic and can improve performance over the WAN.

As a rule, companies use bridges to connect LANs within the same building, especially where network congestion on the LANs is not a problem. Routers work well to connect remote LANs together across a wide-area network, where bandwidth is more costly. However, you can still use bridges to save money if you only have a few sites to connect over a WAN.

In the early days of frame relay, routers and bridges had a more distinct cost difference. As technology evolved and became more efficient, routers became very cost effective, making the need to consider the use of bridges in some situations obsolete.

Messy Politics of LAN Implementations

Many organizational incongruities within firms also exacerbated the problems of LAN internetworking. In many companies, the central IT (Information Technologies) department was rarely consulted or involved in the process of building and connecting LANs. Most of the time, the department(s) needing connectivity took the bull by its horns and ran with it. This resulted in the deployment of new subnetworks in an ad hoc fashion as new networking needs emerged.

In some cases, departmental interference with the network resulted in messy politics. The LAN people distrusted the IT department because of the IT group's unfamiliarity with LANs and PCs. The IT department preferred the mainframe environment for all applications and did not sanction and support LANs; but it also did not want mininetworks springing up all across the company.

Talk of consolidating these disparate applications into a single network only raised political red flags. Many often compared getting the two sides to talk together and work towards a single, highly efficient solution to negotiating Middle East peace. And the language barrier did not help matters. For example, a "host" in the traditional centralized environment means a mainframe, but to a LAN manager, it means any server device on the LAN. To make matters more complicated, a single device can be either a client or server at different moments in time (in a LAN).

Deployment of Parallel Networks

Companies often deployed new parallel networks to connect LANs across distances (Figure 1.4). It was not—and is still not—unusual for a company to already support more than one 9.6Kbps leased line into a remote location to meet the peak requirements of transaction-oriented applications; the LAN connection added yet another leased line, usually a DS-0 operating at 56/64Kbps.

WARNING   The cost of running parallel networks is high. Not only are monthly recurring leased line costs expensive when applications cannot share a single facility but administration and operations costs increase, as well.

FIGURE 1.4

Deploying separate and parallel networks for different applications

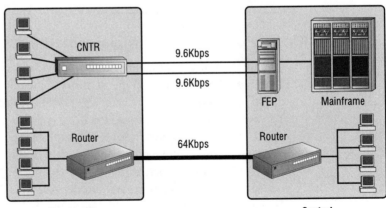

This solution was necessary to keep the LAN traffic from having an impact on the performance of the mission-critical and delay-sensitive SNA traffic. Fortunately, new developments over the past years have resulted in significant changes for both the centralized and the distributed application support groups.

The PC and the LAN are no longer considered rebel devices. IT departments in most organizations now support the deployment and ongoing operation of both PCs and LANs. They also take responsibility for connecting the LANs together, leveraging the existing high-speed backbone network where possible. Both groups have realized that there is a certain set of applications for which the PC and the LAN are very well suited, and there are plenty of other applications that work best in a centralized, mainframe environment. In order to support the LAN internetwork, many IT departments have made staffing modifications by adding new PC and LAN experts and providing training to existing personnel.

LAN users also gained new perspectives. They quickly determined that because of the growing complexity of the applications and the network configuration, they could not support a network on an ad hoc, part-time basis by untrained personnel, so they sought the IT department for assistance. Budgetary pressures forced all departments to consider options for keeping the cost of LAN interconnectivity in check.

As a result, many companies are openly considering or have already implemented common LAN and SNA support and/or network consolidation. Having a single group in charge of network planning, operations, and optimization makes good business sense, especially where cost containment is a corporate objective. Consolidation of LAN and SNA applications can save money, if the resulting network can ensure the integrity of the mission-critical transaction applications.

The Nature of Data Driving Frame Relay

Understanding the nature of data applications, particularly LAN applications, helps substantiate the reasons for frame relay's emergence.

Bursty

Data applications are *bursty* in nature. What exactly does that mean? In a LAN environment, file transfers typically vary in size with each transmission.

Large file transfers and/or peak hour transmissions represent "burst" instances.

No application, including voice and video, is a constant stream of traffic. In fact, the whole theory of voice compression is to take a single conversation, split the speech into its natural "speech bursts," and use the dead space between speech bursts to transport bursts from another conversation.

Intermittent

Besides its bursty nature, data transmissions are also intermittent. This means that sometimes data needs to be sent, and sometimes it does not. This intermittence is similar to your telephone that you use sometimes and at other times allow to sit idle. The PBX (Private Branch eXchange), which ties telephones together and routes calls, only allocates network capacity to phones in use. It does not reserve capacity for phones not in use.

It makes sense to do the same with data. Not all LAN application users send or receive information simultaneously at any given point in time. In fact, there could be long periods of many milliseconds, seconds, or minutes when no LAN traffic goes over the WAN.

Bursty and intermittent data traffic is not the sole property of LAN environments. Bursty and intermittent also characterize transaction-oriented applications, including SNA-based applications, if you eliminate much of the polling that takes place among network devices.

Higher Peak-to-Average Transmission Ratio

In the early days of data transmission over a wide-area network, the average transmission requirement might have been 7.4Kbps and the peak requirement 9.6Kbps. Today, the average requirement for a network site, or even a single application, might be 64Kbps with a peak of several Mbps. The mix of applications is changing, from primarily small terminal-to-host transactions to an even distribution of large LAN-to-LAN file transfers. Larger file transfers introduce greater potential for network congestion. The ratio of average-to-peak requirements has also scaled upward. High-speed public data service can help address these shifts in trends and requirements.

The Shortcomings of Traditional Services

Ideally, the wide-area network that supports bursty and intermittent applications should expand or contract as necessary to meet the needs of the users and application-performance parameters at any given point in time. A look at traditional solutions for the WAN provides insight into why frame relay can offer a better solution for supporting these applications. This section covers private lines and X.25.

Private Lines

To start, we need to look at the history of long-distance networking and traditional point-to-point transmission solutions, or what we call private lines. In this environment, *voice* provides the foundation. Many service providers originally designed the public networks and most WAN services for voice applications. This had an enormous impact on the solutions available today for addressing data-networking challenges.

For example, how is a single DS-0 private line able to transport 64Kbps worth of information? Why not more? Or less? The answer lies in voice. To accurately reproduce a person's speech over an electronic medium requires sampling the speech pattern 8,000 times every second. The sample itself is an 8-bit byte and 8,000 × 8 equals 64,000bps (see Figure 1.5).

FIGURE 1.5

Voice is sampled 8,000 times every second for transmission across the network.

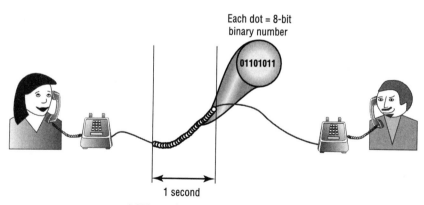

Each dot = 8-bit binary number

01101011

1 second

8,000 samples per second
8 bits × 8,000 samples/second = 64,000

In the U.S. digital hierarchy, for example, 24 DS-0s make up a DS-1, and 28 DS-1s (or 672 DS-0s) make up a DS-3. So you can see that voice provided the foundation for building the wide-area networking infrastructure and today's data applications work in and around these definitions. Today's quality standards for voice require that speech be sampled at 64,000bps (DS-0), which became the basis for the digital hierarchy—DS-0, DS-1, DS-3, etc. Data doesn't have to be sampled at 64,000bps. Therefore, we may not have started with DS-0, DS-1, and DS-3 private lines. Perhaps a network would have looked more like X.25, frame relay, IP, or ATM providing any-to-any connectivity at different line rates and not necessarily in increments of 64,000bps.

TDM (time-division multiplexing) provides the basis for the digital hierarchy for the WAN. With TDM, a multiplexer or channel bank divides a circuit into individual channels, each one dedicated to a specific user's application or communications path. TDM resembles a gun with 24 chambers, wherein each channel has a shot at the transmission barrel on a predetermined rotation basis (see Figure 1.6).

FIGURE 1.6

TDM allocates specific bandwidth or channels for each application.

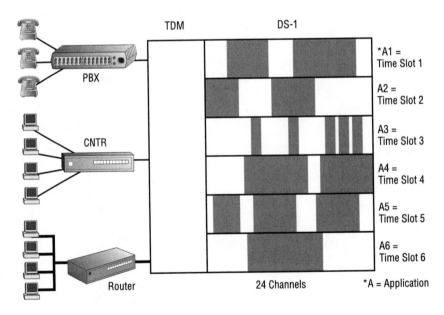

Again using the U.S. standard as an example, TDM equipment divides a single DS-1 link with 1.536Mbps worth of bandwidth into 24 segments to get twenty-four 64Kbps links (24 × 64Kbps = 1.536Mbps). The network reserves each DS-0 for a specific application, regardless of whether the application is active or idle. During idle times, this capacity is essentially "wasted." Other users or applications assigned to other DS-0s cannot access this unused capacity even if these active applications might need additional bandwidth to transmit a very large file or a series of large transmissions. The network cannot statistically allocate capacity to meet the changing requirements of the applications.

As an example, imagine a primary site that communicates with many remote locations. A snapshot of the network usage at any point in time probably shows some of the lines actively transmitting data while others are sitting idle. For the channels transmitting data, the end user might experience slower response times because the channel can only support a specific amount of traffic at any given time. In this situation, it would be ideal if the network had the intelligence to allocate capacity from the idle channels for those applications needing additional bandwidth.

X.25

In the early 1970s, the U.S. government funded work on developing a protocol and networking solution for transporting data over distances. The X.25 protocol was developed to overcome the problems inherent in transmitting data over low-quality copper wires. (Copper transmission facilities have a higher propensity to cause errors on the line and damage data packets.) X.25 uses statistical, not time-division, multiplexing. This allows the allocation of capacity to meet real-time changes in connectivity requirements.

Initially, there was one nationwide network in the U.S.—AT&T's—and it was largely copper-based. MCI was just emerging with its microwave and copper-based network, but it was yet to be a major market force. In addition, network lines had a high degree of background sound generated by the underlying equipment and picked up from outside sources.

Services did not have reliable transmission lines and supporting equipment, and there was a probability of the network damaging the transmissions. Remember that the network transmits information in the form of electrical signals. If an electrical positive pulse is not transmitted as a positive pulse, then the network equipment might interpret a "0" as a "1." In transmitting a voice conversation, a few of these network errors can go largely unnoticed by the parties on either end. But with data applications, changing the value of a digit can have immense repercussions. Therefore, these problems drove the need for a solution for checking transmission accuracy and for recovering any information damaged by the network during transmission to ensure the reliable and successful transmission of data files.

The centralized processing environment provided companies with the most cost-effective means for remote users to access centrally stored data. But the dumb terminals at the remote locations did not have the intelligence to check incoming transmissions for errors or notify the sending device of an error and the need for retransmission.

The X.25 protocol was designed specifically to solve these problems. The protocol operates at the Data-Link layer (layer two) and uses a sophisticated and thorough procedure for determining whether the transmission facilities have damaged a file during transmission. Files are formatted into "packets," with address information indicating the source and destination for that packet. When an X.25 network switch receives a packet, it checks the packet for any damages using an algorithmic equation. This process is called *error checking*. The X.25 switch stores a copy of each packet before it sends the packet to the next switch. The duplicate copy provides a backup that can be sent in case the original copy is damaged. This process is called *error correction*.

X.25 ensured reliable transmission of data over the WAN, with supported speeds of 9.6Kbps, 19.2Kbps, and 56Kbps. The drawback of X.25 was the added overhead (non-user data) and processing the protocol imposed on the transmission to achieve this high level of reliability. However, the benefits more than outweighed the drawbacks at the time.

The U.S. Defense Department was impressed enough with the protocol that it commissioned the ARPAnet, a network based on X.25, to support the transmission of data applications. This eventually evolved into what we know today as the Internet. In addition, the service providers moved to implement nationwide X.25 networks for commercial customers, as more businesses implemented applications requiring a highly reliable and secure underlying data-transmission service.

During the 1980s, more U.S. service providers appeared on the market, and they installed sophisticated fiber-optic networks throughout the U.S. Fiber-optic lines significantly increase the quality of transmission. These transmission lines are clean and very little background noise intercedes the communication path. As networks became more reliable, the fiber-optic networks reduced the likelihood of transmission errors and damaged packets. This resulted in an infrastructure better suited for the transmission of data applications.

Simultaneously, the shift in processing power introduced intelligent desktop devices that can perform error recovery. It placed much less pressure on the WAN to perform this function.

The reliability problems that X.25 initially solved so elegantly are no longer problems, at least in the U.S. This is not to say that X.25 will not be around for a long time or that it does not offer a good solution for some network environments. X.25 remains a cost-effective and viable alternative for applications that require low-speed connectivity among many locations, in the U.S. and worldwide. It also provides an ideal solution for value-added services that require protocol conversion, remote polling, or access control.

For applications requiring lower delay and highly reliable network facilities, X.25's reparations, such as increased delay from higher processing overhead, may be greater than its advantages. Therefore, a new generation of packet-switching protocols has emerged to pick up where X.25 left off.

Frame Relay Stepping Up to the Plate

Frame relay was created to specifically address the changing needs of emerging data applications; dynamic, fast-paced business and computing environments; and the shift in processing power. It also emerged to fill the void created by traditional services, to address changes in business organization structures, and to fulfill the need for faster and improved communications.

Filling the Void Created by Traditional Services

Frame relay does not impose rigid time slots on network connections like TDM does, and it can respond quickly to chaotic transmission needs. This makes it ideal for the support of intermittent and bursty data environments, such as LAN and SNA applications.

Frame relay allows a single physical network interface to support many logical connections. It uses virtual connections that offer the security of a private line but also allows statistical allocation of network capacity, meaning that only active applications get access to the shared bandwidth pool as shown in Figure 1.7. Idle applications do not consume any network bandwidth.

F I G U R E   1.7

Frame relay allows applications to share bandwidth.

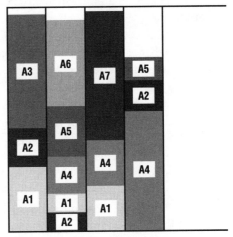

Unlike X.25, frame relay does not perform overhead error correction processing. Instead, it leaves this function to the intelligent devices on each end of the connection and the higher-layer protocols. Frame relay is a streamlined version of X.25. Frame relay only uses layers one and two of the OSI model and not layer three. By eliminating the unnecessary functionality, frame relay can operate more efficiently and more quickly.

The development of the intelligence in desktop devices and the reliance on higher-layer network protocols were critical prerequisites. Although the new implementation still requires the error correction function, it is not necessarily needed within the wide-area network. By pushing this function to the edges of the network, frame relay can process and transmit information faster than X.25.

Frame relay also offers a solution for the problems most companies have with their private-line networks. Private networks based on time-division multiplexing require a high level of up-front investment in equipment, network facilities, and staff. In the '70s and '80s, companies had few available alternatives. The service providers simply did not offer the types and levels of service mandatory for corporate networks carrying mission-critical business applications. Therefore, corporations had to become little phone companies, creating departments designed to build and manage the corporate network. Frame relay allows you to outsource the management of the WAN to the service providers.

Addressing Changes in Business Organizations

Today's business environment is different from what it was in decades past. Companies must be nimble and quick. Global competition and competitive price pressures drive companies to constantly control costs.

The old, hierarchical organizational structure is slowly giving way because of competitive pressures to bring goods to market more quickly, produce products and services more economically, and use resources more efficiently. Companies are embracing the concept of highly mobile cross-functional teams or work groups to facilitate certain business processes, such as new product development. These teams must come together quickly, perform the task at hand, and then disband. It requires quick allocation of resources without regard for distance and geography.

A single team may consist of members from marketing, engineering, sales, management, finance, information systems, and other departments. The members may not all be located in the same city, state, or country. The team members may even work for different companies. This is the true virtual corporation.

Communication is critical among team members. The team members must have an environment conducive to collaboration on a variety of documents, in brainstorming sessions and team meetings, on the development of service definitions and presentations, and much more.

Enabling More and Improved Communications

Communication throughout the whole organization is becoming more critical. Companies depend on the network to support customers, sales people, and internal departments more than ever before. It becomes more difficult to separate the business from the network, but one cannot exist without the other. Once in place, the business and the network feed one another, each causing the other to grow in a synergistic relationship.

The pressures of a slow-growing economy coupled with increased global competition drive businesses to release extraneous costs and focus resources on the core business. LAN interconnectivity, cross-functional work groups, remote database applications, the move towards computer-aided design and engineering, and the shift in processing power all place the traditional corporate network infrastructure under significant stress.

It may no longer be optimal to run a large in-house telecommunications company. In fact, many corporations discover that in-house telecommunications managers are better deployed as strategic resources. They should look forward and develop networking solutions that help the company operate and compete more effectively. The network is becoming a highly strategic resource and someone needs to proactively manage this aspect of the business.

Frame relay services allow you to relegate some or all of the day-to-day management of the network to the service provider. The service provider delivers a more complete network solution and takes responsibility for delivering predefined levels of connectivity, availability, management, and support.

Summary

The term *frame relay* can refer to an interface standard protocol, a switching technology, or a public service, depending on the context of the discussion. Frame relay service is a wide-area networking solution that provides connectivity and enables communication between multiple locations that support a variety of applications. It can help improve network performance, save money, and allow companies to achieve strategic business benefits.

The shift in processing power from a centralized to a distributed structure, the deployment of PCs and LANs, and the need to connect LANs across the wide-area network ultimately all contributed to the emergence and acceptance of frame relay.

Although many companies use traditional services, such as private lines and X.25, for their wide-area connectivity, these services were not designed to transport higher-speed, bursty, and intermittent LAN traffic. Private lines do not allow the sharing of bandwidth, which results in low-bandwidth efficiencies when carrying bursty traffic. X.25's inherent error-checking capabilities within the network compromise speed of transmission. The widespread deployment of reliable fiber-optic networks minimizes the need for error-checking. Frame relay addresses this issue quite well as it relegates error-checking to the end devices or CPE.

CHAPTER

2

How Frame Relay Works—
Its Components and Capabilities

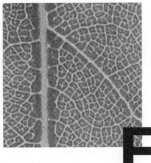

Frame relay service is analogous to a personal computer: you can operate one without understanding the "guts" of the technology or network applications. However, you can make better networking decisions by understanding the basic components and capabilities. Many frame relay customers coast by without fully taking advantage of the benefits that frame relay technology offers.

This chapter covers the networking components common to most public networks. It provides a baseline of information for the discussions on enhanced frame relay features and functions presented later on in this book.

The Composition of a Frame Relay Network

A frame relay network typically consists of three elements: the access link, the port connection, and the associated virtual connections. Although this chapter discusses each element separately, understand that these elements are part of an integrated whole. A port connection without its complementary virtual connections to other port connections is not useful. The elements work together to make up the complete frame relay network, as shown in Figure 2.1.

The Access Link

The local loop or access link provides the connection between your CPE and the frame relay network. It directly interfaces with the port connection, and each access link connects to a port connection. The access-link speed must be equal or greater than the port speed. Refer to Chapter 4 for more information on access links and the different access alternatives.

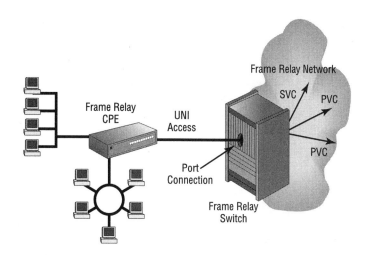

The Port Connection

The port connection is the point of entry into a frame relay network (see Figure 2.2). It is typically associated with an individual site. In most networks, each site only needs one port connection, even though many different users, applications, and protocols may need network access.

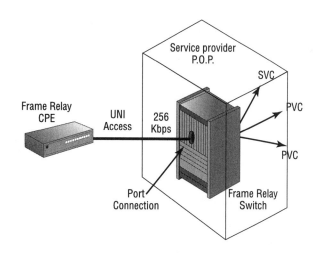

User-to-Network Interface and Network-to-Network Interface

The frame relay specifications outline two types of interfaces or ports—a UNI (User-to-Network Interface) and a NNI (Network-to-Network Interface), as shown in the following figures.

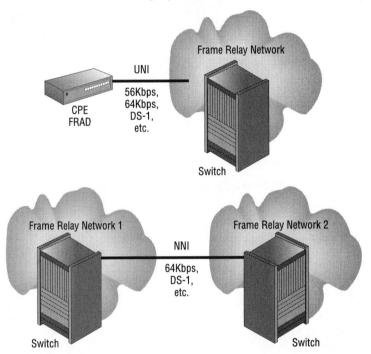

UNI connections provide the interface between customers and public frame relay networks. NNI connections provide the interface between two frame relay service networks. Customers connect to frame relay networks through routers or other FRADs (Frame Relay Access Devices) to FRNDs (Frame Relay Network Devices), such as a frame relay switch, typically through a UNI. An NNI, on the other hand, connects FRNDs together.

Designed as a more effective way to interconnect two public frame relay networks, the NNI allows traffic to pass between the networks. In the U.S., this is particularly useful in connecting local frame relay networks with, for example, those of the intereXchange carriers' frame relay networks. NNIs are equally useful when connecting frame relay networks between different countries. NNIs are not required to connect two frame relay networks, but they do include some added functionality, such as bidirectional polling for network status. This function is performed only unidirectionally with a UNI connection.

A single port connection supports multiple logical connections (PVCs, or Permanent Virtual Circuits, and SVCs, or Switched Virtual Circuits) to many different locations. Once again, all the users, applications, and protocols share these PVCs/SVCs in most cases. The next section describes the different types of logical connections.

Capacity (or speed) defines a port connection. In other words, you choose a port connection's speed on a port-by-port basis. That choice depends upon the amount of information sent to and from that location at any given moment in time. You can typically choose from many different port connection speeds, including 64K, 128K, 256K, 384K, 512K, 768K, 1.024K, 1.536Mbps, and 2Mbps. The frame relay standards now define speeds up to OC-3 and OC-12. However, no service provider offers these higher speeds on a commercially available access speed as of the writing of this book. Design considerations and criteria for selecting the port speed are discussed in Chapter 14.

The capacity of the port connection becomes the gating factor for that location. You cannot send or receive information faster than the port speed at any instant (see Figure 2.3). You cannot receive or send more information to and from the site at any given instant in time than what the port connection allows.

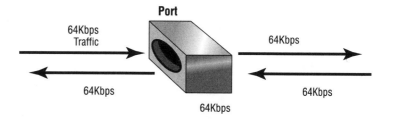

FIGURE 2.3

The port defines the maximum amount of information sent to or from a location.

The port statistically allocates capacity depending on which applications need to send data out onto the network and where to send the data. This means that multiple applications or multiple connections can share the port speed without reserving a percentage of the port speed for specific applications or connections. (The connections in frame relay are called *virtual circuits,* discussed in detail in the next section.) With statistical bandwidth allocation, the port allocates bandwidth to active applications only. For example, if a port supports four applications and all four are running simultaneously, the applications share the port bandwidth. However, if only one application is active, that application gets all of the bandwidth available. This chapter provides more information about statistical bandwidth allocation later.

Virtual Circuits

There are two types of frame relay connections: PVCs and SVCs. Virtual circuits are the logical connections or paths between port connections (or locations) on a frame relay network (see Figure 2.4). They operate similarly to leased lines in connecting locations. However, unlike leased lines, virtual circuits are defined in software rather than physically hardwired. This offers flexibility in the provisioning process, including the initial setup, moves, adds, and changes.

This section discusses the two types of virtual channels as well as their features and capabilities.

Permanent Virtual Circuits (PVCs)

A PVC is permanent, which means that it remains in place and is available for use at all times (except in cases where the network cannot recover from a failure) once it is assigned between two port connections. The frames traveling on a PVC take the same path each time and flow in sequence. The network does not need to resequence the frames in the correct order at the destination.

F I G U R E 2.4

Virtual Circuits provide connectivity between two port connections.

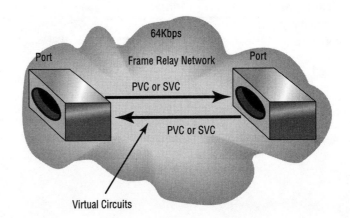

Although the service provider sets up multiple customers on a public frame relay network, each PVC is dedicated to a single customer only. No other company can send information across or intercept information within another company's PVC because each PVC only carries information between a particular company's locations as defined during the provisioning process. These virtual connections are every bit as secure and reliable as a traditional private line. The "virtual" nature of the PVC also means that the PVC does not physically take up space on the port connection or in the network until you need to send information across it. Because it does not take up capacity when idle, the network allocates the capacity to other PVCs, customers, or applications that are active and may need additional bandwidth.

When setting up your frame relay network, you will assign at least one PVC between any two locations on the network that require connectivity. Typically, all the applications at the two sites share this single logical connection, and the connection is designed to adequately support these aggregated transmission needs.

In some situations, you may decide to assign more than one PVC between the same two locations. This is sometimes the case when a network manager decides to keep SNA (protocol A) traffic on a different PVC from the LAN (protocol B) traffic, perhaps for prioritization, performance, or management reasons. In this case, the two PVCs operate independently but still share the same access and port connection, providing better economies of scale than if using separate dedicated connections. Figure 2.5 illustrates these two scenarios.

Switched Virtual Circuits (SVCs)

SVCs operate similarly to PVCs, except that the network establishes and dismantles the connections on a call-by-call basis. SVCs are connection-oriented virtual circuits intelligently negotiated and established between your equipment and a service provider's network when information needs to be sent. Upon completion of the transmission, the network tears down the connection.

There are several uses for SVCs, from support for low-usage sites to handling overflow traffic. SVCs enable spontaneous connectivity between sites already connected to the network and are most useful for applications needing infrequent connectivity to a given network site (although SVCs are still sometimes confused with dial-up access into the frame relay network). Chapter 10 discusses SVCs in detail.

FIGURE 2.5

Ways to provision PVCs to support multiple applications.

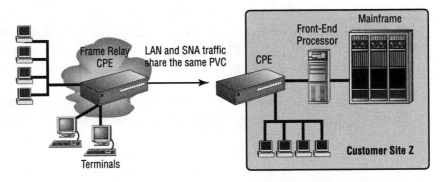

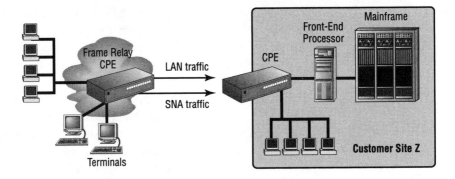

Committed Information Rate

You need to assign each PVC a CIR (Committed Information Rate). The CIR is the speed of transmission for a particular logical connection. The CIR assignment should reflect the expected average traffic volume between the two sites connected (see Figure 2.6). The CIR is not always easy to estimate when first designing a frame relay network. Chapter 14 provides some guidelines for determining the appropriate CIR.

CIR is a statistical measurement of throughput over time. The standard specifies that CIR = Committed Burst Rate (Bc)/Time. The time interval can vary but is typically a few milliseconds or tens of milliseconds.

Deciding on an initial CIR for each PVC can present a challenge in some environments, but one of the advantages of frame relay is better visibility of your network utilization. Once your network is in operation, the average and peak traffic volumes will help you adjust your CIRs accordingly.

F I G U R E 2.6

Each PVC needs a CIR
assignment.

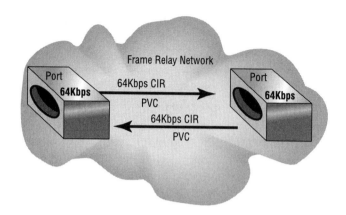

A PVC's CIR should not exceed the lower speed of the port connections *on either end* of the PVC. If you have a 64Kbps port connection at Site A and a 384Kbps connection at Site B, the CIR between the two should not exceed 64Kbps. You should not assign a 256Kbps CIR between these two port connections, because the 64Kbps port connection limits the speed at which this virtual connection may operate. A 256Kbps CIR, in this case, would be a bandwidth goal that the network could not reasonably be expected to meet, because it is limited by the 64Kbps port speed at Site A.

Service providers typically offer CIRs from 0Kbps to the port speed for a given site.

Service providers' frame relay offerings are constrained by the capabilities of the network platform (e.g., frame relay switches). Consequently, some service providers do not offer Zero CIR, and others do not offer user-defined burst rates. For some service providers, the highest CIR that can be assigned to an individual PVC is 1.024Mbps.

Keep in mind that at the instantaneous level a port connection is still a serial connection—the port sends each bit out one at a time. The port transmits the bits at the port speed, not the CIR. PVCs use the port in a first in, first out fashion, each getting its access to the port in the order that packets arrive. Over a given time window, a PVC's transmission is approximately equal to its defined CIR. This is discussed further later in this chapter.

With heavy network use at a site and many PVCs simultaneously contending for port/network capacity, PVCs should effectively transmit at their CIRs. PVCs may also be limited to a transmission rate close to the CIR during network reroute situations when overall network capacity contention increases dramatically on the rerouted section.

Choosing the PVC's CIR is important because the CIR can affect the performance of the network and the experiences of the network users. Do not be afraid of making a wrong decision in choosing the appropriate CIR. Frame relay allows for a high degree of flexibility. Within limits, the service provider can easily change a PVC's CIR. As you gain insight into the traffic patterns of your network, you can modify the PVC's CIR to more accurately reflect the needs of the network users.

Asymmetrical PVCs

Similar to private lines, frame relay is a full duplex service. This means that you can send and receive information across a PVC simultaneously. However, unlike private lines, some service providers give you the flexibility to assign different CIRs for each direction on a particular PVC, as shown in Figure 2.7. A PVC with different CIRs is called an *asymmetrical PVC; a symmetrical PVC* has the same CIR in both directions. The flexibility of frame relay allows PVCs to be sized to meet the needs of the applications in each direction of the connection.

FIGURE 2.7

Asymmetrical PVCs have different CIRs in each direction.

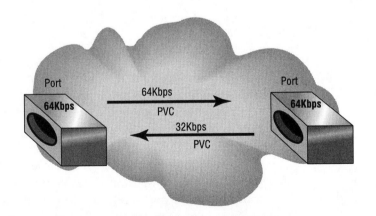

Data applications typically have asymmetrical traffic patterns between two points. Small requests can generate a huge amount of data to send back to the requesting party. Think of an advertising agency's request for a stock photo from a photo-storage library; the request for the photo may be no more than 100 bytes, but the photo itself could be several megabytes.

In a private-line environment, you may need 1.5Mbps in one direction because of the need to transmit large files or large volumes of information but only 256Kbps in the other direction; in this case, you must buy a DS-1 circuit. You end up paying for more capacity in one direction than you really need or use.

With frame relay and asymmetrical PVCs, you can assign CIRs on a PVC such that each direction gets the level of capacity needed to support its applications but no more. In the example above, you can have a 256Kbps CIR in one direction and a 1.5Mbps CIR in the other. This means that you can save money by more efficiently designing your network and not have to pay for more capacity than needed.

The Frame Relay Format

The frame format defines the structure and organization of the information in a frame. All information sent to the frame relay network must use the frame format. The frame relay frame format is shown in Figure 2.8.

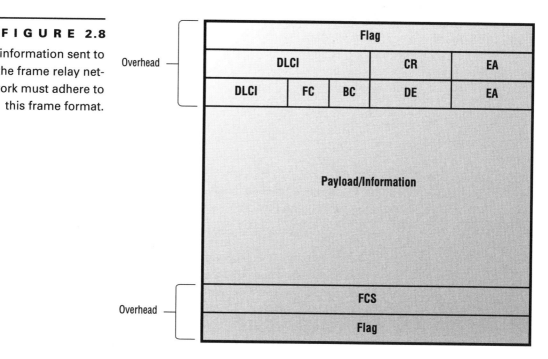

F I G U R E 2.8

All information sent to the frame relay network must adhere to this frame format.

A *flag* is a special sequence of bits that are part of the frame relay standard that precede the beginning of a frame. The front end of the frame has two octets, and the tail end has two, for a total of four octets for each frame plus the flag. All of these are overhead or non-user data. Remember, overhead is similar to the envelope we use when we mail a letter. The envelope itself is not the information we want to send. It simply provides the packaging and information required to deliver the letter to the end destination.

The word *octet* is often used interchangeably with the word *byte*. Both signify eight bits of information.

To further simplify how a frame relay format works, here is the process broken down into sections:

- The flag(s) tells the network equipment that a new frame is beginning/ending or that no frames are being sent.

- The next six bits are the first part of the address of the frame. This address information, called the *DLCI* (Data Link Connection Identifier), specifically identifies a *PVC* (Permanent Virtual Circuit) on the frame relay network. This is a 10-bit field spread across two octets. A frame relay network reads the DLCI, and it is cross-referenced in a routing table to the correct logical circuit that provides connectivity to that port. Certain DLCI addresses are reserved for use by the network, as discussed later.

- The next bit is called the Command/Response bit, and it uses the binary coding of either a 0 or a 1 and currently is not used by the protocol.

- The last bit in the octet, one of two EA (Extended Address) bits, allows the expansion of the DLCI addressing structure to handle more addresses. Again, this is a binary bit.

- The last octet in the header contains the last four bits of the DLCI.

- The next two bits, the Forward and Backward Congestion Notification bits, are known as FECN and BECN (pronounced "feckon" and "beckon"). These bits help with congestion control.

- The DE (Discard Eligibility) bit indicates when frames are sent at a rate in excess of the CIR and helps prioritize frames that may be discarded by the network if there is congestion.

- The last bit is the second EA bit.

After the header fields comes the actual payload (user data). When a router or frame relay device receives an incoming packet, it strips off the MAC or LLC layer protocol overhead (i.e., the Ethernet or Token Ring packet overhead) before encapsulating into a frame. The overhead from layer three and higher, such as the TCP/IP or SDLC overhead information, are left intact. At the destination, the process is reversed. The frame relay overhead is stripped away, the packet overhead for the LAN protocol is again added, and the packet is forwarded to the correct address.

The last two octets in the frame are again overhead.

- These two octets are called the FCS (Frame-Check Sequence). The network discards damaged frames and does not transmit them.

- Following the last octet, another sequence of one or more flags signal the end of that frame and the beginning of the next one.

Frame relay supports variable-length packet sizes. In other words, the frame size may be as large or as small as needed to transmit the information. (Actually, the frame information field is limited to 8,189 bytes by the standards, but few applications benefit from sizes that large; the default maximum frame size is 1,600 bytes.) By having variable-length packets, frame relay can be a very efficient protocol (low overhead) when you use "large" packet sizes as shown in Figure 2.9.

In practice, frame sizing depends on higher layer protocols and LAN protocols that impose their own packet-size restrictions. For example, the largest Ethernet packet size is 1,500 bytes. Therefore, the largest frame size in an Ethernet environment is also 1,500 bytes, even with larger file sizes. For large file transfers, the file breaks down into 1,500-byte or smaller units for transmission. The CPE adds the frame relay overhead to each Ethernet frame.

FIGURE 2.9
Overhead percentage increases with smaller frames.

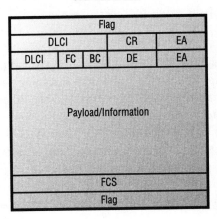

Overhead is 30%

Flag				
DLCI			CR	EA
DLCI	FC	BC	DE	EA
Payload/Information				
FCS				
Flag				

Overhead is 10%

Flag				
DLCI			CR	EA
DLCI	FC	BC	DE	EA
Payload/Information				
FCS				
Flag				

Virtual Circuit Identifiers

DLCIs—logical pointers, or addresses—identify a virtual connection. The DLCI is a label for the virtual connection but is not the connection itself— like a Route 66 sign identifies the name of the road in the U.S. but is not the highway itself. Often, however, you hear DLCI used interchangeably with PVC. With 10 bits available in the address, each port can recognize up to 1,024 different DLCIs.

The DLCI address holds local, not global, significance, meaning that the same DLCI number can be reused throughout the network at different port connections. Every port can have 1,024 other remote ports it can iden- tify and communicate with. The current 10-bit address does not pose a practical address limitation for most networks.

The number of unique addresses can be increased with the use of the EA bits, if frame relay networks grow large enough to require this level of addressing. However, not all equipment vendors support the EA bit.

The DLCI tables in your router or other CPEs will cross-reference a destination address (e.g., LAN address) with a DLCI. The DLCI points to a particular destination port on the network. The frame relay switch reads the destination DLCI and uses its own table to cross-reference the appropriate PVC to which the frame should be allocated. At the far end, the receiving frame relay switch puts the origination DLCI into the DLCI address slot, so that the receiving CPE knows the frame's origination point on the network. In setting up your frame relay network, you cannot actually use all of the 1,024 DLCIs at each port. Some are reserved for network-related signaling, such as the LMI (Local Management Interface), leaving 992 DLCIs for user connections. However, most of the DLCIs are available for your use. There is no secret or logic in choosing DLCIs. Just start with a number and work your way up. Some people use area codes, cost center numbers, or a variety of other number assignments.

Frame Relay Features and Capabilities

Most frame relay services support the following features and capabilities. There may be slight differences in implementation depending on the service provider. Therefore, it is best to check with the service providers and have them explain in detail the features and capabilities of their individual service offerings.

Automatic Rerouting

Most frame relay services build redundant physical network paths into the underlying network architecture so that in the event of a physical line failure, the PVCs provisioned over a failed line has an alternate route available, as shown in Figure 2.10. The path of the virtual connection is constant, unless a major network failure occurs along that path. In this case, the PVC is given an alternate route around the network failure, and it maintains that route until the primary route is recovered (or for some networks, until the PVC is manually returned to the primary route).

Retransmission may be necessary if a network failure occurs while a PVC is transmitting information. However, for many frame relay networks the

FIGURE 2.10

The frame relay network can automatically reroute PVCs around failed network components.

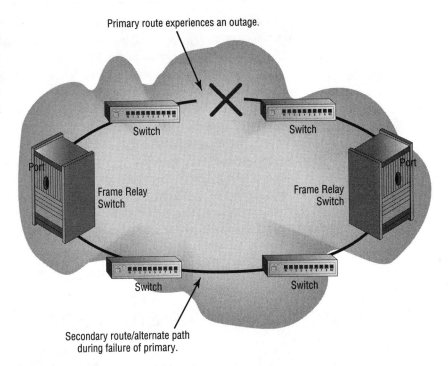

Primary route experiences an outage.

Switch   Switch

Port   Port

Frame Relay Switch   Frame Relay Switch

Switch   Switch

Secondary route/alternate path during failure of primary.

PVC reroute takes place very quickly, usually in a few seconds (i.e., less than one to seven seconds after the failure occurs). If a few frames of data are lost, the end equipment simply asks for a retransmission. The user of the application may never realize that a service-related problem has occurred on the network.

Bursting

A PVC can exceed its assigned CIR when transmitting a large file or a large volume of information and with excess capacity on the port connection and network (see Figure 2.11). This is called *bursting*. Bursting can only happen if the service provider lets you and there is spare bandwidth on the network.

The burst results in two network-performance benefits. It allows you to send information across the network more quickly, thus improving the response time of the application. It also eliminates congestion at the port connection more quickly, freeing up the port and the PVC to handle more incoming data.

The availability of excess capacity and the amount of excess capacity depends on the number of active PVCs and the CIRs of the PVCs sharing the port. The level of traffic or congestion on the public network also affects the ability of the PVC to sustain a burst above its CIR.

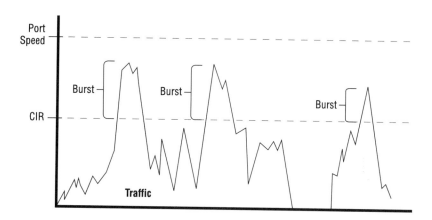

FIGURE 2.11

A transmission that exceeds the CIR is called a *burst*.

The frame relay specification calls for the network equipment to mark all data transmitted in excess of the PVC's CIR as DE (Discard Eligible), as shown in Figure 2.12. In the event of network congestion, the network discards DE frames first in an attempt to alleviate congestion. The standard also specifies ways to avoid congestion and to decrease congestion as it begins to occur but before a problem arises.

It is obviously better for the network to proactively avoid congestion all together. Some equipment vendors have designed sophisticated algorithms to do this, in addition to supporting the mechanisms defined by frame relay standards. But even with additional avoidance capabilities, the network may not be able to avoid some congestion situations and must try to minimize or eliminate problems. In these cases, the network discards the DE frames first. Think of it as jettisoning ballast to save a sinking balloon.

Each vendor's platform handles bursting differently. Some support unlimited bursting, others allow a temporary burst, and others allow service providers to implement their own unique bursting policies. Be sure to talk to service providers about their bursting policies.

Bursting has had its share of controversy, because you could theoretically design a network with less CIRs than the applications require, with the intent of letting the burst capability of the PVC handle the brunt of the data transfer.

FIGURE 2.12

The network marks frames transmitted above the CIR as DE.

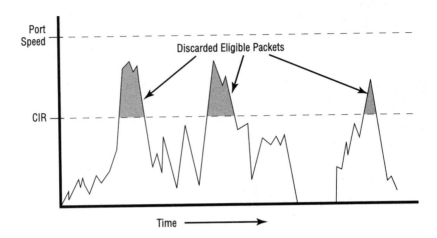

This is often what companies do when ordering Zero CIR services. Although you can save some money by subscribing only to a small amount of CIR, keep in mind that all frames transmitted above the CIR have a higher probability of getting discarded when the network has to drop frames. In the case of Zero CIR, the network marks all frames DE. Therefore, you need to balance cost savings and the criticality of the application.

Statistical Bandwidth Allocation

The effects of exceeding your CIR and of statistical bandwidth allocation depend greatly on the network platform your service provider uses.

To begin this discussion, here are a few examples of statistical bandwidth allocation of a port's capacity. These examples do not yet take into account the serialization output from the router or windowing of higher-level protocols.

First, consider a port connection with four different PVCs, each connecting with a different remote location, and each with a CIR of 64Kbps as shown in Figure 2.13.

In the first instant in time, T^0, the users do not send any information. In the next instant in time, T^1, each of the four PVCs simultaneously sends exactly 64Kbps worth of information to its respective remote location. The result is that all four PVCs are 100 percent active, each at the full CIR at time T^1. At the next instant in time, no information needs to be transmitted. Figure 2.14 shows how the port connection allocates the port capacity.

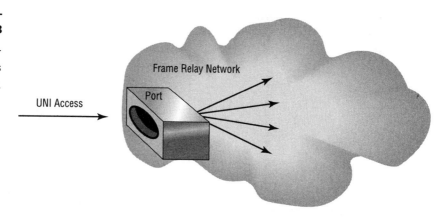

FIGURE 2.13

A sample configuration with four PVCs sharing a single port.

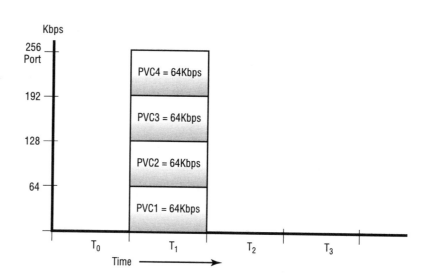

FIGURE 2.14

Example 1 of how the network statistically allocates port capacity.

Now take another example. Again at T^0, the users do not send any information. In the next instant in time, PVC1 needs to send a 32KB (256Kb) file. At time T^2, when the transmission begins, no other PVCs need the capacity of the port connection, and network congestion is also low. In this case, the port connection allocates the full capacity—256Kbps—to PVC1 (see Figure 2.15). The entire file transmits in time T^2. This not only improves the response time for that application but also immediately clears the network port connection of congestion and frees it up completely to accept more data. Of course, transmissions in excess of CIR are marked as discard-eligible.

FIGURE 2.15

Example 2 of how the
network statistically
allocates port capacity.

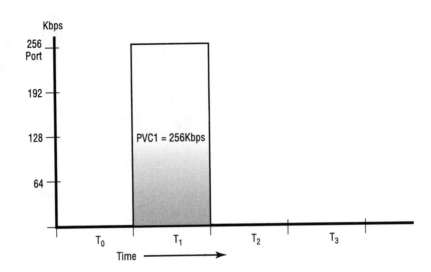

One last example. Assume that four different users are preparing to send data across the network, each using a different PVC. The first user uses PVC1 and needs to send a 48KB (384Kb) file beginning in time T^1. The second user needs to send a file also, but it is only 4KB (32Kb), and it does not begin transmitting until T^2 over PVC2. The third user has a 16KB (128Kb) file that begins transmitting in time T^3 over PVC3. The fourth user has a 32KB (128Kb) file that begins transmitting in T^4 over PVC4, but at the same time the second user begins sending another 32KB (128Kb) file over PVC2. Figure 2.16 illustrates how the port connection will change the allocation of capacity to the PVCs in each time period.

After working through three conceptual examples, the description of the bandwidth allocation method is not entirely accurate. These examples represent the network bandwidth spatially. However, bandwidth is really a measure of network speed. When just considering information coming to the port connection from a router, the following concepts apply: router ports are serial interfaces, and higher-layer protocols break up files into smaller segments and use sliding windows to control the flow of transmission.

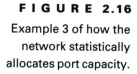

FIGURE 2.16

Example 3 of how the network statistically allocates port capacity.

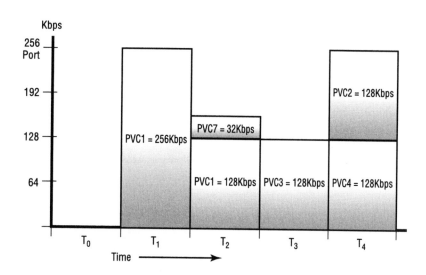

Oversubscription

Chapter 1 points out that most leased-line connections have an average use of 30 percent or less. This means that 70 percent or more of the time an individual dedicated connection is idle—a very inefficient use of bandwidth.

Frame relay services typically let you exploit this intermittent characteristic of data by *oversubscribing* the port connection. You can assign more PVCs and *total* CIR to a port than the port connection's speed. (The CIR of any individual PVC is still limited by the port connection speed on either end.) Consider using oversubscription for ports that support bursty traffic and applications that are used occasionally.

Oversubscription allows more cost-effective network connectivity, which is accomplished in two ways. First, because of oversubscription, you can choose a lower port-connection speed in a frame relay environment than what you would need in a dedicated environment.

Take the example of a headquarters location with 32 remote locations. All remotes need at least one direct connection to the headquarters site at 64Kbps. Using private lines, the primary site would need two DS-1 local loops, one for the first 24 DS-0 connections and one for the remaining eight connections (see Figure 2.17).

F I G U R E   2.17

Private-line configuration at the headquarters site for a star network with 32 remote sites.

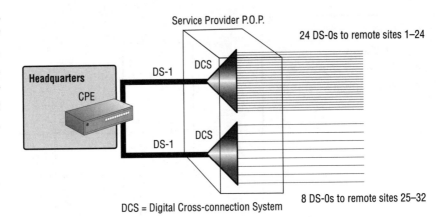

F I G U R E   2.17

Private-line configuration at the headquarters site for a star network with 32 remote sites.

Frame relay oversubscription allows you to purchase a single port connection and a single DS-1 local loop with all 32 remote sites sharing the capacity (see Figure 2.18). In fact, depending upon the likelihood of all the sites sending information into the port connection simultaneously and the size of the port's buffers, you may determine that you don't even need a full DS-1 port connection. Instead, you might need a 1.024Mbps or lower port speed.

F I G U R E   2.18

A frame relay configuration using oversubscription at the headquarters location.

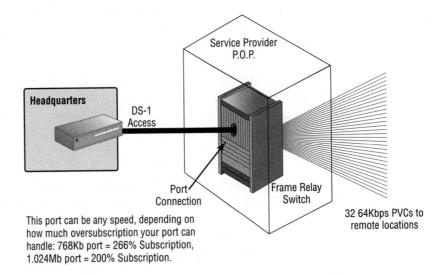

Oversubscription allows you to also save money on local access, ports, and CPE (WAN ports on the router and CSU/DSUs or NTUs). It takes advantage of the statistical multiplexing of frame relay and the ability of the port connection to statistically allocate capacity.

Additionally, oversubscription also allows you to provide direct connectivity to and between remote sites that would probably not cost-justify a connection in a leased-line network.

When combined with statistical bandwidth allocation, oversubscription allows the sharing of port capacity among a larger number of individual network connections than would be possible in a private-line environment. Because PVCs do not take up capacity until the user needs to transfer information, the ability of the port connection to statistically allocate its capacity across a large number of PVCs can result in significant cost savings.

Increasing the amount of direct connectivity between remote locations reduces the congestion at primary and hub locations because less overall traffic goes through those sites. This increases the performance of all the applications on the network.

Oversubscription offers many advantages, but not all situations can benefit from it. Keep in mind that the chances of oversubscription negatively affecting application and network performance increase with higher subscription rates and/or with a higher number of active PVCs at any given time.

High-Speed ATM Backbone

Many frame relay services today do not exclusively use frame relay switches. Some frame relay service providers have deployed cell-based (e.g., ATM) backbones (see Figure 2.19). The network equipment divides up incoming frames into fixed-length cells, switches the cells across the network, and reassembles the cells back into frames at the receiving end. Cell relay enables greater network speed, traffic aggregation, efficiency, as well as other benefits. All conversions from frame to cell and vice versa happens within the service provider's network and are transparent to you.

The term *cell* indicates a fixed-length packet, whereas *frame* depicts variable length. Because the cell has a fixed length, the size is totally predictable. Some functions, such as cell switching, can be done efficiently and quickly. With cell switching, as soon as the network equipment receives enough of a frame to fill up a single cell, it begins the forwarding process to the destination. Cells are relatively small. The well-known ATM cell has 53 octets. The network equipment can quickly process small cells.

F I G U R E 2.19

Using cell-based
switches for providing
frame relay services

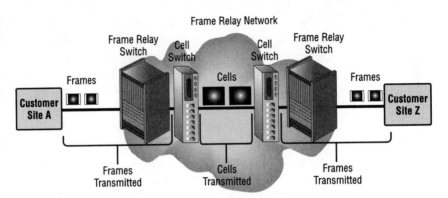

Even though the rest of the frame has not arrived yet, part of the information is already on its way. This increases overall network efficiency because the network fills up capacity in a "tighter" manner than possible if the network has to wait for an entire frame to arrive before forwarding the information.

Overhead is the biggest disadvantage of using cell relay. Overhead represents 10 to 12 percent of each ATM cell. Cell switching introduces a higher percentage of overhead on the backbone network compared to frame switching, where there are 5 bytes of overhead for the entire frame regardless of the frame size.

However, this increase in overhead does not directly affect your applications or your expenses as the service provider is responsible for the efficiency of the backbone network. The service provider may need to allocate more capacity to the network backbone to accommodate the increased overhead.

Congestion Management and Avoidance

As stated previously, a frame relay service uses a shared network among multiple customers. In certain situations, the network hits temporary periods of congestion and not all data can get through. You should have a basic understanding of how the service providers manage their networks and avoid congestion.

Many people get nervous about using frame relay because the network discards their data during periods of congestion. However, understanding congestion management will help minimize your concern, help you better determine the appropriate design of your network, and help you in selecting a service provider.

So let's begin with a description of the congestion management approach designated in the frame relay specifications. This is not the whole answer and only serves as a launching point for further discussion in this book and with your service providers.

The frame relay specifications are simple. If congestion occurs, get rid of it. This means discarding DE frames. These are the frames that are in excess of a PVC's CIR and are marked as DE. This assumes that the service provider has designed the underlying network to support the aggregate CIR and discarding frames in violation of the CIR will bring the network back to stability.

The standards specify several ways for dealing with congestion before it occurs. If the network becomes congested and discards some frames, the user applications recognize that frames have not been received and implement correction procedures. In other words, the frame is retransmitted. It is the responsibility of the higher-level protocols, not frame relay, to retransmit discarded frames.

Everything discussed so far may lead you to believe frame relay network congestion is binary: either it is congested or it is not. But you can have a partially congested network. Regardless of the level of congestion, the frame relay switches have ways to alert you and your CPE of the congested state.

Because frame relay networks are shared networks, a network can reach higher than desired congestion levels but not high enough to warrant dropping all DE packets. The service providers have mechanisms to control congestion in the public network. However, your best bet for complementing these capabilities and controlling the flow of your own applications in response to network congestion is through the flow-control mechanisms provided in your level three and higher functions.

FECN (Forward Explicit Congestion Notification) and BECN (Backward Explicit Congestion Notification) play a role in managing congestion in a frame relay network. The FECN and BECN bits are designed so that the network has a mechanism for communicating the existence and direction of congestion to the CPE. The CPE then notifies the application of this congestion, and the application/traffic source restricts the rate at which it releases information for transmission. The frame relay switch in the network sets the

FECN bit to indicate congestion in the same direction of the received frame. The frame relay switch sets the BECN bit to indicate congestion in the opposite direction of the received frame. Figure 2.20 shows how the network uses the FECN and BECN bits.

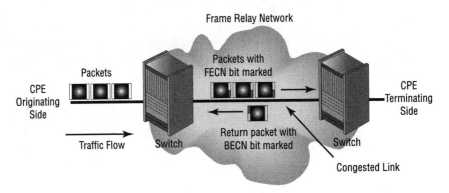

FIGURE 2.20

Setting FECN and BECN bits across the frame relay network.

Although this works great in theory, one big problem occurs in practice. The network takes no action (e.g., dropped packets); it simply alerts the originating and terminating CPE that the link is experiencing congestion. It is now up to your CPE to decide how you want to handle this knowledge.

The CPE can ignore this information and continue to send frames at the speed you normally would, or it can throttle the speed and stop sending frames in excess of your CIR. Even if the equipment can recognize the FECN and BECN bits, a mechanism for communicating this to the traffic source— the user or application—has not been well established. Also, higher-layer protocols do not have standardized procedures for interpreting the FECN and BECN bits to make a change in the window size. See the sidebar "Implicit Flow Control," later in the chapter, for more information on controlling the window size for higher-layer protocols.

Some equipment vendors have established router mechanisms that respond to FECN/BECN messages upon receiving them from the network, at least for certain protocols. If a particular network path is congested, the router can temporarily hold the packets destined for that path, lowering the effective throughput rate. This becomes a prioritization technique for traffic within the router. After being buffered in response to FECN/BECN messages, the packets then released are more likely to be within the CIR;

therefore, the network would not mark them as discard-eligible. It should be noted that the primary flow-control management still stems from the higher-layer protocols.

Some network-backbone equipment uses proprietary algorithms that build upon the congestion-management specifications within the frame relay standards. The algorithms monitor the state of network congestion continuously and adjust the ability of the port connections to statistically allocate excess capacity to PVC bursts (e.g., to let a PVC exceed its CIR). Doing so allows the network to actively avoid a state of congestion.

Frame and cell relay use statistical multiplexing by allowing more aggregate CIR than the available network resources to gain the network efficiencies. Service providers approach shared network designs in this manner because of the Service providers have been using this same approach for designing voice networks for a long time. Most voice customers only notice problems with network capacity on such days as Mother's Day and Christmas. In these cases, network congestion may cause a delay in your voice application or cause an "all circuits are busy" message.

Frame- and cell-relay services work in the same way. Service providers design the backbone network to support all of the CIRs but rely on conservative design parameters to allow for the efficiencies of statistical multiplexing. The service providers benefit from the intermittent nature of data applications, as well, which is one reason why they can afford to offer frame relay services at attractive rates.

Understanding how the network approaches congestion situations will help you figure out how the network handles your data in periods of congestion, such as network reroutes. This can have an impact on some of your decisions when designing the network.

The Role of the CPE

The frame relay CPE formats LAN, SDLC, X.25, TCP/IP or other data packets into frame relay frames. This is usually a router, bridge, multiplexer, concentrator, or FRAD. The following discussions use a router with a frame relay interface.

Implicit Flow Control

The frame relay specification has inherent congestion indicators built in, although not all equipment vendors or higher-layer protocols support these options.

To establish flow control in your frame relay network effectively, your applications should use layer three and higher protocols. Nearly every off-the-shelf protocol, such as TCP/IP, IPX, DECnet, etc., has its own mechanism to control the flow of information over the WAN. These protocols accomplish this step by timing the rate at which acknowledgments to transmitted frames are received and adjusting the window size accordingly.

The window size refers to the number of outstanding frames that can be sent out onto the network before an acknowledgment must be received. With larger windows, the application can send more frames and achieve better throughput. If a higher-layer protocol senses congestion, it decreases the window size, sending fewer frames out at once and waiting for an acknowledgment before more are sent. In this way, the protocol controls the flow of information.

For example, if frames are being acknowledged at a rate during the beginning of a transmission that indicates an effective throughput rate of 128Kbps and then the acknowledgments begin to slow down, the protocol interprets this as congestion on the network. It reacts by reducing the window size.

Frame Formatting

The router reads the destination address from the overhead of the incoming packet to determine where it needs to send the frame. The router encapsulates incoming data-packet frame relay frames by adding the necessary flags, 2-byte header, and 2-byte trailer. It then uses a look-up table to cross-reference this address information to a frame relay DLCI. The correct DLCI number goes into the DLCI address field of the frame header. The network equipment forwards the frame across the appropriate PVC, based on the DLCI, to deliver the information to its destination CPE. Once the frame reaches the destination CPE, the CPE strips off the frame relay format, reads the local-area destination address, and forwards the packet to its ultimate destination. Figure 2.21 shows the role of CPE in frame formatting.

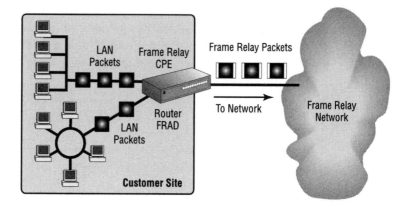

The frame relay equipment in the service provider's network reads the DLCI and places the frame on the correct PVC.

Buffering

Frame relay CPE has a serial interface into the network over a local loop. The equipment can only send information out one bit at a time. The equipment is clocked at the port-connection speed, and it probably does not recognize an underlying CIR on a PVC. The result is that transmissions are typically sent to the port connection at the port speed.

Depending upon the network equipment, the port and PVCs might have buffers that temporarily hold incoming frames that exceed the CIR. Some network platforms implement congestion management schemes that provide feedback to a switch and throttle a PVC's output to the CIR so that DE frames are not allowed to go through the network in a congestion situation where the likelihood of dropped frames increases. The network equipment holds the frames in the buffer until the equipment can send out the frames as non-DE traffic. Other network platforms operate more in keeping with the frame relay standards, in which the network allows violating traffic but drops this traffic during congestion situations.

First Come, First Served Transmissions

When you send simultaneous file transfers across different PVCs that share a single port, the role of the frame relay CPE becomes critical in understanding what happens to your traffic and how the CPE treats it.

If the router receives several files at once, it treats the files on a first come, first served basis, unless you program prioritization guidelines into the router. The CPE handles each transfer independently by sending the first file, then the next, and so on. Because of this serialization, the PVCs out of the port connection are not active all at the same time, even when all applications are sending simultaneously.

Traffic Prioritization

Instead of the simple first come, first served approach to processing incoming data, many routers allow you to set prioritization parameters by incoming port, protocol, and even packet size.

This mechanism allows you to prioritize critical traffic, such as SNA transactions or voice communications, in front of other file transfers. This book covers this topic more in Chapter 9.

Network-to-CPE Communications

The LMI (Local Management Interface) enables communication between your equipment (e.g., the router or other access device) and the service provider's frame relay network.

DLCIs 0 and 1023 are reserved for the LMI, depending on the version of LMI used. The router can use this path to request network status information from the service provider's switch to which it is directly connected.

The initial LMI was developed as a keep-alive signal between the router and the frame relay network. A second generation of LMI called ANSI T1.617 Annex D by ANSI and an LMI called Annex A by ITU-T build upon this framework by adding features that provide information on the health status of the network. The ITU-T and ANSI are two standards bodies that contributed to the development of the frame relay standard.

Routers use the LMI to

- Request the status of active and inactive (or removed) DLCIs.

- Request the status of the local loop connection between the router and the port connection.

- Download network addresses to simplify network configuration.

You should choose premises equipment that supports LMI, and you should enable the functionality within your network. LMI is an important part of implementation. For example, if you enable LMI when you add a new connection, the network automatically notifies the two CPE it connects of the presence of the network connection. When LMI is not enabled, each CPE (and the network switch) must be manually updated.

Putting the Pieces Together

You can see the end result of all these elements and the effect on your traffic and throughput by walking through one file transfer example.

1. User sends a file using the TCP/IP.

2. TCP/IP breaks the file into smaller packets and sends out the first set.

3. The sending router receives the packets, encapsulates the information into a frame relay frame, and sends each out serially over the network to the port connection at the port-connection speed.

4. The port connection places the incoming information onto the correct PVC after reading the address information.

5. If the PVC's CIR is less than the port speed and the incoming frames violate the CIR, one of two things happen:

   - The information is transmitted at the port speed, but some of the frames are marked as discard-eligible.

   - The network signals the port connection that congestion is occurring on the path. Then the frames in excess of CIR are buffered.

6. The destination router acknowledges receipt of the frame, and the acknowledgments are sent back over the network (or if some frames have been discarded, it signals for a retransmission).

7. The protocol calculates the effective throughput of the network based on the time interval of acknowledgements and adjusts the window size accordingly.

Summary

The three main components of a frame relay service are local access, ports, and virtual circuits. The access link connects the CPE to the port on the frame relay network. The port is the port of entry to the frame relay network and defines the maximum amount of information that a location can send to or receive from the network. A single port can support multiple virtual circuits. Virtual circuits provide logical connectivity between two ports (locations). There are two types of virtual circuits: PVCs and SVCs. PVCs are available at all times once the service provider offers the connections. SVCs on the other hand are established on a call-by-call basis and are torn down at the end of each transmission.

Frame relay features and capabilities include automatic rerouting, bursting, statistical bandwidth allocation, oversubscription, high-speed ATM backbone, and congestion avoidance and management.

Frame relay works in the following manner: the sending CPE encapsulates the information into frames. The network receives the frames and forwards the frames over the appropriate virtual connection based on the address information on the frames' headers. At the destination, the receiving CPE strips the frame relay header and delivers the information to the end computing device.

The next chapter discusses in detail the different access alternatives available on frame relay.

CHAPTER

3

Why and When to Use Frame Relay

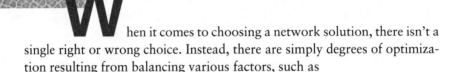

When it comes to choosing a network solution, there isn't a single right or wrong choice. Instead, there are simply degrees of optimization resulting from balancing various factors, such as

- The level of satisfaction with the existing network's performance

- The investment in your current implementation

- The current network ability to meet your present and future needs effectively

- The impact of migration from your existing networking solution to frame relay or another solution

- IT resource and expertise constraints (people)

- The capital budget and your company's financial objectives

This chapter takes a closer look at the benefits of using frame relay and offers some guidelines for determining the most ideal situations for a frame relay implementation.

Is Frame Relay Right for You?

The list below provides some characteristics of networks and companies that may benefit from frame relay. You can use this list to evaluate frame relay the suitability of your networking environment.

- Do you need to connect many sites in a partial- or full-meshed environment?

- Do you have star networks that require more than one DS-1/E-1 local loop at the primary site?

- Do you operate separate and parallel private networks for one or more applications, such as LAN, SNA, and intracompany voice applications?

- Do you have small offices, remote offices, telecommuters, and mobile workers who need access to corporate resources?

- Do you have geographically distributed LANs that need connectivity?

- Do you have mainframes, front-end processors, and cluster controllers?

- Do you use a public X.25 network service today but need higher speeds?

- Do you currently manage a network composed of private lines and intelligent multiplexers?

- Are you unhappy with the response times and performance of the current network implementation?

- Do you need a highly available, highly reliable, and highly secure network to support mission-critical business applications without having to invest in redundant network facilities?

- Do you need the flexibility to rapidly change the network to keep pace with constantly changing business and end-user requirements?

- Do you want to implement new business applications but cannot cost-justify the additional bandwidth?

- Do you have minimal in-house networking expertise and desire to relegate the management of the network to a service provider?

- Do you have a limited networking and capital budget?

Public frame relay services combine some of the best attributes of public and private network architectures. Unlike private lines, a public frame relay network uses virtual connections for connectivity. Virtual connections are defined logically in software rather than hard-wired physically. This means that a connection between two locations does not need a dedicated physical facility in a frame relay network. There is, of course, a physical infrastructure that supports the frame relay network, but the connections between locations are defined logically to traverse over the physical infrastructure. The virtual connections do not consume network capacity until you need to send information.

But like private lines, these virtual connections offer security and reliability with added flexibility and increased network availability. These features allow many end users and applications to share the network connectivity and to achieve performance and throughput equivalent to a private-line solution at a lower cost, or they allow increased throughput while maintaining current cost.

Frame relay services were originally designed to support data applications, although it is possible to run both voice and video over a frame relay network. The PSTN (Public Switched Telephone Network) provides a similar analogy. Although equipment such as analog modems were not designed for data, they could convert a digital data signal into an analog data signal that the PSTN could then use to transmit data. Standards for running voice over frame relay were developed later in frame relay's development.

When evaluating the potential advantages of a frame relay solution for your company, consider both the tactical and strategic benefits you can achieve by using frame relay.

Tactical Benefits of Frame Relay

Tactical benefits include those advantages that interest most data-communications managers or MIS directors. These include decreased network and operating costs, improved performance, higher network availability, increased flexibility, and simplification of the network architecture.

Frame relay services can provide an opportunity to achieve savings in at least four areas: equipment, local access, interconnections, and operating costs.

CPE (Customer Premises Equipment) Savings

With private lines, each connection generally requires its own physical interface on the CPE, such as routers, bridges, integrated access devices, and others. As the number of interconnections increases, the CPE investment grows. Frame relay allows many logical connections or virtual circuits to share a single network interface on the CPE. The frame relay solution requires fewer WAN CPE ports, even when many locations have direct connectivity to each other. It also translates into a reduction in the number of CSU/DSUs (Channel Service Unit/Data Service Units) or NTUs (Network Termination Units) needed.

The reduction in CPE ports and CSU/DSUs or NTUs also reduce the number of single points of failure on the network from end to end. This improves total network reliability.

See Figures 3.1a and 3.1b for a comparison of a private-line and a frame relay implementation.

FIGURE 3.1a

Typical private-line implementation using multiple CPE at each location to connect to other locations

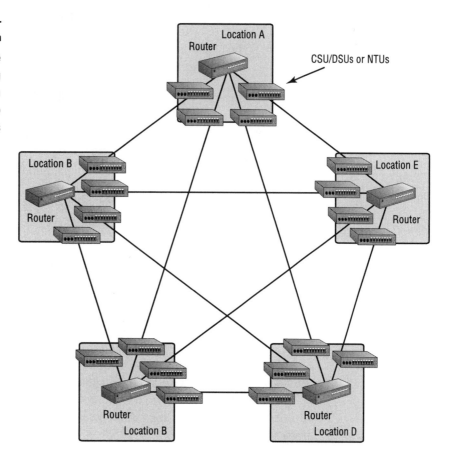

FIGURE 3.1b

Frame relay configuration with a single CPE at each location supporting multiple connections

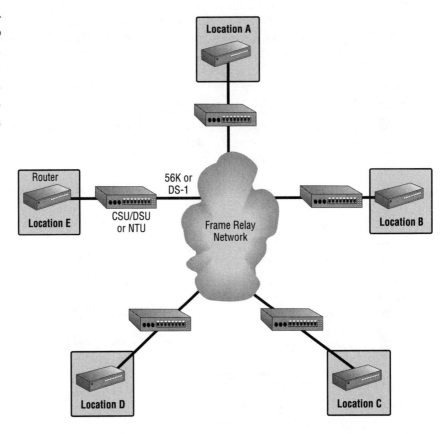

Local-Access Savings

Because many logical connections share the same physical interface into the frame relay network, this often significantly reduces the number of dedicated local loops needed. This applies at both remote locations and at the primary location(s).

At remote locations, you can consolidate separate low-speed private lines into a single frame relay network connection. Even different applications, such as LAN, SNA, and intracompany voice and fax, can share the same connection into the frame relay network. This situation often results in a reduction of two or more dedicated loops down to a single loop. See Figure 3.2a for a remote-site local-access solution using leased lines and Figure 3.2b for a solution using frame relay.

F I G U R E 3.2a

A private-line implementation may require multiple local loops to support different applications at each remote site.

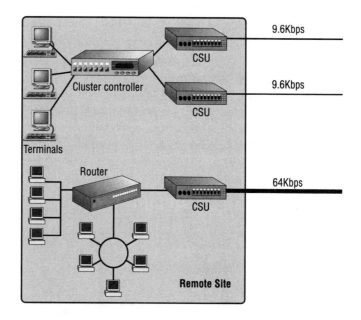

F I G U R E 3.2b

Each remote site only needs one local loop to access frame relay.

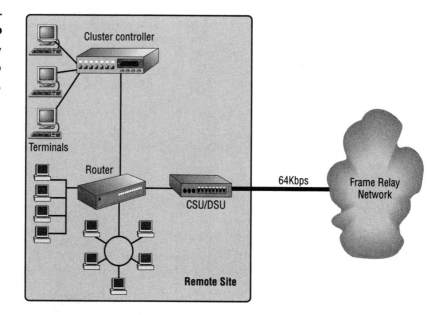

Primary locations typically need a DS-1 local loop for every 24 remote locations in a private-line environment, but it is not uncommon that only 50 percent or less of these remote locations are active at any given time. Frame relay allows you to take advantage of the intermittent nature of many data applications and allows a single DS-1 local loop to support more than 24 remote locations. (This assumes the frame relay service provider allows over-subscription of the port connection, as nearly all providers do. See Chapter 2 for more information on oversubscription.)

Frame relay saves on local access bandwidth and cost through statistical multiplexing of incoming and outgoing frames and results in a more efficient allocation of access bandwidth. See Figure 3.3a for a primary site access solution using leased lines and Figure 3.3b for a solution using frame relay.

FIGURE 3.3a

The local loop at the primary site must have enough capacity to support the dedicated connections to each remote site.

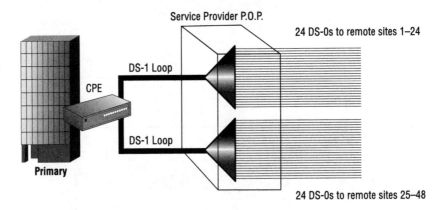

FIGURE 3.3b

The same number of remote sites can be supported with less bandwidth required on the primary site's local loop with frame relay.

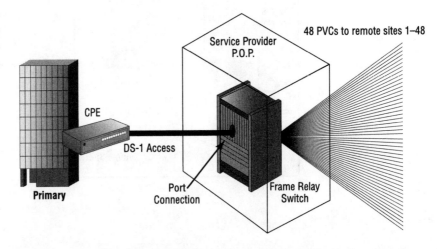

Most service providers initially offered dedicated access to frame relay only. Later enhancements to some services included support for a more comprehensive set of access alternatives. Some access alternatives available today include analog dial-up or modem access; ISDN BRI and PRI (Integrated Services Digital Network Basic Rate Interface and Primary Rate Interface); Switched 56/ 64Kbps; frame relay access (to interexchange frame relay networks); xDSL (Digital Subscriber Line); and even cellular access. Refer to Chapter 4 for more details on the different frame relay access options available.

These access options allow you to choose the most appropriate and most cost-effective access solution on a location-by-location basis. For example, locations that generate lower traffic volumes that normally would not be able to cost-justify dedicated access can now take advantage of frame relay without being forced to buy dedicated local loops.

With the availability of dial-up or switched-access alternatives, frame relay also becomes a viable solution for mobile and semipermanent locations. You can also use dial-up access for disaster-recovery purposes. Chapter 7 covers disaster recovery in greater detail. Some of the dial-up and switched-access alternatives have usage rather than fixed-rate charges. Service providers measure usage based on connect time, time of day, number of packets/frames sent, number of megabytes sent, or other parameters.

Dial-up and switched-access alternatives of pricing structure allow you to pay only for what you use and/or when you use the service.

Network Interconnection Savings

Frame relay can significantly reduce network interconnection (local, regional, national, or global) expenses, as well. These savings can emerge in many different circumstances, depending upon network requirements. Some frame relay services have non-distance-sensitive pricing structures, which means a 100km connection costs the same as a 1000km connection. This option can result in significant savings for geographically dispersed networks. In general, frame relay also offers less expensive, incremental connectivity compared to private lines, hence offering a more cost-effective solution for star, partially meshed, and fully meshed network topologies.

As mentioned in Chapter 2, bursting is defined as frame relay services that allow users to temporarily send data at a rate above the CIR. Bursting translates into transmission savings because you can purchase lower-capacity transmission paths, even though you may occasionally exceed this amount during peak hours. This advantage works well in conjunction with frame relay's ability to allow multiple applications to share the same virtual circuit, reducing the number of dedicated connections required between any two sites. However, don't forget that you need to balance the number of applications and the bandwidth requirements of each application sharing a virtual circuit with the performance parameters required by each application. As the number of applications and as the bandwidth requirements increase, the probability of performance degradation and dropped frames increases.

Most service providers designed their frame relay networks with the ability to automatically reroute traffic around network failures. The inherent self-healing capabilities of public frame relay networks mean you do not have to purchase diverse network connections for the sole purpose of providing an alternate backup path between locations. You can avoid having to purchase redundant private lines used solely to construct ring network configurations for survivability.

Although most service providers have fixed-rate virtual-connection charges, some service providers offer usage-based options. Usage billing is ideal for locations that have low volume and sporadic transmissions. Many companies associate usage-based pricing with SVCs and fixed rates with PVCs. However, a few service providers also offer fixed rate and usage options for SVCs and PVCs, respectively. Most usage plans have minimum and maximum (or cap) charges. The caps protect you from unexpectedly accumulating large network charges. However, keep in mind most service providers typically set the cap charges higher than the fixed-rate charges for the same amount of bandwidth. Therefore, if you have high traffic volumes and fairly dense traffic patterns, some of the fixed-rate options may prove to be more cost effective.

These examples represent only a few of the ways frame relay can help save on recurring network charges for network connections. Other cost-saving features include the ability to specify asymmetrical CIRs on a single virtual circuit so that it more closely matches the underlying traffic patterns.

Reduced Operating Costs

Network architectures are typically simplified with a frame relay network implementation. For example, the ongoing administration and operating costs for managing and maintaining networking facilities naturally decrease as you reduce the number of leased lines and separate and parallel networks. See Figure 3.4a for an implementation using separate and parallel networks and Figure 3.4b for a single frame relay network supporting multiple applications.

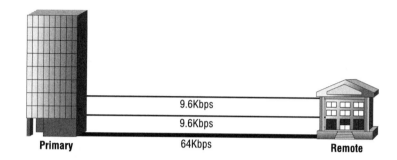

Primary   9.6Kbps   9.6Kbps   64Kbps   Remote

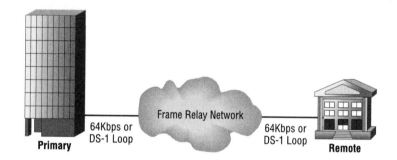

Frame Relay Network

64Kbps or DS-1 Loop   Primary   64Kbps or DS-1 Loop   Remote

Reducing the amount of CPE and equipment ports attached to the WAN also helps to lower operations expenses. Some frame relay services offer the option for packaging the network and the CPE together. These services are sometimes referred to as *managed network services*. These services can minimize or even eliminate your concerns about equipment interoperability, in-house networking expertise, technology obsolescence, and migration strategies. Using a single vendor to provide the complete network solution reduces the number of vendors you have to manage. The service provider is responsible for all coordination with the various equipment vendors and partners involved in providing the service. Chapter 12 provides additional information about managed network services.

With a public frame relay network solution, the service provider assumes the responsibility of operating, managing, and planning for network growth. For example, it becomes the service provider's responsibility to maintain diverse network paths to ensure the network can tap into excess resources in case of a failure. Refer to Figure 3.5a for a redundant leased-line solution and Figure 3.5b for a self-healing solution using frame relay.

FIGURE 3.5a

Private line users need to purchase redundant facilities for backup purposes to improve network availability.

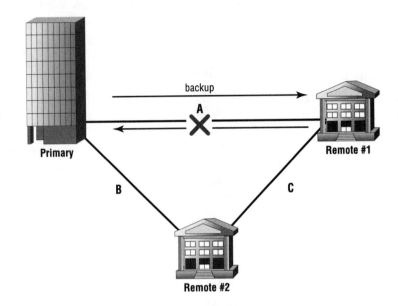

FIGURE 3.5b

Public frame relay services have an inherent automatic rerouting or self-healing capability without requiring the user to buy backup facilities.

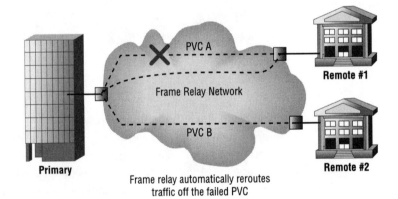

Frame relay automatically reroutes
traffic off the failed PVC

Improved Performance

A frame relay solution can help improve network performance in many different ways. For example, in a traditional, private-line network topology, remote sites may need to communicate directly with each other, and they may do so by tandeming through a primary or headquarters location. Most end users typically build star networks to save money on CPE, access, and network connectivity, but when there is remote-to-remote traffic, star networks can cause network congestion for all users with traffic going to, from, or through the primary site. This situation can result in longer network-response times and application-level delays or even session timeouts. See Figure 3.6a for an example of the traffic pattern between remote sites before the implementation of a frame relay solution.

Frame relay allows you to design more cost-effectively a network with a higher level of *direct* connectivity between remote locations. Each site needs a single port connection to the frame relay network supporting virtual circuits to other locations. You can typically add more virtual circuits at a relatively low cost. See Figure 3.6b for remote-to-remote connectivity with frame relay.

By providing a greater level of direct connectivity between remote locations, frame relay benefits nearly all network users because it reduces network congestion at the primary location (and other network hubs) and improves response times.

FIGURE 3.6a

The primary or hub location becomes the bottleneck from remote-to-remote traffic in private-line, star-network configurations.

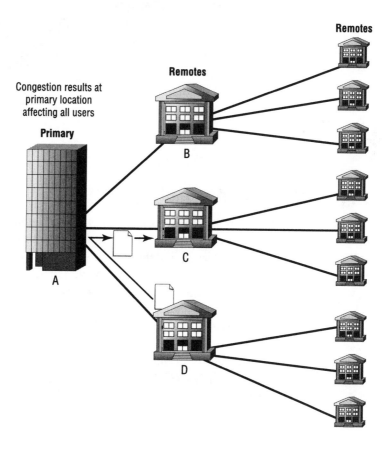

FIGURE 3.6b

Frame relay can pro-
vide more direct con-
nectivity between
remote locations.

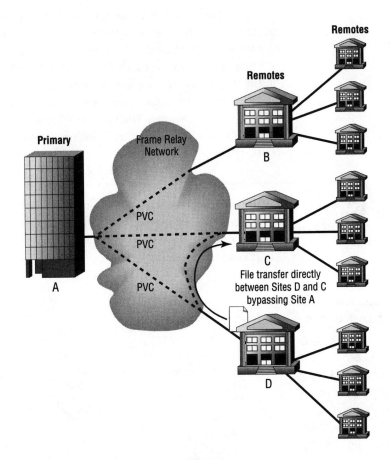

FIGURE 3.6b

Frame relay can pro-
vide more direct con-
nectivity between
remote locations.

Higher Network Availability

Most public frame relay networks have the ability to automatically reroute virtual circuits around a network failure. Depending upon your current network architecture and the amount of redundancy you have already built into the network, frame relay can help you increase your overall network availability. And that means keeping the users happy and business applications up and running.

Many network topologies today consist of multipoint circuits or tandem (or hub) architectures. Companies typically implement these topologies to save money on distance-sensitive private-line costs. Figures 3.7a and b and Figure 3.8 help to illustrate how frame relay can help improve network survivability and result in greater availability.

The problem with the tandem architecture shown in Figure 3.7a becomes clearer when you ask the question: What would happen to site C's and site D's ability to communicate with primary site A in the event of a network failure between sites A and B?

In the network configuration shown in Figure 3.7b, a network failure at site B not only affects site B's ability to communicate with the primary location but also affects communications to and from sites C and D. In this example, a single network failure disrupts communications at three locations.

FIGURE 3.7a

This figure depicts a typical multipoint leased-line circuit.

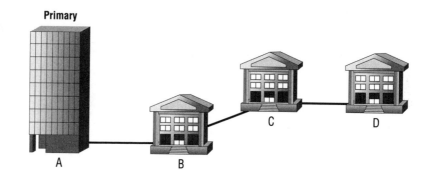

FIGURE 3.7b

Failure at site B affects A-to-B, A-to-C, and A-to-D communications using private lines.

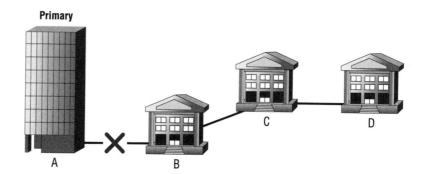

As shown in Figure 3.8, frame relay can provide a greater level of direct connectivity between remote locations cost-effectively. This, combined with frame relay's ability to automatically route around a network failure, can greatly improve network survivability.

A network failure between locations A and B would not affect the ability for locations B and C to communicate with the primary site. Site B would most likely maintain its connectivity with location A as well because the network would automatically route the connection around the failed connection.

F I G U R E 3.8

Failure at site B does not affect communications between A and C or communications between A and D with frame relay.

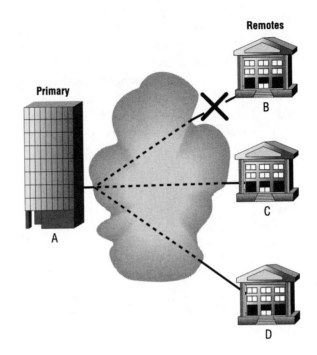

Greater Flexibility

The logical nature of frame relay connections allows you much greater flexibility when reconfiguring the network architecture for changing business requirements, end-user needs, and traffic patterns. Adding new locations, adding new connections, and changing the capacity between existing locations is easier and faster than with traditional private-line networks.

For example, when a new PVC is needed between two locations already on the frame relay network, it typically takes three to five working days to install the new connection (depending on the service provider). Intervals for international services may take longer. Some service providers can provision the new PVC within minutes or hours.

This interval also applies to any changes to existing PVCs, such as modifying the CIR. Some service providers have real-time management tools that let you control the modification of CIRs (bandwidth) on existing PVCs. The change occurs in near real time.

If you are using SVCs, the process is even simpler. Any of your corporate locations that already have access to the frame relay network can communicate with each other. The SVCs are established at the time of transmission, allowing "any-to-any, anytime" communications. Unlike PVCs, SVCs do not need to be predefined hours, days, or weeks ahead of time.

Another simple task is adding a new site to the network. The time it takes to install the local access typically drives the installation interval for the new location. Therefore, you would probably not see any difference in implementation intervals compared to leased lines when connecting a new site to your frame relay network.

However, frame relay allows you to quickly establish connectivity from the new site to existing network locations. You can assign new PVCs between the new site to any of the existing sites without adding new CPE, access lines, and port connections at the existing locations. The service provider simply assigns a new logical connection between the new site and an existing site.

Many businesses find this improved flexibility especially advantageous as businesses move to implement virtual-project workgroup concepts. An example might be the assembly of a cross-functional team designed to conduct research, develop a product, or improve business processes. The members of the virtual-project workgroup change on a project-by-project basis. This may result in changes in connectivity needs.

One early user of frame relay service accomplished a major network reconfiguration in less than a week. The company estimated that the same reconfiguration in its previous leased-line network would have taken approximately four to six months to implement.

Simplification of Network Architecture

Frame relay allows you to consolidate separate applications and separate parallel networks onto a single network infrastructure. This consolidation of applications and circuits results in a simplified network architecture. Depending upon the existing environment and the applications supported, frame relay can also streamline the equipment infrastructure. Simplification has many benefits, including reduced costs, improved reliability and performance, and simplified planning, engineering, and operations processes.

Strategic Benefits of Frame Relay

Y ou can also achieve strategic business advantages using a frame relay solution. These benefits are of primary interest to members of the executive management staff. Some of these benefits include providing your company with a competitive business advantage, introducing products and services to market more quickly, cost-justifying new business applications, improving worker productivity, and increasing profitability.

You can refocus or reallocate much of your time to defining the strategic direction of telecommunications within the corporation. There is a growing trend of companies that want to outsource the day-to-day management of WAN and spend more time evaluating how telecommunications can better support strategic business objectives. Frame relay enables this shift in mindset from an operational to a strategic perspective.

As mentioned previously, service providers offer managed or outsourced solutions for end users who prefer to stay focused on their core business. These solutions typically include some combination of the frame relay network, CPE, equipment configuration and installation, monitoring and maintenance, network management, LAN management, and ongoing network optimization.

As the structure of the organization begins to change in an effort to become more fluid, dynamic, and flexible, it becomes more critical that the network enhance and not hinder this modified business climate. Many organizations, for example, have begun to explore faster and more flexible methods for new product development. Companies use small, quickly assembled, cross-functional teams or ad hoc work groups, with representatives from many departments and even different companies. This approach enables the introduction and launch of new products and services to market more quickly, giving the business a strategic, competitive advantage.

Geographically dispersed team members can put new and unusual strains on the corporate network. Network flexibility, scalability, and connectivity become critical business requirements. Frame relay can support this new organizational structure—helping and not hindering this movement toward greater organizational responsiveness and productivity.

Competitive Business Advantage

There are many ways a frame relay network can improve your company's market position. As with the example in the previous section, your company may choose to design a new product collaboratively by bringing together a single team with representatives from different departments around the country, around the world, or from different companies. This approach can speed up development time and introduce products and services to market more quickly. The corporate network—the vehicle for communications and information flow between team members—then becomes an integral part of the development-and-launch process.

You may use the network to provide salespeople, field engineers, and other customer-support people with better and more advanced business and competitive tools. This can increase your ability to penetrate new accounts and improve customer retention.

New Business Applications

Many new business applications within an organization are often key ingredients to greater productivity, better quality work, improved worker relations, etc. However, some companies may not implement these applications due to high costs associated with the network that supports these applications.

Frame relay typically allows you to add incremental network capacity more cost effectively than in a leased-line environment, often making it easier to justify the implementation of these new ideas and applications.

For example, an engineering consulting firm that implemented a frame relay network found that the quality of its proposals improved significantly when the company used the network for collaboration between the experts at the headquarters and in other offices. The company directly attributed a 15 percent increase in the firm's proposal success ratio to the vast improvements of the proposals generated. Network capacity, connectivity, and budget constraints had prohibited the company to adopt this application with its previous private line–based network.

Improved Productivity

Again, the way improved worker productivity manifests itself is a function of your business environment. By increasing the level of direct connectivity between locations within the network and increasing capacity through statistical bandwidth allocation, you can achieve better network response times with a frame relay network.

One manufacturing company that migrated a pure SNA network using private lines to a frame relay network found that average response times per screen dropped 12 to 15 seconds to 0.4 seconds. The company estimated that this contributed to a 4 to 6 percent productivity improvement in its field offices. Because these offices were responsible for customer support functions, the company believed that customer satisfaction increased, as well.

The consulting firm mentioned previously also achieved an unexpected benefit in increased worker productivity. Before the implementation of frame relay, the firm's workloads were unevenly distributed across the country. In any given week, one office might be overburdened with work and new proposals, while another office might have a much lighter workload. The frame relay network enables the company to more evenly distribute work to experts across the country, thus allowing the company to secure a greater level of work from its employees and improve overall productivity.

Increased Profits

One of the most important objectives for any executive officer is to increase corporate profits. Although a president or CEO may not get very excited about local-access consolidation or increased direct connectivity, he or she can understand the bottom-line impacts of reduced expenditures, lower operating costs, and greater worker productivity. The benefits of a frame relay network often have a direct impact on the company's bottom-line.

Public vs. Private Frame Relay Implementations

The decision to implement a private, public, or hybrid private-public network depends on several factors as each of the options has its own pros and cons. In this discussion, a private network does not necessarily refer to just a frame relay implementation. The private network can use other technologies, such as private lines, X.25, ATM, IP, etc. The public- or private-implementation decision may not be as obvious or as simple for some companies because the trade-offs of one do not overwhelm the other. In fact, the hybrid solution often makes the most sense. The following are examples of situations where you may need to carefully weigh the trade-offs before making a final decision.

Cost Savings and Performance

A virtual solution using a public frame relay service might offer increased availability, improved flexibility, and long-term cost savings. However, if you already have a sizable investment in private-line equipment and training and you are satisfied with the network performance, you should consider the cost break-even point and the overall performance improvement you can achieve with frame relay.

Assume your analysis shows a break even within six months, a 10 percent monthly network cost savings, and a 5 percent improvement in overall productivity due to decreased application response time. Keep in mind that although frame relay may offer these benefits, the level of cost savings and performance improvement may not justify the time and resource investment as well as downtime risks during the migration. However, as your business and networking needs change, conduct regular analysis to determine whether cost savings and performance levels have shifted to justify migration to a public frame relay service.

Network Control

As mentioned previously, the service provider invests in the frame relay equipment and in the diverse interswitch trunks (i.e., facilities between frame relay switches) with public frame relay services instead of you having to buy intelligent time division or statistical multiplexers and redundant leased lines. The service provider passes on many of the inherent features and advantages of these sophisticated frame relay networks to you without you having to make the investment directly. However, this environment also means you lose some direct control over your network because you have to work with the service provider to make any networking modifications. This can also result in decreased responsiveness to your end users. Depending on your situation, this may not be acceptable for your network or for some locations in your network, or this could free your resources to concentrate on core business issues.

Hybrid Solution

You may find that some of your locations or applications exhibit characteristics ideal for private lines, whereas other locations may lead you to choose a public data solution. In these cases, you should consider having both types of implementations in the same network. Choose the solution that works best at each site.

As an example, one large computer manufacturer uses a private-line network between its five largest sites and then uses a public frame relay network service for connectivity to all other remote locations. In this example, the company happens to use a multiplexer that has frame relay inputs as well as standard voice and data interfaces. However, not all hybrid implementations require this type of equipment.

Another company, a major multinational software developer, uses a similar hybrid network configuration and uses standard time-division multiplexers to support international connectivity and leased lines between primary and backup host sites. The company uses frame relay services everywhere else.

Mixing and matching different services within the network allows you to provide each location with the service that best meets the users' and applications' needs at each site. Frame relay is not the Holy Grail of networking. It is, instead, an attractive networking alternative that, when applied correctly, can reduce the total cost of ownership and improve network performance.

Comparing Frame Relay to the Alternatives

Service providers originally positioned frame relay as an alternative to traditional private line networks and X.25 packet-switched networks. Frame relay provides the best attributes of each, combining the security, efficiency, and quality of private lines with the flexibility, statistical bandwidth allocation, and any-to-any connectivity of X.25. Figure 3.9 below summarizes the benefits of frame relay compared to private lines and X.25.

Most discussions in this book use private lines and X.25 as a reference for comparison and for evaluation of competing services as a large number of companies around the world use these traditional services. However, this book will discuss newer and emerging services, such as ATM, IP-based services, and VPNs (Virtual Private Networks). Consider these emerging services when evaluating other alternatives to frame relay and/or migration strategies.

Table 3.1 provides an overview of the different WAN services in the following areas: pricing structure, available speed, type of traffic supported, geographic availability of the service, method for creating connections, and typical network topology. This table should help you determine how the different services compare with each other and the situations where one may be better suited than another.

F I G U R E 3.9

Benefits of Frame
Relay Compared to
Private Lines and X.25

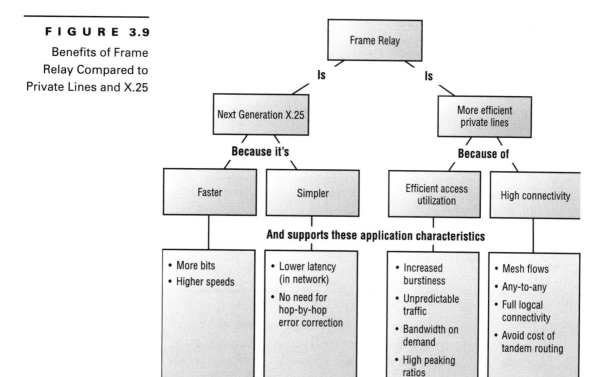

F I G U R E 3.9

Benefits of Frame Relay Compared to Private Lines and X.25

T A B L E 3.1: Comparison of Different WAN Services

	X.25	SMDS	Frame Relay	ATM	IP	Private Line
Typical Price Structure	Usage	Flat Fee	Flat Fee or Usage	Flat Fee or Usage	Flat Fee or Usage	Flat (May Be Distance Sensitive)
Speed	9.6Kb–2.048Mb	56Kb–34Mb	56Kb–45Mb	1.5Mb–622Mb	2.4Kb–622Mb	56Kb–622Mb
Traffic Type	Data	Data	Data, On-net Voice, and Video	Data, Voice, and Video	Data, Voice, and Video	Data, Voice, and Video

T A B L E 3.1: Comparison of Different WAN Services *(Continued)*

	X.25	SMDS	Frame Relay	ATM	IP	Private Line
Availability	Worldwide	Very Limited	Widely Available in North America; Limited Elsewhere	Available in North America and in Select Industrialized Regions	Widely Available	Worldwide
Path Selection	Connection-oriented	Connection-less	Connection-oriented	Connection-oriented	Connection-less	Connection-oriented
Typical Topology	Star	Any-to-Any	Full Mesh, Partial Mesh, and Star	Full Mesh, Partial Mesh, and Star	Any-to-Any	Point-to-Point, Multipoint, Multidrop, and Star

Although these services may compete with each other in some instances, they may be complementary in other circumstances. In situations when two or more services complement each other, you can use these services together in a single network. You can use the most appropriate service on a location-by-location basis.

Connection-Oriented Versus Connectionless

A connection-oriented service requires a predefined connection between communicating locations before transmission of information. Although frame relay does not consume any network resources unless there's information to send, it still requires a predefined, logical path before you can transmit information. Therefore, frame relay is a connection-oriented service. On the other hand, connectionless services do not have predetermined paths across the network. Each information packet finds its own way through the network; the path taken by the information may vary in different instances in time between the same two locations. IP-based services and SMDS (Switched Multimegabit Data Service) are examples of connectionless services. In the case of IP, routers in the network forward the information.

If you decide to pursue further examination of a frame relay solution for all or part of your network, you need to gather information about and/or better understand the following issues:

- The company's business and financial objectives

- The current and future business functions and applications

- The current network configuration, topology, network size, and equipment implementations

- The frequency and number of network moves, adds, and changes

- Traffic patterns, distribution, and densities

- The internal networking resources and expertise

- The networking budget

This information will be critical in evaluating whether frame relay offers the best solution for you. The rest of this book aims to give you the right tools to evaluate frame relay, design a network, and implement the solution effectively.

Summary

Frame relay is best suited for networks that need connectivity between multiple locations in a partial- or full-meshed configuration, support multiple applications, need improvement in network performance, need higher speed connections, and need higher network availability.

Frame relay offers many tactical and strategic benefits. Tactical benefits include those advantages that interest most datacom managers or MIS directors. These include decreased network and operating costs, improved performance, higher network availability, increased flexibility, and simplification of the network architecture.

You can also achieve strategic business advantages using a frame relay solution. These benefits are of primary interest to members of the executive management staff. Some of these benefits include providing your company with a competitive business advantage, introducing products and services to market more quickly, cost-justifying new business applications, improving worker productivity, and increasing profitability.

When deciding whether to implement a private or public frame relay solution, consider the trade-offs in cost saving, performance, and level of network control. Remember, you can have a hybrid private-public solution in which you implement the most appropriate option depending on the location's requirements.

Frame relay is not the only networking solution. Consider and evaluate alternative services, such as private lines, X.25, ATM, IP, and SMDS. Although these services may compete with each other in some instances, they may be complementary in other circumstances. In situations when two or more services complement each other, you can use these services together in a single network. You can use the most appropriate service on a location-by-location basis.

CHAPTER

4

Connecting to the Network

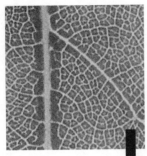

In the early days of frame relay, service providers offered dedicated access only. This limited the use of frame relay to locations that could cost-justify dedicated local loops with large traffic volumes or those companies who expected an increase in traffic volumes. Moreover, frame relay did not address the needs of mobile workers. Although frame relay can address the needs of almost any location that has data applications, it only offered a viable solution for static corporate locations because of the limited number of choices in access alternatives at that time. Therefore, it was not unusual to find less optimal, but more cost-effective, hybrid networks. Companies used frame relay for the larger sites and/or static sites and other technologies for the smaller locations and/or mobile users.

As frame relay matured, service providers introduced more access alternatives to address other user needs and demands. This allows you to build larger and homogeneous frame relay networks. With the variety of access methods available, you can use frame relay for large and small locations, static and mobile locations, as well as primary and backup locations.

Access Options

Because frame relay services do not address the full spectrum of users' access requirements, much of the service providers' product development efforts in the last few years have focused on providing a comprehensive set of access alternatives. Multiple access options allow you to choose the most appropriate access method on a location-by-location basis. All or most of your corporate locations can then achieve the benefits of connectivity over a single frame relay network.

The access alternatives covered in this chapter include dedicated, dial-up, and frame relay gateway access.

Dedicated Access

With dedicated access, you can choose DS-0, channelized (can be segregated into 24 DS-0) DS-1, integrated, nonchannelized (a single high-speed transmission stream) DS-1, N × DS-1 (i.e., multiple DS-1s with N representing the number of DS-1s), DS-3, fiber, and DSL (Digital Subscriber Line) access to the frame relay network. Most service providers typically price the local access based on the distance from your premises to the service provider's nearest CO (Central Office) or POP (Point of Presence). A few service providers offer flat-rate access regardless of distance in areas where they own the local-access facilities. Previous chapters discussed frame relay's ability to automatically reroute around network failures. However, this ability does not necessarily mean that your data is safe from network failures once it leaves your premises. Unfortunately, automatic rerouting works only for facilities between two frame relay switches and only if the service provider has at least two geographically diverse paths out of its frame relay switches. The service provider also needs to have enough excess bandwidth to accommodate all rerouted traffic. Therefore, the self-healing capabilities of frame relay do not cover the dedicated local loop.

Backhaul is also vulnerable to network failures. Assuming that the CO or POP nearest your premises does not have a switch, backhaul is the facility from that CO or POP to a frame relay–capable CO or POP. Keep in mind that not all COs and POPs have frame relay switches, including the one closest to your premises.

For highly mission-critical applications with very low tolerance for failures, consider a back-up or diversity plan for the dedicated access. The succeeding sections discuss these dedicated access alternatives in more detail.

DS-0 Access

The most popular port connection speed in terms of number of units sold is 56/64Kbps. 56/64Kbps ports represent 60 to 70 percent of all public frame relay ports in the world today. The most common way to access this port connection is through a dedicated DS-0 circuit.

There is only one downside to this approach. If you should ever need to increase the port connection speed beyond 56/64Kbps, you need to disconnect the DS-0 local loop and order a higher-speed access connection, such as a DS-1 or E-1. In some areas, you can also order fractional DS-1 or E-1 access. If you are using a stand-alone CSU/DSU (or NTU), you will most likely need a new CSU/DSU (or NTU), as well. You would then need a DS-1/E-1 or fractional DS-1/E-1 CSU/DSU (or NTU) rather than a 56/64Kbps CSU/DSU (or NTU).

You lose some of the advantage of rapid scalability and flexibility. Depending on the service provider, you might not have to buy a new CSU/DSU (or NTU) because the service automatically includes the appropriate type of terminating equipment.

However, if you think a 56/64Kbps port with a 56/64Kbps local loop can adequately serve a particular location for at least six months, you may want to start with a DS-0 local loop. The savings gained from starting with this configuration are probably well worth the hassles of upgrading the circuit should this become necessary.

In the U.S., the typical pricing range between DS-0 local loops and DS-1 local loops is two or three DS-0s. *Crossover* represents the number of DS-0s that would have a price equivalent to the price of one DS-1, making it more cost effective to buy a DS-1 local loop. The crossover increases as the distance increases for distance-sensitive, local-access pricing structures. This means that if you need a number of DS-0s beyond the crossover point into a given location, upgrading to a channelized or nonchannelized DS-1 loop may save you money.

Channelized DS-1/E-1 Local Access

Channelized refers to the process of breaking a DS-1/E-1 circuit into 24 DS-0/30 DS-0 channels, with each operating at 64Kbps. A channel bank, fractional CSU/DSU (or NTU), or multiplexer performs this channelization function at your location. On the service-provider side of the channelized connection, the circuit goes through a channel bank or DCS (Digital Cross-connect System) before connecting to the frame relay network. A DCS maps low-speed channels of a high-speed channelized connection to low-speed channels on another high-speed channelized connection.

 A channel bank refers to equipment used to break down a DS-1 into multiple DS-0s.

In the U.S., DS-1 local loops can support sub-DS-1 (i.e., less than 1.5 Mbps) frame relay port connections. The service provider sets up only the appropriate number of DS-0 channels required to support the sub-DS-1 port connection. For example, a 128Kbps port only uses two of the 24 DS-0 channels available on the channelized local loop, 192Kbps uses three, 256Kbps uses four, and so on. With a channelized DS-1, you can more flexibly increase or decrease the port connection without installing new access facilities or CPE. As you add more applications and as your traffic volume increases, your appreciation of this flexibility will increase, too. For example, you may want to increase your port connection to support on-net or intracompany voice and fax, in addition to your data applications.

Some service providers offer fractional DS-1/E-1 local access to provide access speeds between 64Kbps and 1.5/2Mbps. These services typically cost less than buying full DS-1/E-1 local access. However, fractional services are not available in all regions of the world.

Integrated Access

Many companies limit their initial expenses with frame relay by making use of unused channels on existing DS-1/E-1 local loops. In fact, one of the advantages of using channelized local access is the ability to share loop capacity between different services, such as frame relay, traditional private lines, Internet access, and the PSTN (Public Switched Telephone Network). Most service providers call this *integrated access*.

Integrated access is a function of both your CSU/DSU (or NTU) or multiplexer and equipment in the service provider's POP. Many CSU/DSUs (or NTUs) today offer the capability to support a DS-1/E-1-1 WAN port and two or more V.35 ports on the end-user side. This means you can achieve an integrated-access solution without having to invest in a multiplexer because each V.35 can support a particular application. A multiplexer is more expensive, but it allows you to have a greater degree of flexibility in allocating the 24 or 30 DS-0 channels to different applications because it has more end-user ports available.

By using integrated access, you can economize on loop costs. You can use a single local loop at each location to access the service provider's frame relay network, private-line network, IP network, and the PSTN simultaneously. The service provider terminates the loop into a channelization device, such as a DCS. The DCS allows the service provider to partition groups of DS-0s and direct them to the appropriate service platform. Figure 4.1 shows a sample integrated-access solution.

Using integrated access requires careful planning. For example, some applications may require contiguous slotting of the DS-0s to work optimally. *Contiguous slotting* refers to placing individual DS-0 circuits in contiguous or adjacent channels. Contiguous slotting limits the delay variation between information arriving across different DS-0s. An application requiring 256Kbps, for example, needs four DS-0 circuits (4×64Kbps = 256Kbps).

FIGURE 4.1

Integrated access allows you to put multiple services over a single access link.

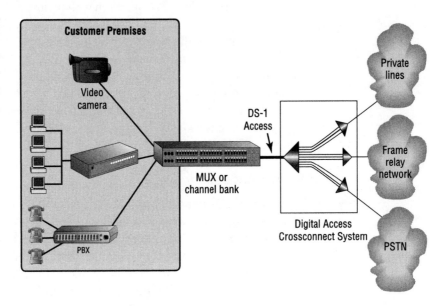

Using adjacent DS-0 time slots, such as channels 5, 6, 7, and 8, can reduce delay variation, as opposed to using channels 5, 9, 14, and 24. Some service providers recommend contiguous slotting for the DS-0s supporting the frame relay port connection.

In this situation, you need to think about future network growth trends and perhaps plan for the expansion of contiguous channels for one or more applications. In doing so, your initial DS-0 slotting on the DS-1 might look like Figure 4.2.

In this situation, your loop will be underused until the predicted growth occurs. Then, when an application requires higher capacity, you can easily and quickly add bandwidth without a major reengineering effort.

Contiguous slotting of DS-0s and planning for this network growth require coordination with your service provider(s). To help prepare, you should acquire a circuit layout record to verify that the slotting meets your requirements prior to actual service installation. Developing this setup will keep your future application- and growth-related problems to a minimum.

Before the introduction of voice-over frame relay CPE, companies generally used integrated access to support intracompany data over frame relay and intracompany voice over a separate but parallel network, such as private lines for tie lines (dedicated connection between two PBXs or key systems) or

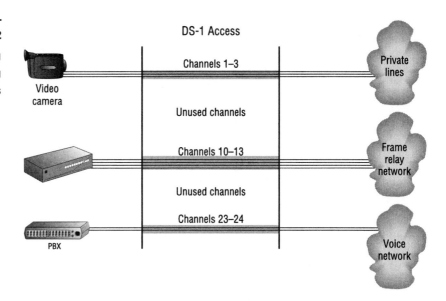

FIGURE 4.2

Contiguous slotting and growth planning on local loops

DS-1 Access

Channels 1–3

Private lines

Video camera

Unused channels

Channels 10–13

Frame relay network

Unused channels

Channels 23–24

PBX

Voice network

the PSTN. Because frame relay CPE is capable of supporting voice and data, you can combine both voice and data traffic over the frame relay network. All voice and data intracompany applications can now ride the same frame relay network, eliminating the need for integrated access for voice and data delivery over separate networks. However, you should consider integrated access for applications that originate from a location connected to the frame relay network but do not terminate on a location on the same frame relay network (or vice versa). You should also consider integrated access if quality, cost, or other business considerations support the need for different networks.

Integrating several applications onto the same local-access facility has its advantages and disadvantages. Consider both sides carefully for each location before making your decision.

The positive aspect is obviously the cost savings you can achieve with this approach. Sometimes cost becomes the overriding decision factor, especially for less critical remote sites.

On the negative side, integrated access increases vulnerability to failure of multiple applications at the same time. With all your eggs in one "access" basket, the location becomes vulnerable to a single access failure that affects all the communications to and from that location.

Nonchannelized DS-1/E-1 Local Access

Nonchannelized DS-1/E-1 loops are typically used for 1.536Mbps/2.048Mbps port connections. With a nonchannelized DS-1/E-1 loop, the entire local loop supports a single application or multiple intracompany applications on the frame relay network.

NxDS-1 Access

As end users became more comfortable with the technology of frame relay, the traffic volumes, number of end users, and number of applications on frame relay networks increased, as well. This resulted in larger frame relay networks and port connections. Although most remote locations only need 64Kbps ports, the headquarters office typically requires fractional DS-1/E-1 or DS-1/E-1 ports, particularly in large star networks. In large star networks, the headquarters site has to support all remote-to-headquarters traffic as well as tandem traffic created by remote-to-remote communications. This means that for some companies, the headquarters site can easily outgrow a DS-1/E-1 port.

Another situation requiring a very large port might be the need for headquarters connectivity to a secondary host site, in addition to the remote-site connections. The connection to the secondary host site might be required to download large amounts of back-up information. The secondary host site basically mirrors all functions and information at the headquarters. This ensures that the remotes are not isolated if a catastrophic failure occurs at the headquarters.

Headquarters locations aren't the only ones that need high-speed connections, however. Regional and branch locations that share large files in a peer-to-peer environment may require very high-speed ports, as well.

When a location outgrows a DS-1/E-1 port, you can subscribe to multiple DS-1/E-1 ports using multiple DS-1/E-1 local loops. Alternatively, you can take advantage of high-speed frame relay ports (higher than 1.5Mbps) using multiple DS-1s/E-1s, fractional DS-3/E-3, or DS-3/E-3 access.

NOTE Subscribing to multiple DS-1/E-1 frame relay ports for a particular location means that you need multiple DS-1/E-1 local loops and CPE (typically a router or FRAD) with multiple WAN ports (one for each of the terminating DS-1/E-1 loops). To decrease the load on the original DS-1/E-1 port and to even out the traffic load distribution, the service provider may need to reterminate or reassign some of the virtual circuits on the new DS-1/E-1 port(s). Reterminations typically require reconfiguration of the CPE routing tables.

Because local access is the segment of the network most vulnerable to failures, you may want to consider ordering geographically diverse DS-1/E-1 local loops and DS-1/E-1 ports terminating in different switches. Geographic diversity means that the service provider sets up the DS-1s/E-1s over different physical and electronic facilities, which decreases the likelihood of a single failure affecting all DS-1/E-1 connections at a location. The service provider may or may not charge extra for geographic diversity. If you can't afford the cost of geographically diverse facilities, ask about electronic diversity. With electronic diversity, the service provider sets up the local loops over separate electronics or equipment but over the same physical path. Check with your service provider about the diversity options available and associated charges.

Some service providers offer ports, more commonly referred to as *high-speed frame relay* service. NxDS-1/E-1 is similar to having multiple DS-1/E-1 ports on the access segment; the difference is in the terminations at your premises and at the service provider's POP. The DS-1/E-1 local loops terminate at a single high-speed port on the frame relay switch at the service provider's POP and at a single high-speed port on the router at your premises.

How are multiple DS-1s/E-1s terminated on a single port at both sides of the local loops? Actually, the DS-1s/E-1s terminate on an IMUX (Inverse MUltipleXer) before delivery of traffic to the frame relay switch at the POP and the high-speed port on the router. In the U.S., most NxDS-1 IMUXs can typically support up to eight DS-1 inputs from the WAN. On the backside of the IMUX is a high-speed interface, such as a V.35 or HSSI (High Speed Serial Interface). The service provider configures the interface to run at the aggregate speed of all the DS-1 inputs. For example, the IMUX inverse multiplexes two DS-1s into a single 3Mbps port, three DS-1s into 4.5Mbps, four DS-1s into 6Mbps, and so on. The high-speed interface on the back of the IMUX connects to the high-speed interface on the frame relay switch and the router. A frame relay implementation using N × DS-1 access is shown in Figure 4.3.

FIGURE 4.3

NxDS-1 access to frame relay fills the gap between DS-1s and DS-3s.

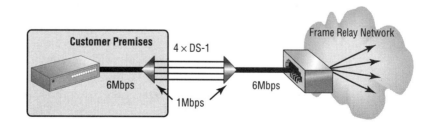

Unlike having multiple DS-1/E-1 frame relay ports, you do not have to provision the virtual circuits on specific DS-1/E-1 ports with corresponding DS-1/E-1 local loops. All virtual circuits go over the single high-speed port.

You can also have diverse DS-1/E-1 local loops for this high-speed solution. Although diversity may cause some DS-1s/E-1s to take a longer path than the other DS-1s/E-1s on the same IMUX, IMUXs can synchronize within a differential delay range. Some can tolerate differential delays equal to the time it takes for information to travel halfway around the world or longer. With most IMUXs, if one of the DS-1s/E-1s fails, the high-speed interface throttles down to a speed equal to the aggregate speed of the remaining DS-1s/E-1s. The IMUX throttles back up to full speed once the failed DS-1/E-1 becomes active again.

When evaluating the cost-effectiveness of multiple DS-1 ports versus a single high-speed port, consider the cost of the frame relay ports and the cost of the inverse multiplexers (if not included as part of some frame relay component charge). As of the writing of this book, the Frame Relay Forum is working actively to complete an implementation agreement for MLFR (Multi-Link Frame Relay). MLFR is a software-based inverse multiplexing solution. It can support not only N × DS-1/E-1 but also N × 56/64Kbps. With MLFR, the inverse multiplexing function will reside with the frame relay switch at the POP and within the CPE (CSU/DSU, NTU, router, FRAD, etc.), eliminating the need for external inverse multiplexers at the POP and at your premises. The typical pricing crossover range between DS-1 local loops and DS-3 local loops is 10 to 12 in the U.S. If you need bandwidth beyond the pricing crossover point, consider buying a DS-3 local loop.

Fractional DS-3s/E-3s offer another alternative to N × DS-1/E-1 and MLFR where the service provider provides a single access link with speed options between DS-1/E-1 and DS-3/E-3. However, similar to fractional DS-1/E-1 services, these fractional DS-3/E-3 services are not as common, and it's best to check with your service provider.

DS-3/E-3 Access

In the U.S., you can subscribe to a high-speed frame relay service using a DS-3 local loop if you need speeds greater than 12Mbps (the top speed supported by an inverse multiplexed solution with eight DS-1s). While the DS-3 local loop can run up to 45Mbps, the service provider configures the frame relay port at speeds less than 45Mbps. Evaluating which is cheaper, a DS-3 access or inverse multiplexed N × DS-1 access, depends not only on the local access pricing crossover points but also on the types of CPE required. With DS-3 access, you need a DS-3 CSU/DSU and a high-speed interface on your router or FRAD.

Fiber Access

Some access solutions involve metropolitan fiber rings. These networks offer fiber into and out of select buildings—usually in the business districts of cities—with geographically diverse points of entry and exit as shown in Figure 4.4.

F I G U R E 4.4

Metropolitan fiber rings have geographically diverse points of entry.

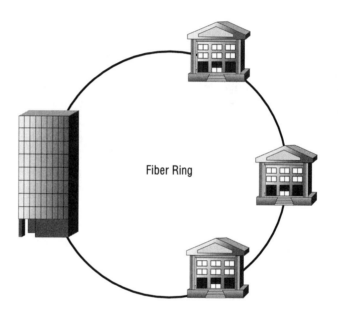

Fiber Ring

The services available on these rings vary by service provider but often include speeds as low as 1.5Mbps up to 45Mbps. You can expect higher speeds as frame relay switch vendors integrate OC-3 (155Mbps) and OC-12 (622Mbps) ports on the switches.

There are several advantages to this type of access. The fiber facility offers higher quality. Service providers using SONET (Synchronous Optical NET-work) rings can recover from fiber cuts with subsecond response times, offering higher network availability. Scaling up in speed is also easier. Once the connection is in place, providing your application with more capacity is usually a logical assignment, not a physical one. This speeds up installation intervals for incremental capacity additions.

Digital Subscriber Line

DSL is a relatively new technology that can support high-speed transmissions over existing copper facilities. There are different flavors of DSL, and the industry generically refers to the different flavors as xDSL, using x as a placeholder. The different types of DSL vary in speed, upstream and downstream transmission speeds, and distance limitation. *Upstream* refers to the transmissions from the end user to the service provider, whereas *downstream* refers to the transmission in the other direction. Because DSL takes advantage of existing copper wires, it allows service providers to offer high-speed services at cheaper rates.

Only a few service providers currently offer frame relay services using DSL access, but the number continues to grow. The most common DSL types used include Asymmetrical Digital Subscriber Line (ADSL), Symmetric Digital Subscriber Line (SDSL), and High Speed Digital Subscriber Lines (HDSL). ADSL supports up to 8Mbps downstream and 1Mbps upstream. SDSL and HDSL provide 1.5Mbps in both directions.

Some service providers make the underlying access technology transparent to the end users. Therefore, you may not know or realize that you may be running 1.5Mbps over DSL. This situation makes it simpler for you because you don't need to worry about the technicalities and various underpinnings of DSL.

Dial-Up Access

With the introduction of dial-up access, locations that generate lower traffic volumes and occasional transmissions can now have cost-effective access to a frame relay network without having to subscribe to expensive dedicated local loops. Additionally, telecommuters or workers who need access to corporate resources after office hours can dial in to send and receive information. Dial-up access solutions are also ideal for mobile workers or traveling salespeople who need connectivity to the corporate LAN.

Dial-up access to frame relay allows you to relegate part of the management of a remote LAN-access solution to the service provider. Although you may have to make decisions on some network design parameters, such as the number of users-to-modem port ratios, you do not need to manage access servers, modem banks, authentication servers, and security servers to support a remote LAN-access solution. The service provider is responsible for all WAN equipment and software features that will ensure that connectivity is provided only to authorized users. Of course, you have the option to implement your own dial-up solution to a public frame relay network if you have the resources, expertise, and budget to do so and/or want to have more direct control of your dial-up solution.

Analog Access

Analog dial-up access means that an analog modem on your PC, laptop, or terminal dials in to establish a connection between you and the network prior to transmission. It uses the PSTN as access to the frame relay network. Service providers use a variety of network implementations to support analog dial-up access. Each implementation has its own pros and cons. However, rather than concentrating on the strengths and weaknesses of the implementations, let's discuss some of the most important selection criteria when evaluating analog-access services.

Available Access Speeds   Make sure that the service provider can support an access speed equal to the highest (and lowest) modem speed used for your remote PCs/terminals and laptops. Your modems need to synchronize with the service provider's modems. The modems synchronize to the lower of the two modem speeds. Most service providers can provide access up to 28.8Kbps (V.34 standard); some go up to 33.6Kbps and 56Kbps.

You can increase the effective throughput achieved over the network by using compression schemes. For example, V.42 bis is a compression standard that can yield up to 115.2Kbps on a 28.8Kbps modem. V.42 bis modems are more expensive than regular modems that do not support compression.

Supported Protocols   The most common protocol supported by service providers is IP. Some service providers also support IPX. If you are running IP, you need PPP (Point-to-Point Protocol) or SLIP (Serial Line Internet Protocol) on your PC or laptop. PPP is a protocol that allows a computer to transmit TCP/IP or IPX information with a standard telephone line and a high-speed modem. SLIP is the predecessor of PPP but is still in use today.

Other protocols, such as AppleTalk and SNA, can be supported by encapsulating, or wrapping, the protocols in IP. Telnet is a process by which PCs with terminal emulation software can establish an SNA session with a host using TCP/IP to exchange character-oriented terminal data.

Access Number Options   Service providers typically offer a toll-free and/or local-number access options. In the U.S., some service providers charge more for toll-free access, but it is usually available nationwide. Although local-number access offers a cheaper alternative, it may have limited availability in some remote or rural areas. Most services offering toll-free and/or local-number access work for static as well as mobile users. Depending on the pricing structure and rates, a particular solution may be more applicable to mobile users than to static locations. There are mainly two implementations supporting toll-free or local-number access for remote and mobile users today. One implementation uses an X.25 network to access the frame relay network; the other uses access servers to terminate the dial-up sessions and then delivers the information to the frame relay network.

Some service providers allow you to use an on-net number on your voice VPN (Virtual Private Network) to access frame relay (i.e., if you already subscribe to the service provider's voice VPN service). Voice VPNs are software-defined services designed to replace private voice networks and to interconnect corporate locations, similar to frame relay replacing some private data networks. The corporate locations have dedicated or switched access to the voice VPN. These locations are generally referred to as *on-net* because they are part of the voice VPN. Locations not part of the voice VPN are *off-net*.

For example, if a caller to an on-net office in New York wants to talk to someone in an on-net office in Los Angeles, the caller dials an on-net voice VPN number (typically seven digits) instead of a long-distance phone number. The PBX (Private Branch eXchange) in New York sends the call over the dedicated or switched access to the voice VPN. The network then determines if the call is on-net or off-net. An on-net call, in this example, is routed to the voice VPN POP serving Los Angeles and terminated using a dedicated or switched access facility in Los Angeles. Off-net calls, on the other hand, are routed over the long-distance network. On-net calls over a voice VPN are significantly more cost effective than calls routed over a long-distance network.

This implementation is ideal for remote locations that are part of a VPN service for voice applications but need occasional data connectivity. It is, however, not a viable solution for mobile users. Rather than using a different and separate access facility for data, you can use the voice VPN to access the frame relay network. The service provider provisions a gateway between the voice VPN and the frame relay network. An on-net VPN number, and perhaps an authorization code, gives you access to the frame relay network.

Modem Pool Sharing The service provider can assign modem ports in various ways. Some service providers allow you to subscribe to a specific number of modem ports or groups of modem ports. The ports are dedicated to your corporate traffic only, giving you direct control over the design and optimization of your network. Your ability to gain access to the network is influenced only by your company's traffic and not by anybody else's.

Other service providers share all modem ports on their networks among all their dial-up customers. This can be an advantage or disadvantage, depending on the user-to-modem port design ratio used by the service provider. In the Internet community, some service providers offer "no busy" guarantees. Check with your service provider about SLAs (Service Level Agreements) and credits for nonconformance. Chapter 13 discusses frame relay SLAs.

Also, determine when the network delivers a busy signal back to the user. When the user calls, the network can automatically return a busy signal if there are no available ports at that time. The network can also hunt in a round-robin fashion for an available port. The network returns a busy signal after a specified time frame or after several hunting sequences.

Flexibility in Modifying Access Lists When subscribing to a dial-up service, you would normally subscribe to a set of usernames. The service provider typically assigns usernames to each of your corporate end users who need access to the frame relay network.

You should consider the flexibility and ease of modifying the user access list. In a dynamic networking environment, the capability to easily add and delete usernames to the access list is important. Some service providers require that you call them to modify the access list. This can become cumbersome as your network changes. Others give you read-and-write access to the list through a Web or terminal interface. In addition to modifying the access list, the service provider may also give you the capability to view the users logged into the network at any given time.

Client Addressing Choices Service providers implement different client addressing schemes in assigning IP addresses and mapping usernames to IP addresses for dial-up users. Some offer a set of options. The addressing scheme determines the setup for PCs or laptops, the types of services available to each user, and the level of accounting required.

IP addresses can be assigned to dial-up uses in three ways: dynamic from an address pool, dynamic based on username, and static. Using an address pool, the service provider dynamically assigns an IP address to the user when the call is established. This IP address is taken from a pool of available IP addresses. Upon completion of the call, the IP address goes back in the pool. With each call, a particular user may get different IP addresses. With this method, you don't need to assign and program IP addresses to each PC.

The service provider can also dynamically assign a specific IP address for specific usernames. A user is always assigned the same IP address with each and every call. The service provider maintains a database that correlates IP addresses with usernames. Some service providers use this scheme to offer workgroup services. A workgroup can be an internal department or organization, such as Engineering, Human Resources, Operations, or Legal. A workgroup can also be an ad hoc group composed of representatives from the internal departments organized to perform a special function, such as new product development. The service provider can define workgroups based on the IP addresses of the users. The service provider can also define different levels of service, levels of accessibility, and other unique services for the workgroups. Similar to the first method, there is no requirement to program PCs with addresses.

Last, you can configure a static IP address for every PC laptop. However, this creates security issues: a hacker can use a stolen laptop to generate the entire address for your company. Similarly, unauthorized parties can copy the address to other machines that emulate the original source.

Network Response Time   Depending on the service providers' different network implementations, you may not achieve the same throughput levels even though they may have the same access speed. Using an X.25 network as access to the frame relay network can introduce incremental network delays. These delays can be attributed to several factors, including interswitch latencies (i.e., transmission delays between switches), X.25 encapsulation and de-encapsulation process of PPP (Point-to-Point Protocol) packets, hop count, etc. The impact on throughput and response time may vary on a case-by-case basis. Some may detect significant variances and others may not. You might want to consider testing the different implementations on one or two of your remote locations before making a decision for your entire corporation.

Hop count is the number of switches the frame traverses minus one.

The network response time can also affect the cost of connectivity. Inherent delays introduced by the network increase the time for sending and receiving information. More time on the network translates to higher monthly bills with usage-based pricing.

Security Service providers can implement different levels of security. The first level is based on network addressing, and the second level is based on user passwords. The first level ensures the network device (PC, terminal, or workstation) can access the network, but it does not protect the network from unauthorized users on an authorized network device. Some service providers use level one and two security measures in tandem.

The network may consult a database of authorized IP addresses or caller phone numbers, typically referred to as ANI (Automatic Number Identification), to allow or deny access.

The two most common ways to authenticate incoming calls using passwords are *PAP* and *CHAP*. PAP (Password Authentication Protocol) uses unencrypted passwords; CHAP (Challenge Handshake Authorization Protocol) uses encrypted passwords. CHAP passwords are more difficult for hackers to decode.

Pricing Finally, consider your pricing options. Service providers generally have a usage component to their pricing structures based on the length of time you are connected to the network. Some have a flat rate per minute of usage. Others have nonlinear pricing structures where the rate per minute decreases as the minutes of use increase. The pricing may also have monthly minimums and maximums or caps. The minimum is a flat-rate charge that you pay if you have usage levels less than the service provider's minimum usage level. Your monthly bill will have at least this amount. The maximum, on the other hand, is the flat-rate charge for usage levels higher than the service provider's maximum usage level. Your monthly bill will never exceed the cap. The service provider typically charges based on the aggregate minutes of use if your usage level falls anywhere between the minimum and maximum. Usage charges over a voice VPN may also have a distance-sensitive component, depending on the service provider. This is generally implemented using distance bands.

In addition to the usage charges, some service providers have flat-rate, monthly recurring pricing components. These may include prices for groups of modem ports, number of users, port connection to the frame relay network from the dial-up access server, and the virtual circuit(s) to the headquarters site.

What Happens in the Network?

Service providers implement various solutions to offer analog dial-up access to frame relay. The following example highlights one of many solutions and helps illustrate what goes on within the network.

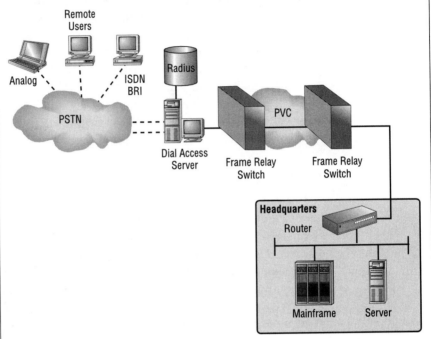

The typical client software required at the remote sites supports the following features: PPP (Point-to-Point Protocol) or SLIP (Serial Line Internet Protocol), PAP/CHAP (Password Authentication Protocol/Challenge Handshake Authentication Protocol), and dynamic IP addressing. PAP and CHAP are protocols used for user authentication. Dynamic IP addressing provides simplified routing and address administration.

The user initiates a call by dialing a local or toll-free phone number. The network routes the call to an idle port on the service provider's dial-up access server located in its POP. The access server hunts for an idle port and returns a busy signal if there are no available ports. The access server dynamically assigns a source address when a remote site dials in to the network. Once the connection is established to a modem port, the dial-up access server forwards the PPP username to an authentication server. Using CHAP, the access server generates and sends a challenge (or encoding scheme) to both the user and the authentication server. The user sends an encoded password in response to the challenge, and the password is presented to the authentication server. Based on the username and password, the authentication server determines whether or not to authorize the call. Access is provided only if the call is authorized.

Once the user gets access, the user sends the information to the network using PPP. The dial-up access concentrator accepts the incoming packets on one of the idle ports. The dial-up access concentrator terminates the PPP session and sends the information to the gateway via an Ethernet connection. The gateway (typically a router) determines the destination of the information and encapsulates TCP/IP in frame relay. The network then forwards the frame to the appropriate destination on the frame relay network.

ISDN BRI, ISDN PRI, and Switched 56/64 Kbps Access

ISDN BRI is a subscriber line consisting of two 64Kbps B channels, or *bearer channel*, and one 16Kbps D channel, or *data channel*. The D channel is generally used for signaling or for low-speed data transmission. You can use both B channels for data or voice, or one B channel for each. ISDN PRI offers 23 B channels and one D channel. Some service providers support ISDN BRI and/or PRI, but not all allow you to use all B channels available.

Switched 56/64Kbps is primarily a data-only access technology that offers 56/64Kbps on demand.

Service providers support ISDN and Switched 56/64Kbps access to frame relay by using access servers or voice VPNs, similar to analog dial-up support. Some access servers can terminate analog, ISDN, and Switched 56/64Kbps calls on the same device. Most VPNs also support analog, ISDN, and Switched 56/64Kbps on the same network.

Pricing is similar to analog dial-up. In the U.S., if you subscribe to an IXC's frame relay service, you may get a separate bill from the LEC (Local Exchange Carrier) for the access charges. The IXC charges you for the usage on the frame relay network and other flat-rate components (if any).

Cellular Access

Few service providers offer cellular access to frame relay today, but cellular access can support any application other dial-up methods support. It is ideal for mobile workers.

One of the service providers offering cellular access developed a service designed for Telnet. The cellular access is processed over an X.25 network prior to delivery on the frame relay network. Figure 4.5 shows an implementation using cellular access.

FIGURE 4.5

Using cellular to access the frame relay network

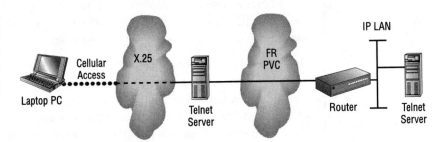

To implement the cellular access, the remote user dials an access number, and the X.25 network prompts the user to log in with a username and password. Based on this login information, the X.25 network creates a switched virtual circuit to the Telnet server. The Telnet server presents a menu to the asynchronous terminal indicating the different applications of hosts that the user can access. The user indicates the appropriate destination, and the Telnet server initiates a Telnet session with the destination host. The character stream sent by the asynchronous terminal to the Telnet server is encapsulated in TCP/IP and then in frame relay before being presented to the frame relay network.

Frame Relay Gateway Access

This section uses the U.S.-based frame relay services as an example because frame relay access is more widely available in the U.S. In the U.S., you can use a local frame relay service to access an IXC frame relay service. The "gateway" between the two frame relay networks is typically an NNI (Network-to-Network Interface) connection. The standards bodies developed NNI to connect distinct frame relay networks. The NNI uses bidirectional signaling for monitoring network status on either side of the connection, and it helps create a larger frame relay network from two smaller ones. The NNI gateway consists of a frame relay port on each of the interconnected networks and the facility that connects the two ports. All virtual circuits between the two networks traverse the gateway. Figures 4.6a and 4.6b illustrate a frame relay implementation using dedicated access compared with one using frame relay access.

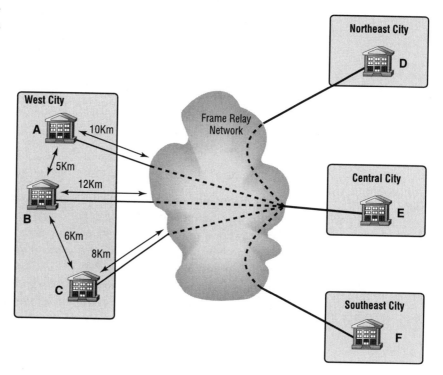

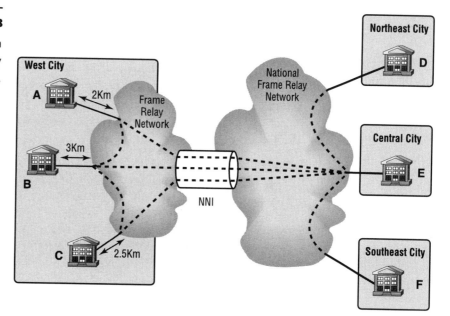

Some service providers give you a choice of dedicated or shared gateways. A dedicated gateway only supports your company's traffic. On a shared gateway, you share the gateway connection with other companies' virtual circuits. Although shared gateways offer a cheaper solution, dedicated gateways give you some level of direct control over the design and performance of your frame relay network. Depending on your service provider, you can change the size of the gateway as your traffic volumes change.

Local Frame Relay Access

Some of the benefits of using frame relay gateway access are as follows:

Higher Access Survivability   Most LEC and IXC frame relay networks in the U.S. have automatic rerouting capabilities. Therefore, using frame relay gateway access to an IXC's frame relay service gives you self-healing features on both the LEC and IXC segments of your network. This can potentially result in higher network availability overall compared with a solution using dedicated access to an IXC's frame relay network. However, this still leaves the facility between your premises and the nearest frame relay switch from the LEC susceptible to network downtime. Additionally, the gateway does not have inherent rerouting capabilities.

More Cost-Effective Local Access   As a rule, local frame relay service in the U.S. becomes a cost-effective access alternative when there are at least three locations within a LATA (Local Access Transport Area). (A LATA defines the boundaries in which the local provider can offer services. Local providers offer intra-LATA services, whereas IXCs offer inter-LATA services. LATA boundaries have begun to slowly disappear with deregulation.) This means you need connectivity from three (or more) sites within the same LATA into an IXC's network. You may be able to cost-justify local frame relay service with two locations within a single LATA if you also need intra-LATA connectivity. Figure 4.7 depicts a network with intra- and inter-LATA connectivity.

Although local frame relay access is typically not cost effective for a single location within a LATA, you may still want to consider it for long local loops (minimum of five miles, depending on the region). Local frame relay charges are generally nondistance sensitive. Determine the crossover distance where frame relay access becomes more cost effective than dedicated access.

FIGURE 4.7

IntraLATA and Inter-LATA Frame relay Service Connectivity

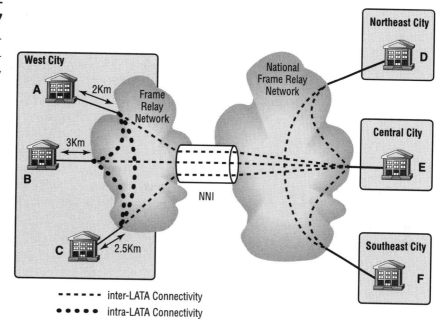

Another consideration for pricing frame relay local access is backhaul. Most service providers do not charge for backhaul; they assume every CO or POP has a frame relay switch. But others charge for it. If there are charges for backhaul, then local frame relay access for a single location within a LATA may not be cheaper than dedicated access.

In addition to the local access and the IXC frame relay charges, some IXCs may charge "gateway" charges. These charges cover the interconnection between the LECs' and the IXCs' frame relay networks.

NNI Challenges

The operational issues present some of the biggest obstacles for service providers to overcome in providing frame relay services over interconnected frame relay networks. Local and IXC frame relay service providers need to establish and agree on provisioning, installation, and maintenance procedures.

With dedicated local loops, an IXC has visibility to the local loop, all the way to your CSU/DSU. The IXC can evaluate the performance of the local loop in real time and identify potential problems. The IXC can remotely control the CSU, putting it into a loop-back mode for circuit testing, if needed.

This level of control and visibility diminishes with interconnected frame relay networks, making coordinated procedures between the service providers even more critical. The service provider on either side of the NNI has visibility to the virtual circuits that originate on one network, go through the NNI, and terminate on the other network. However, each service provider does not have visibility to virtual circuits that are wholly provisioned on the other network—these are virtual circuits that never cross the NNI. For example, the IXC will not have visibility to the virtual circuits between two locations within a single LATA on the LEC's frame relay network. The NNI specification defines bidirectional signaling that only provides the up and down status of the connections. Without coordination procedures and tools, it is difficult to isolate the problem and identify the cause.

If the IXC is your single point of contact for all problems, then communication between the IXC and LEC becomes the critical link. To their credit, many local, regional, and long distance service providers have done a good job developing communications channels and putting procedures (manual or automated) in place. You can order your own frame relay local loop and coordinate with the IXC, but it is highly recommended that you pick either the IXC or the LEC as the single point of contact. These service providers have developed procedures to create a more efficient environment and to minimize customer confusion.

Summary

Multiple access options allow you to choose the most appropriate access method on a location-by-location basis. All or most of your corporate locations can then achieve the benefits of connectivity over a single frame relay network.

Service providers offer dedicated access options, including DS-0, channelized DS-1/E-1, integrated access, nonchannelized DS-1/E-1, N × DS-1, DS-3/E-3, fiber, and DSL access. The dedicated solutions are ideal for static locations that have bandwidth requirement as low as 56/64Kbps and up to 45Mbps.

Smaller locations that generate low traffic volumes, telecommuters, and mobile workers can benefit from dial-up access solutions. When evaluating dial-up access solutions, consider the available speeds, protocols supported, access number options, model pool sharing, ways to modify the access lists, client addressing schemes, impact of network implementation on response time, security, and pricing.

Some service providers also offer ISDN and Switched 56Kbps access. A small number of service providers offer cellular access.

You can also use a local frame relay service to connect to a national or international frame relay service. Frame relay local access provides higher network availability on the local loop and a more cost-effective solution compared with dedicated access in some situations.

Now that you have a good grasp of the technology, the features and benefits, the components, and the wide variety of access options, the next chapter ties together many of the concepts you've already learned and provides information about what you can expect from your service provider and its offerings.

CHAPTER

5

What to Expect from Frame
Relay Services

Getting the most out of your frame relay network means understanding how public services are structured. In some cases, the most cost-effective solution is to implement a hybrid private-line/frame relay network, whereas in others, the optimal solution is to use one homogeneous network service. If you understand the structure and marketing of typical frame relay services, you will better comprehend the design issues discussed in later chapters.

No discussion of frame relay services can possibly provide an all-encompassing view; frame relay services change so quickly that information becomes obsolete before it goes to print. Instead, this chapter outlines what general service characteristics to expect from long-distance U.S., local U.S., and international frame relay services.

U.S. Long-Distance Services

The frame relay services currently available in the U.S. bear little resemblance to the first services introduced in 1991. U.S. IXC (Inter-eXchange Carrier) frame relay services make up the majority of revenue in the global frame relay market. The fast-growing and constantly changing IXC frame relay market includes all the major IXC service providers as well as smaller providers. Competition is fierce due to the large number of providers in the market.

U.S. IXCs were the first frame relay service pioneers and still tend to be the first with new features and service options. Today, U.S. long-distance frame relay services offer more service options than they did just a few years ago. Typically, you can choose from the following options:

- Dial access, either 1-800 or local dial

- DS-0 or DS-1 local access (perhaps DS-3 access)

- Integrated access supporting private lines and frame relay

- Customer network-management system options

- Managed CPE

- Internet connectivity

- Ports ranging from 56Kbps up to 1.544Mbps (in some cases up to 45Mbps)

- CIR speeds from 0Kbps up to 1.024Mbps (in some cases up to 10Mbps)

- Disaster recovery

Some providers continue to work on wireless access and other enhanced, applications-based service options. An increasing number offer support for connecting to other providers' frame relay service via a NNI connection. Competition in the IXC frame relay service market continues to force providers into offering more economical and enhanced services to meet customer demand.

Most IXC frame relay services are structured to be cost effective for certain types of network configurations—based on the number of sites, distance between sites, and/or number of connections. For example, if you have a two- or three-site network, chances are that frame relay will not be the most cost-effective solution. Private-line services are still the primary service for small, star networks. But for five-or six-site networks, with each site potentially connected to two or more sites, frame relay service generally becomes more attractive. In general, the larger the network and the greater the connectivity, the more attractive frame relay services become.

Comparing frame relay service providers can be a tricky business. Service providers implement unique features or offer them in slightly different ways, making direct comparisons difficult. A direct comparison of price between providers is one of the most difficult to make, and the variety of pricing structures also makes it tough.

For example, although most services use fixed-rate billing, there are providers offering usage-based billing options. Most direct comparisons require network assumptions, so if those assumptions change, the most economical provider may change, as well.

In addition to traditional frame transport, IXCs often include basic CPE support options, consisting of either purchase or lease options for equipment—for example, routers, FRADs, probes (devices that are located at the customer site and are used for monitoring traffic), and CSU/DSUs. The equipment support is handled through either a third party, a joint marketing arrangement with the vendor, or a special integration group (discussed in detail in Chapter 12). Maintenance and monitoring support may also be available under many of these arrangements. By ordering CPE support services or managed network services, you can outsource some or all of the WAN responsibilities to the provider.

U.S. Local Services

Designed to support customer networks with locations within a LATA (Local Access Transport Area), local public frame services typically lag behind interexchange services by one to three years. For example, most local services do not yet offer dial-up access as an option. As deregulation and competition expand, local providers must enhance their services to compete. In addition, many IXCs have entered the local frame relay market via acquisitions or via local network builds. This now allows you to choose a provider with a single network end-to-end (assuming you are lucky enough to have your building located on-net on both sides).

Most local service providers, especially the regional Bell operating companies (RBOCs), have integration units that provide the CPE with maintenance and monitoring options. If you choose to lease equipment from one of these companies, you will likely receive two bills—one for the equipment management and one for the frame relay network service. This is due partially to regulatory restrictions but mostly to internal system limitations.

Local services have one major attractive feature: pricing. Because local providers must transport services only a short distance, aggressive pricing is common. Consider a local provider if your network is concentrated in a small area, because they tend to be half the price of the national IXCs. The limits of local provider networks are generally less than 100 miles, compared with 2,000 or more miles for national IXCs. Service pricing components can include any or all of the following: access, port, PVC, DLCI, total CIR, and backhaul. There is one major issue: pricing bumps for out-of-region connections. If you decide to order service from a provider with in-region and out-of-region services, you will likely pay one price for in-region and another for out-of-region. Therefore, you may have to pay an "out of region" port fee for a port that has many in-region PVCs and few out-of-region connections (see Figure 5.1).

FIGURE 5.1
Local and long-distance connections.

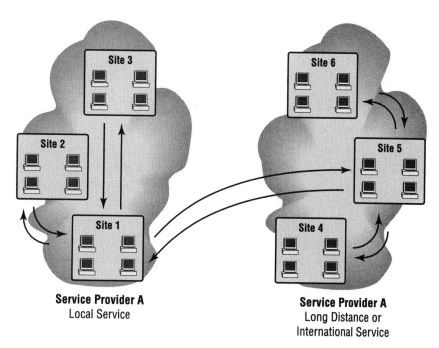

Service Provider A
Local Service

Service Provider A
Long Distance or
International Service

Frame Relay Services Outside the U.S.

International frame relay services did not have a strong presence in the market until U.S. services had matured significantly. Most foreign services lagged in development relative to U.S. services for several years but have since gained ground. Although differences have become less pronounced, you should expect a slightly more limited selection of access, port, PVC speeds, and some value-added service options. Many non-U.S. providers do not currently offer luxuries, such as dial-up access, short installation periods, or even timely installation. In some countries, your local access charge will be more than the frame relay service charges!

With that information, you may think non-U.S. services are less sophisticated and less desirable, but nothing could be further from the truth. An area where non-U.S. providers lead is managed network services. Often a basic service includes management and monitoring when offered from a non-U.S. provider. Pricing can be difficult to come by and comparison shopping extremely time consuming. Frame relay connections between international locations are most often priced-based on each country. You will typically have a port charge, charges for PVCs based on their CIRs, and an international surcharge or zone charge.

Pricing Structures and Alternatives

Pricing structures of frame relay services have few constants and many variables. The vast majority of service providers use a flat monthly fee per connecting location. In this scenario, distance does not have an impact on pricing; instead, pricing is based on the port connection speed and either the CIRs of the PVCs or the number of PVCs. Flat rates make it easy for you to budget network costs because costs do not fluctuate. This also makes it easier for serevice providers with inflexible billing systems to invoice customers.

Some services charge you based on the number of PVCs, others on CIR. With CIR pricing, the price for three PVCs, with each at 64Kbps, would cost the same as a single PVC at 192Kbps. This encourages increased connectivity because you can have connections to multiple sites economically instead of routing traffic through a central or intermediate site.

The design of a private-line network often proves most cost effective when you aggregate traffic to a few hub locations and buy larger and faster leased lines to connect these sites. However, this is usually not the case with frame relay. As discussed earlier, more direct connectivity can result in better network performance for all users.

Most carriers allow you to oversubscribe the port connection, and some even charge less once you have reached the 100 percent subscription level, which allows for two things. First, you cannot send more information into the network than your port connection speed allows. For many connectivity requirements, you don't need to connect two given sites all the time, but you need the ability to connect anytime information needs to be sent. This is an important distinction. Once you oversubscribe a port connection, you cannot connect to every location at the full CIR, all at the same time. With oversubscription, you leverage the fact that connectivity itself is valuable—the ability to connect when needed. The higher the level of port oversubscription, the greater the risk that there will be contention for the port's capacity among PVCs. Carriers recognize the additional risk, but they also recognize that the connection is still valuable. Therefore, capacity can be assigned over 100 percent, but you still pay a charge for this capacity. However, it costs less incrementally (meaning it costs less per Kbps than the Kbps under 100 percent), reflecting the higher risk that an application could be delayed. The result is that both you and the carrier should come out better than you would in a dedicated environment. You get a connection that you wouldn't be able to cost-justify in a leased-line network, and the carrier gets at least some revenue for giving you the ability to connect to this site.

Second, the value of having a connection to some locations is much less than the value of having a direct connection to other locations. The same is true for all goods, and has long been recognized by economists as a downward-sloping demand curve. Take water, for example. If water were limited in supply, the water you need to drink to survive would be very valuable, and you would be willing to pay a lot of money for it. However, the water that you use to wash your dog and your car is much less valuable. Even though it is exactly the same water, its value is less.

The same holds true in networking. You are probably willing to spend more for a connection from a remote site back to the primary site than you are for a connection between remote sites. For the most part, private-line costs do not decrease, even though the relative value of the connections do. The decreasing cost of incremental network connectivity in a frame relay environment is a recognition of this fact.

Carriers are becoming very creative with service and pricing options. For example, some carriers allow you to designate Zero CIR services on a PVC. (All the frames are eligible for discard.) This is similar to buying a general admission ticket to a baseball game but knowing there is no guarantee there will be enough seats to accommodate all the general admission fans. Although this would not be recommended for high-volume sites or mission-critical applications, it does provide a cost-effective solution for connectivity between remote locations or for low-volume sites with non-mission-critical applications.

Other carriers are allowing usage-based pricing. You have to pay only for the amount of traffic that you generate on the network. There are pros and cons to this approach. The majority of sites actually generate significantly less traffic than what most network managers estimate. Usage-based charging could significantly reduce your overall costs. The downside is that costs are not predictable. Again, the ability to quickly modify your decision means that you have the flexibility to change your mind if your first decision ends up being less optimal than another approach.

Some carriers add a distance-sensitive element. Although many network managers prefer the simplicity and cost-effectiveness of non-distance-sensitive pricing, networks that are concentrated into a tight geographical area can benefit from this mileage-sensitive alternative.

With all these options, you will probably have to compare bottom lines. This is easy if every carrier is asked to price out exactly the same network with the same ports, CIR, PVCs, etc. If you allow each carrier to design its own network and provide pricing based on a unique design, comparing prices between carriers will be a bit more difficult than what you might like.

It also means that elements other than price will probably figure into your final selection. These might include your comfort with the carrier as well as the carrier's ability to reach your network locations, offer the highest degree of network reroute protection, offer CPE and CPE support, provide configuration management, and provide other ancillary services and support options.

Enhanced Frame Relay Features

Ports, PVCs, bursting, oversubscription, automatic rerouting, and access alternatives combined typify a baseline frame relay service. End users demanded more than the baseline as the networks became more distributed, as the number of locations grew, and as more applications were integrated. These needs required additional network intelligence, more sophisticated frame relay capabilities, added flexibility, and a higher level of support and management from service providers.

The list below offers an overview of these enhanced features. These capabilities may depend on enhancements in CPE and/or the frame relay network. The succeeding chapters cover these features and capabilities in more detail.

SNA-Over Frame Relay   Service providers originally designed frame relay services for data applications, particularly for bursty and delay-tolerant LAN traffic. However, advancements in CPE implementations allowed end users to integrate highly predictable, time-sensitive SNA applications. This eliminated the need to run separate and parallel networks for LAN and SNA. It also provided SNA applications some added flexibility in network reconfigurations while maintaining a high level of network availability.

Voice- and Fax-Over Frame Relay   Although data applications still dominate most frame relay networks, voice- and fax-over frame relay are experiencing continued growth. Some end users have been able to run voice for "free" on their frame relay networks that were initially cost-justified for data. One of the more recent standards completed by the Frame Relay Forum offers an implementation agreement for voice-over frame relay. This standard legitimizes the technology and ensures some level of interoperability between voice Frame Relay Access Device (FRAD) vendors.

PVC Priorities and Classes of Service   Although CPE identified and serviced SNA and voice applications differently than LAN, the type of application was transparent to the network. The frame relay network treated all frames equally. The introduction of PVC priorities and classes of service on the frame relay network ensures that the network distinguishes between the different applications. With PVC priorities, the network services high-priority, mission-critical traffic before lower-priority traffic. Classes of service guarantee delay, frame loss, and availability service levels to meet the unique needs of each application.

Switched Virtual Circuits (SVCs)   Unlike PVCs, SVCs are established on demand when you have something to send, and the network disconnects the SVC at the end of the session. Companies with any-to-any connectivity requirements, low volume, occasional remote-to-remote communications, and intracompany voice traffic can benefit from SVCs. SVCs also allow service providers to offer call-by-call usage billing based on connect time or number of frames sent. With this pricing structure, you only pay for what you use.

Frame Relay-to-ATM Service Interworking   Frame relay and ATM can coexist and work together with interworking. You can seamlessly interconnect a frame relay site to an ATM site over the public network. The network is responsible for translating between the two protocols. For example, traffic from low-speed, frame relay remote sites can be aggregated at the headquarters with a high-speed ATM port using service interworking. Interworking offers a good migration path from frame relay to ATM.

Disaster Recovery   Disaster recovery services allow you to maintain connectivity to valuable network resources when a failure occurs on the network or at your headquarters. Frame relay already offers high network availability with its inherent automatic rerouting capabilities. However, this does not protect you from failures of host systems, local loops, and backhaul. Some disaster recovery options include dual PVCs, PVC redirects, growable PVCs, dial backup, and others.

Managed Network Services   In addition to transport facilities, some service providers offer managed network services as solutions. These services include CPE, LAN integration, network monitoring and maintenance, management reporting, on-site support, and even ongoing network evaluation and consulting. Most service offerings include different levels of services or options, depending on your applications, requirements, and comprehensiveness of support services.

Summary

After reading this chapter you should realize there are certain features and capabilities common to most frame relay services in the U.S. long distance, U.S. local, and international markets. But also realize that talking about typical frame relay services is like talking about typical cars. There are certain things almost all cars have in common, such as four wheels, windows, brakes, etc., but when you look at a specific car, the general discussion doesn't describe it very well. Some cars have leather seats, CD players, and other features that make them unique or of higher quality than others. Frame relay services are similarly difficult to generalize due to disaster-recovery services, unique access options, classes-of-service, etc. Also keep in mind that frame relay services continue to evolve, and there are undoubtedly new services since the writing of this book.

The main consideration for selecting a frame relay service provider is not for all the features and enhanced services it has, but for all the ones you need today and in the near future at an economical rate. If you think you may require some of the enhanced services discussed in this chapter and want more information, many of these are discussed in detail in later chapters.

CHAPTER

6

How Frame Relay Supports
SNA Traffic

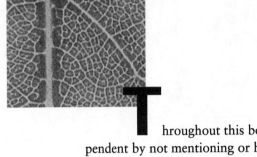

hroughout this book, we have attempted to be vendor independent by not mentioning or highlighting specific carriers or equipment
vendors, although we have tried to cover both the standard and unique
capabilities of the leading players. We are not making an exception in this
chapter, although we will specifically discuss IBM here. We are interested
more in addressing "IBM" in terms of its network architecture and set of
widely used protocols, because of the high number of installed SNA networks worldwide.

This chapter covers the primary migration paths and alternatives for SNA
and LAN/SNA traffic using a frame relay network service. The focus on the
SNA protocol is necessary because at least half of all frame relay customers
have some SNA traffic. Keep in mind that there is no single "best" solution
for transporting SNA across frame relay because the optimal network configuration and migration strategy depends on several factors, including

- The legacy networks and equipment you already have in place

- The percentage of SNA/transaction applications compared with LAN/
  file sharing applications

- The relative speed of growth in each area

The purpose of the chapter is to present IBM's set of alternatives for
migrating traditional SNA architectures and consolidated SNA and LAN
traffic to frame relay. This chapter assumes you are familiar with legacy IBM
SNA equipment. If not, then you probably do not have any SNA traffic going
across your network.

Frame Relay Support in the Controller Family

The controller family is IBM's bread-and-butter networking platform. The family consists of three primary products: the 3174 cluster controller, 3172 cluster controller, and the 3745 front-end processor (FEP).

IBM now supports direct connections into a public frame relay network on the entire controller family(see Figure 6.1). IBM also supports frame relay on the AS/400 and the RouteXpander card, which fits within a PC. These devices can directly interface with a frame relay network without being front-ended by a device such as a router. (We will cover this topic in detail later in this chapter.)

FIGURE 6.1

Direct frame relay support by IBM SNA equipment

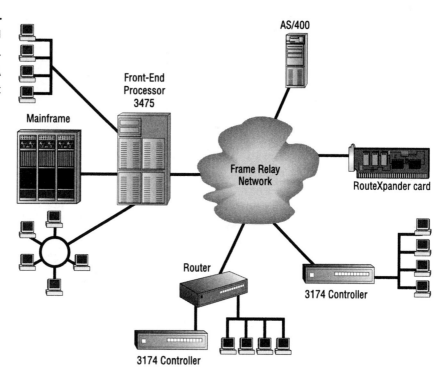

APPN: Routing SNA Traffic

APPN is IBM's *Advanced Peer-to-Peer Network* protocol, which supports any-to-any connectivity on a network and is the architecture for routing SNA traffic. It is simpler than the NCP (Network Control Program) used by FEPs for traffic routing. APPN can therefore be accommodated by smaller, and less expensive, networking devices. The result of migrating to APPN can be a reduced cost of network ownership and operations. In addition, the APPN protocol is open so non-IBM vendors can either duplicate or purchase the code and therefore develop equipment using APPN.

Today, IBM's FEP and 3174 controller are APPN network nodes. Both also support frame relay, as stated before. The end result of APPN is that SNA traffic can be routed over a frame relay network. This is discussed in a later section of this chapter

APPN has some weaknesses, such as the inability to route around network failures and the inability to provide improved congestion or flow control. As you move to high-speed networking, congestion must be tightly managed; these issues are being addressed by IBM with APPN's successor protocol, HPR, which is discussed next.

Second Generation APPN—HPR

High Performance Routing, HPR, is an extension of APPN and is sometimes referred to as *APPN+*. It is an "industrial strength" version of APPN suitable for tomorrow's interworking environment. It adds significant improvements to the protocol in much the same way that frame relay improved upon X.25.

Although APPN provides both error-checking and error-recovery services, it assumes that the underlying transmission facilities are not reliable, in much the same way as X.25. Each APPN NN (Network Node) must store a copy of each packet it transmits until it receives a positive acknowledgment from the network node. This takes time and space and is not necessary for digital networks.

HPR moves error correction to the edges of the network (usually the FEP or controller), making it faster and more efficient than APPN. This provides a significant architectural advantage. HPR operation is like a link-state routing protocol, in that each network node holds a topology map of the entire network. HPR is part of RFC 1490 (multiprotocol encapsulation over frame relay), allowing it to run in parallel with other protocols over a frame relay network. This multiprotocol environment is discussed in the remainder of the chapter.

Integrating LAN and SNA Traffic over Frame Relay

There are several alternatives for integrating LAN and SNA traffic over the same frame relay network. If one of the consolidation solutions available today makes sense for your network, you might be able to finance SNA equipment additions or upgrades from the network savings achieved from the consolidation. These consolidation and migration issues and options are discussed in this section of the chapter.

Getting Started with Spoofing

In delving into the issues of topology and migration, it is necessary to start with one of the core principles of SNA: polling. Polling represents a critical element of an SNA network, and the issue of how to handle the polling over an integrated LAN/SNA network must be considered. This isn't specifically a frame relay issue; you would face the same trade-offs if you decided to use a private line–based router internetwork.

The SNA equipment relies on polling to inform other network equipment of the status of each device and whether or not it has something to transmit. Therefore, a significant amount of "data" is transmitted across the network simply to allow devices to know the status of other devices. If no steps are taken to reduce the amount of polling that traverses the WAN, then a large portion of your network bandwith may be needed for polling.

If you allow the polls to travel the wide-area network, you will increase network congestion and impact application response times. The alternative is local termination of most of the polls, a procedure known as *spoofing*. Spoofing improves network response times because most of the polls do not actually travel across the WAN. For example, if a FRAD or router is handing SDLC traffic at a remote location, the requests to send information from the attached concentrator (or 3270 emulator) are acknowledged by the router instead of being sent across the network in response to the FEP poll. The router/FRAD plays the role of a local (or remote) FEP in this respect.

The router attached locally to the FEP at the other end of the connection is performing the same function. It is responding to the FEP polls as if it were a remote cluster controller, sending information or replying that no information needs to be transmitted.

A small percentage of actual polls are allowed through the network to ensure that devices remain attached and operational—a "heart beat" monitoring process. However, the majority of the polls are kept off of the WAN.

The benefits of spoofing are that WAN congestion is decreased and response times on the network are improved. Most of the consolidation approaches available today, using either routers or FRADs, offer the ability to spoof the polling.

Consolidation via Routers and FRADs

The CPE vendors offer several alternatives for consolidating LAN and SNA traffic over a single frame relay network, and the sophistication and breadth of these options increases each month. The basic configurations discussed in the following sections include Token Ring bridging, SDLC tunneling, data link switching (DLSw), and APPN network node support. Although we will discuss the basic configurations, you should be aware that no single "best" configuration works for all network environments. Each has its pros and cons, and you will probably use a combination of solutions within your network.

Is a FEP Always Necessary?

Can a router/FRAD replace a front-end processor? The answer seems to be both "yes" and "no," depending upon which FEP functions you rely upon and for which you have replacement strategies. The answer also depends not only on the functions you require but also which equipment vendord's router/FRAD you install. In the end, you may be able to achieve significant network savings through the elimination of at least some remote FEPs from the network.

Token Ring Bridging and LLC2

In the Token Ring bridging/LLC2 solution, SNA devices (either controllers or 3270 emulators) are LAN-attached. The SNA traffic gets translated into LLC packets. The router then takes the LAN packets and handles them as it would any other LAN packet on the network (see Figure 6.2).

This approach is appropriate in networks where routing on the WAN is not needed and where devices are LAN attached. The advantage is that because the SDLC packet is actually converted to LLC2, traditional SNA

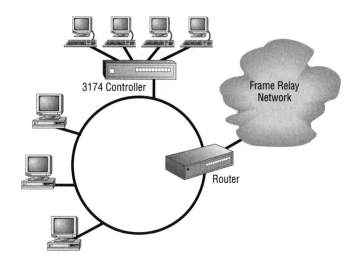

network management—via NetView—can be performed. It can also reduce
some of the uncontrollable time delays that characterize TCP/IP-based routing
alternatives. This solution also preserves your IBM system investments. However, there are downsides. This bridging solution does not recover well from
link failures, and the number of hops is limited to between two and seven,
depending upon time-out sensitivities. Although this is a less-than-ideal solution in large networks with high traffic volumes and high levels of polling
overhead traversing WAN, it is a good interim solution, especially in smaller
networks.

SDLC Serial Tunneling and Data Link Switching

SDLC tunneling is another alternative for consolidating LAN and SNA
traffic over a single frame relay network. Router vendors initially developed
their own approaches to serial tunneling, but several router vendors currently also support DLSw (data link switching).

Most serial-tunneling implementations provide local termination of SNA
polls. The SDLC packet is then encapsulated into a TCP/IP packet. This allows
the router to handle all of the flow-control and standard error-recovery processes as it would with any other TCP/IP packet. The TCP/IP packet is then
encapsulated into frame relay and sent across the frame relay network (shown
in Figure 6.3).

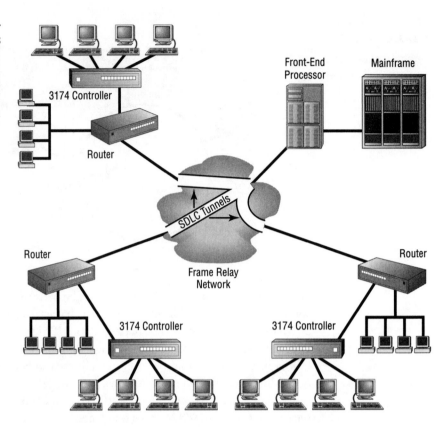

FIGURE 6.3

SDLC tunneling and
Data Link Switching
across a frame relay
network

The biggest disadvantage of tunneling and DLSw is the unpredictability of response times, which is a function of the TCP/IP environment. This problem can be partially overcome, if you implement prioritization techniques within the router or with segregated and prioritized PVCs (see Chapter 9). In relatively small networks, session time-outs caused by unpredictably high response times are less of a factor because the number of intermediate network hops can be kept at a minimum. In larger networks, frame relay can offer a greater level of direct connectivity than leased lines, due to lower-cost connections (PVCs). Thus, the number of hops can be minimized and so too can potential problems with session time-outs.

A disadvantage to this configuration is the added 40 bytes of overhead the combination of TCP/IP and frame relay add to each packet. However, a new method of TCP/IP overhead compression has been defined in RFC 1144, which decreases the TCP/IP overhead to 5 bytes.

DLSw is an IBM-developed approach to encapsulating SNA and NetBIOS within TCP/IP. It can be found under RFC 1434. The link controls are terminated locally (i.e., spoofed) to enhance overall network performance and keep wide-area network congestion down. Serial tunneling was initially developed by several router vendors as a mechanism to transport SNA traffic over an IP backbone, but each vendor had its own approach. An RFC should be available soon that standardizes DLSw.

The router is directly connected to the 3174 controller and creates a TCP/IP packet from the SNA or NetBIOS packet. This is done by placing the SNA packet into the payload of a TCP packet, then into the payload of an IP packet, and finally into the payload of a frame relay frame. At the other end of the connection, a router is also attached to the FEP, as shown in Figure 6.4. (If the router and the FEP are both running APPN, then the remote router could directly communicate with the FEP.)

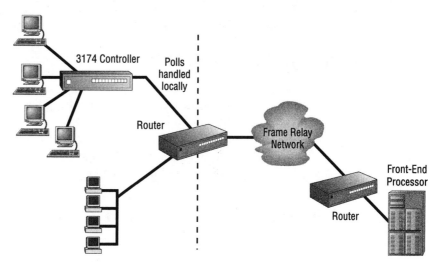

FIGURE 6.4
Data Link Switching locally terminates polls

The TCP/IP layer controls the session and assumes full responsibility for delivering the packet. If a packet is dropped by the network, the router, not the SNA devices, assumes responsibility for error recovery. The TCP/IP protocols will take responsibility for routing the packet, ensuring transmission integrity and even routing around network problems. Do not consider an implementation for tunneling in which a protocol other than TCP/IP is used unless it has the same error correction capabilities.

This approach allows the router to consolidate the traditional SNA traffic onto the frame relay internetwork without modification to the underlying SNA architecture. A standard controller can be directly attached to the router, and the router will perform protocol encapsulation. The advantage to this approach is that you can replace parallel leased-line networks with a single frame relay infrastructure that is probably faster, more easily reconfigured, and less costly, while deferring decisions on upgrade paths for the SNA network itself. Controllers are also upgradeable to support direct interfaces into a frame relay wide-area network, providing an alternative path.

The disadvantages of tunneling and DLSw apply mostly to large SNA networks with a fairly heavy level of SNA traffic and response-time sensitive applications. You may have difficulty scaling up your system to very large networks with this configuration, and the unpredictable response times can cause session time-outs. However, if you can engineer your network so that you do not exceed two hops per logical link carrying the DLSw traffic, this solution can provide a viable alternative. When you tunnel SDLC through IP, you can lose sight of the SDLC management information.

SNA over LANs with DLSw

A combination of the above solutions is also a possibility, especially where LANs and multiprotocol routers are already in place. The SDLC frame can first be converted into LLC2 and then encapsulated into TCP/IP. This allows the packet to be routed (not bridged) across the WAN and provides for automatic link recovery from failure. This has become a very popular solution with both equipment vendors and end users.

Routers FRADs and APPN Support

Routers and FRADs that support APPN, and eventually HPR, can be configured as a standard APPN NN and as such are capable of "routing" SNA/APPN traffic. Acting as NNs, the devices function as peers to other IBM devices directly attached to the frame relay network. This means that a router at one site can communicate across a frame relay network to an APPN FEP at another site.

If the router or FRAD is also equipped to support dependent LU requester (DLUR), it can support the SNA traffic alongside the APPN traffic for consolidation over a frame relay network. The APPN traffic is routed, while the traffic is tunneled to a specific VTAM. The handling of polls in both cases is local.

Some of the benefits associated with APPN include "routing" SNA traffic, allowing peer-to-peer communication, dynamic configuration and reconfiguration of the network without having to regenerate the NCP, and the ability to dynamically route around network problems. It should be noted that many of these benefits can be achieved through a migration to an internetwork environment without having to actually upgrade to APPN. You can do this by using one of the alternatives we've discussed for transporting SNA traffic over frame relay, and in the process, buy time to plan the upgrade paths and to upgrade sections of the network in a phased approach.

Multipoint/Multidrop Replacement

Because many SNA networks currently use multipoint/multidrop solutions, it is necessary to address how these can be migrated to frame relay. One solution is to swap out the old multipoint/multidrop leased lines for the more flexible frame relay virtual connectivity. You can accomplish this by defining logical groups of PVCs and presenting the PVC group to the front-end processor as a string of sites on a multipoint line. Because everything in the frame relay environment is "virtual something," this could be termed a *virtual multipoint*.

Native SNA Services

Several frame relay service providers have incorporated carrier-grade devices into their offerings. For these solutions, end users do not need to modify their existing SNA solutions. Instead, all frame relay conversions and issues are addressed once the traffic enters the service providers network (see Figure 6.5).

The advantage of this configuration is that if you have a large number of traditional devices, such as asynchronous terminals, you can directly interface these into the frame relay network without any upgrades, additional equipment, or modifications at your site.

Each remote location's traffic is given a single PVC back to a central site, which is also connected into the frame relay network. The advantages of this

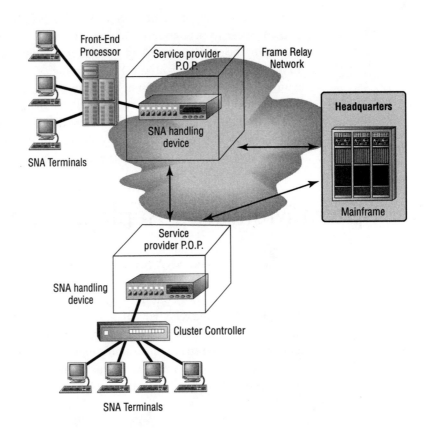

FIGURE 6.5

A typical native SNA
Frame Relay Service

approach are that you gain speed, and thus performance, on the network; the
ability to automatically route around network failures; the ability to dynamically reconfigure the network topology; and network savings associated
with the change without any investment or modifications on your part. In
addition, you do not have to learn how to manage a frame relay network.

Network Management

Network management is covered in detail in Chapter 12, although a
quick discussion of NetView and NetView for AIX (formerly called NetView/
6000) is appropriate here. Regardless of the migration and convergence
approach(es) you choose, you will probably find that you will continue to use

NetView to manage the SNA/APPN/HPR devices and traffic. Then you may use another LAN management solution, such as NetView for AIX, for the LAN/SNMP devices. These solutions can also work together to create a hybrid management solution for LAN and SNA networks.

The NetView management system uses SNA protocols for communication with network devices. You will continue to need NetView to manage the traditional IBM devices, including the controller family.

Most routers are monitored via SNMP (although configuration of the device is typically via a vendor-specific application). There are many network management alternatives for managing SNMP devices, including NetView for AIX, SunNet Manager, and OpenView. You will need one of these solutions for managing the routers and other SNMP devices in your network.

IBM has enabled the NetView and NetView for AIX systems to exchange information, with NetView assembling the data into a single integrated view of the network. Several leading equipment vendors are developing NetView for AIX interfaces to allow the NetView for AIX (and thus NetView through an information exchange) to view alarms and monitor the health and status of SNMP network devices.

Some IBM equipment, such as the controller family, can be configured to support monitoring using SNA protocols, SNMP, or both. In fact, parts of the device can be monitored using NetView, and other parts, such as the IP routing functions, can be monitored via NetView for AIX (or another system) using SNMP.

The downside is that you may need different management system components as well as another system that allows you to remotely configure your routers and other internetworking equipment if these are non-IBM devices. NetView and NetView for AIX can be tied together through command-and-control functions so that you can create a single focal point for management. Recent innovations with NetView, such as the Resource Object Data Manager, include layering additional intelligence on top of data collection functions to provide automation for responding to alarms and other network situations.

Summary

It's clear there are several solutions for migrating SNA traffic to a frame relay network. Each has its own advantages and disadvantages based on your specific goals and existing infrastructure. Many of these have been around since frame relay's introduction back in 1991, while others are relative newcomers. The expanded capabilities of IBM's controller family of products, routers, FRADs and other CPE makes tuning the performance of your network possible.

Although SNA has been around for over 20 years, frame relay is one of the first transport services capable of supporting the unique needs of this time-sensitive, mission-critical protocol. Many companies have already migrated to frame relay. Other companies, perhaps yours, are still considering the move. The topics discussed in this chapter have provided you the necessary information to determine whether frame relay can provide you a better solution than what you have today.

In addition to all the CPE-based solutions, there are other issues, such as network delay, that must be addressed in order for SNA to perform as needed. We will cover these issues in detail in Chapter 9. With all these solutions and options, making a decision can be a bit overwhelming. Be sure to discuss these options with your service provider and equipment vendors; they probably know which one will be "best" for you. Chances are they have helped deploy SNA over frame relay for numerous companies in situations similar to yours. Remember, over 50 percent of all frame relay customer networks are transporting some SNA traffic.

CHAPTER

7

Protecting Your Network
from Failures

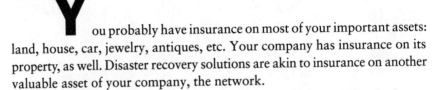

You probably have insurance on most of your important assets: land, house, car, jewelry, antiques, etc. Your company has insurance on its property, as well. Disaster recovery solutions are akin to insurance on another valuable asset of your company, the network.

A disaster refers to the inability to communicate and exchange information due to an unexpected and undesirable interruption or failure in the network. The disturbance can come from many sources: natural disasters, such as fires, tornadoes, hurricanes, and floods; man-made disasters, such as a backhoe cutting a buried cable or a terrorist attack; or they can be electronic disasters, such as power supply and switch component failures. How a disaster occurs is not as important as how your company's network survives the disaster.

Because many service providers promote the inherent self-healing capabilities of their frame relay services, you may think that you do not need to have a disaster-recovery plan. Although most service providers have taken responsibility for building more fault-tolerant frame relay services compared to their standard private-line services, you shouldn't assume that your network can withstand any kind of network failure. In general, your risk of downtime theoretically decreases with frame relay. However, the reality is that you still have some risks. Frame relay networks can and do fail. When frame relay networks fail, as with any service, the service providers will attempt to fix the problem as quickly as possible. You need to evaluate your business and the financial risks associated with network outages when deciding whether you need a disaster-recovery plan.

This chapter discusses the points of failures or areas vulnerable to network outages and the potential impact on your network. It also provides different disaster-recovery options that help reduce your network's risk of failure and minimize or eliminate downtime. We will highlight the various factors to consider when choosing the most appropriate disaster-recovery option for your company.

Inherent Fault-Tolerant Networks

Service providers need to have some standard level of fault-tolerance or self-healing capabilities in their frame relay networks to be competitive and considered a legitimate player. With frame relay, you automatically get the inherent automatic rerouting feature when you subscribe to the service. The service providers typically do not charge for this standard level of fault tolerance. But beyond this standard level, the service provider may charge you for additional disaster recovery features.

The standard service typically has the capability to reroute traffic around failures *within the network*. The network generally includes the frame relay switches and the physical transmission facilities (or trunks) between the switches. The following are some ways service providers design their networks to provide a self-healing network.

Implement Hardware Redundancy in the Switches Most service providers have hardware redundancy in their frame relay switches. Hardware redundancy protects a network from downtime due to switch hardware failures. For example, the interface modules (i.e., a physical component in the switch on which end-user connections or trunks terminate) may have 1:1 or 1:N protection. 1:1 means that the switch has a redundant (or backup) interface module for every active interface module. The redundant interface automatically takes over when the primary interface module fails. In a 1:N protection scheme, a single backup module protects multiple actives interface modules. The backup module can protect any one of the N active modules at any given time. Given that it can only protect one module at a time, multiple module failures can result in a network outage. The 1:1 or 1:N protection scheme also applies to other components of the switch, such as power supplies, processor modules, etc.

Deploy Switches with Rerouting Capabilities A frame relay switch typically has the intelligence to track the network's topology; to know the location of other switches and how the switches are connected to each other; to track the utilization, latency, and speed of various trunking facilities; to detect a network failure; and to reroute the traffic around the failure.

If the service provider designs the network properly with enough bandwidth to support rerouted traffic and geographically diverse trunks, the switches can often reroute the traffic when failure occurs on a trunk. Of course, the network's ability to recover from the failure depends on the severity of the failure and the number of simultaneous failures for which the service provider has designed the network. For example, the network may take longer to recover from a fiber cut that affects multiple trunks compared with an equipment or electronics failure on a single trunk.

During the rerouting process, the switches use various parameters to choose the most appropriate alternate route. These parameters include highest bandwidth, lowest utilization, least number of hops, etc. In some cases, the service provider has the ability to override the default algorithm and specify an alternate path. Some switches can also load-balance. With load-balancing, if the switch has multiple alternate routes it can choose from, it evenly distributes the traffic between the different routes.

Network failures most often affect the virtual connections. This is why service providers promote their services' ability to automatically reroute PVCs.

Have at Least Two Paths out of Each Switch Ideally, the service provider should have at least two geographically diverse paths for trunking out of each frame relay switch. Geographic diversity refers to separate physical paths. With two separate physical routes from a switch, a single fiber cut will not completely isolate the switch. A fiber cut should only affect one of the routes if the routes are truly on two different rights of way. If one of the trunks fail, the traffic can go over the remaining active trunk.

Have Enough Capacity in the Network to Support Rerouted Traffic Depending on the network design, the network may only be able to reroute some but not all of the traffic affected. Some service providers design their networks for recovery from multiple simultaneous failures rather than just one failure at any given time. Even in situations in which there is only a single failure, there can be capacity issues. If the alternate path is already 60 percent utilized and traffic is rerouted from another trunk to this path, it may become overutilized. This will cause packets to be dropped and performance to suffer. In cases such as this, some providers have the ability to reroute traffic to multiple alternate paths and therefore have a lesser impact on your network performance.

In general, most public frame relay networks can reroute PVCs around trunk failures, assuming that the service provider has designed the network to do so. When a reroute occurs, your applications may or may not detect it, although most networks can recover within a few milliseconds. Keep in mind that the reroute time depends on a number of parameters, including the number of switches in the network, complexity of the network topology, network design, severity of the failure, number of logical connections to reroute, etc. For most LAN applications, the end users are often not aware that the network just rerouted their traffic; however, the higher-layer protocols (IP and TCP) might have detected a problem in some situations. For example, TCP/IP expects an acknowledgment within a certain time interval for each packet it sends. If it does not receive an acknowledgment within the time allotted, it assumes that it got lost, or the network experienced some problems. The higher-layer protocols retransmit the information. This retransmission occurs transparently to the end users. However, for more time-sensitive applications, such as voice, video, and SNA, extended reroute times can have a negative impact on the performance of the applications.

As mentioned previously, switches usually have some level of hardware redundancy. But what happens when an entire switch fails? The failure of an entire switch results in a loss of connection for locations directly connected to that switch. You lose traffic originating or terminating on that switch. On the other hand, pass-through traffic can potentially survive this type of failure. Pass-through traffic depicts transmissions that do not originate or terminate in the failed switch. The failed switch is simply an intermediate point in the transmission. If the intermediate switch fails, the other switches in the network know to bypass the failed switch and reroute the traffic over a different path using a different intermediate switch (see Figure 7.1).

FIGURE 7.1

Pass-through traffic gets rerouted around the failed intermediate switch.

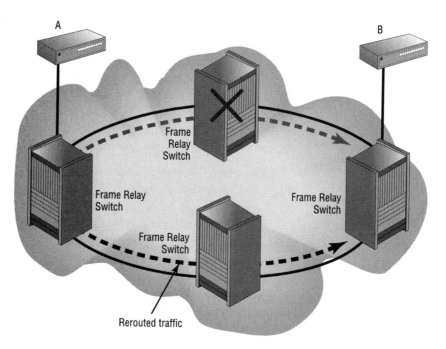

Points of Failure

Although the switches and the facilities between the switches combined give you some level of protection, other parts of the network are left unprotected with a standard frame relay service. The following network components can fail and cause a network outage without a supplementary disaster-recovery plan.

Local access   The vast majority of failures occur on the local access or local loop. The local access connects your location to the service provider's POP or CO closest to your location. In general, your risk of failure increases with longer local access. You can have dedicated, analog dial-up, ISDN, Switched 56/64Kbps, and even wireless access to the frame relay network. Chapter 4 discusses in detail the different types of local access.

Most disaster-recovery plans revolve around having a backup plan when the dedicated local loop fails. Dedicated local loops tend to carry more traffic and applications compared to other local-access methods.

Backhaul   The POP or CO closest to your location (where the local loop terminates) may or may not have a frame relay switch, but all locations need to eventually connect to one. Backhaul refers to the facility between that first non-frame-relay POP and the frame relay–enabled POP (i.e., a POP with a frame relay switch). Some people refer to backhaul as local-access extension. The backhaul facility may be only a few kilometers, but some may be hundreds of kilometers. As with local access, the risk of failure increases with longer backhaul stretches.

CPE   CPE includes routers, FRADs, CSU/DSUs or NTUs, terminal adapters, and other equipment at your locations that connect to the WAN. You may own, install, maintain, and manage the CPE, or the CPE may be part of the provider's managed service offering. See Chapter 12 for more information on managed network services.

Host (or site)   Another potential point of failure is the computer, mainframe, or server that stores content, houses the applications, or responds to end-user requests. In an SNA environment, the remote sites communicate with the host site in a star configuration. In a LAN environment, any location on the network may perform server or host functions as the intelligence is distributed throughout the network. For the purposes of this chapter, a host failure and the complete loss of a location (such as due to a natural disaster) have the same negative impact on the network, and so require the same level of disaster recovery.

Entire frame relay network   A major software problem can propagate through all the switches and brings an entire network down to its knees. Although the probability of this happening in low, it has happened in the past and can happen again in the future.

Disaster-Recovery Solutions

In this section, we will discuss some of the network designs and implementation options that can minimize your risk for problems that might occur in the local loop, backhaul, CPE, host (site), or the entire frame relay network. Remember that no network is 100 percent fail-proof. However, you can build a more robust network with some *insurance*.

For the purposes of discussion, many of the examples cited below implement a disaster-recovery solution for the headquarters or host site. Most users tend to implement disaster recovery for the headquarters location because it typically supports the largest amount of traffic, supports many applications, and houses the company's computer resources. However, you can implement any of these disaster-recovery solutions for any location on your frame relay network. In addition, you can mix and match the options to better meet your network survivability plans.

Local-Access and Backhaul Protection

Local-access failure completely alienates a location from the rest of the network. That location cannot send or receive information from other locations on the network. You can protect your network from local-access and backhaul failures by using A/B (or toggle) switches, SONET rings, or frame relay dial-up access.

A/B or Toggle Switches

Figure 7.2 depicts one way to protect a location from local-access failure. It uses two local loops and an A/B switch at each end of the two local loops. But you use only one CPE port and one frame relay port for a particular location. One of the local loops is designated as "primary" and the other as "backup." Traffic goes over the primary local loop during normal conditions. The backup local loop provides an alternate path for the traffic if the primary loop fails.

The A/B switch or toggle switch simply switches from the failed loop to the backup loop. You can use only one local loop at any given time. Therefore, you cannot load-balance between the two loops.

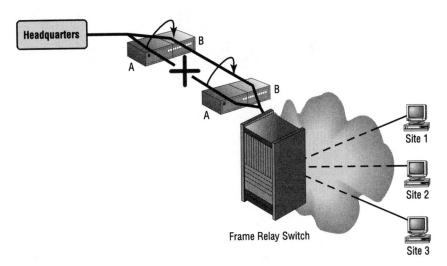

FIGURE 7.2

Local access protection using A/B switches

You can also extend this protection scheme to include the backhaul by connecting each local loop to a separate backhaul facility and connecting the A/B switch (on the network side, not the one on your premises) in the frame relay–enabled POP, as shown in Figure 7.3.

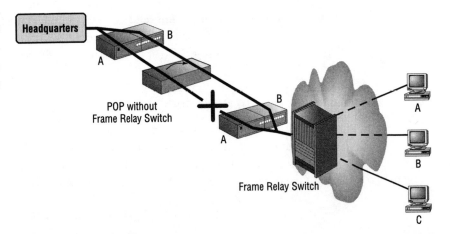

FIGURE 7.3

Local access and backhaul protection using A/B switches

Consider using two diverse local loops (and backhaul). Ideally, you want complete geographic diversity for local access (and backhaul), meaning that the two local loops (and backhaul facilities) traverse entirely different rights-of-way and POPs or COs. There are, of course, shades of geographic diversity. In some situations, the service provider may not have multiple POPs or COs that serve your location. This means that both local loops go through the same POP or CO from your location but may go over diverse facilities as they move out. In the common POP or CO, you can request that the local loops run on different electronic equipment. In this case, you limit your vulnerability to complete failure of that common POP or CO.

Keep in mind that service providers will charge you for both local loops. Some may also have an additional charge for geographic diversity. This additional charge may be substantial, particularly when construction is required. The service provider may need to dig new trenches, build a new POP, lay fiber, and so on to provide extensive geographic diversity.

Most service providers generally do not charge extra for backhaul. However, geographic diversity requirements can change this status.

If you can't obtain or can't cost-justify geographically diverse local loops (and backhaul), consider electronic diversity. Electronically diverse facilities typically traverse the same route and same POP or CO but are provisioned over separate equipment. Electronic diversity protects you from equipment failures but not from POP disasters or cable cuts. Also ask you service provider for the best combination of geographic and electronic diversity possible.

You should note that this disaster-recovery solution does not require any changes in the CPE routing configurations because the same interface on the CPE and the same frame relay port support the traffic in normal and disaster modes. Therefore, communications to and from the location use the same IP address and DLCIs in both modes.

However, you may need to call the service provider to flip the A/B switch when a problem occurs and again when the problem clears. The service provider can operate the A/B switch remotely and does not have to send someone on-site. It generally just takes the service provider a few minutes to make the change once contacted, but you should get a Service Level Agreement (SLA's are discussed in Chapter 13) that includes support for disaster-recovery solutions to ensure this.

SONET Rings

If your location happens to have access to a service provider's SONET (Synchronous Optical NETwork) ring, you don't need to buy a backup local loop. (Locations on a SONET ring are sometimes referred to as *on-net* locations.) Most SONET ring implementations have automatic rerouting capabilities. The nature of SONET allows it to reroute around a failed segment on the ring. Assume that traffic flows in the clockwise direction on the SONET ring during normal conditions. A failure on the ring will cause the ring to reroute the traffic in the counterclockwise direction to avoid the failed segment (see Figure 7.4). This solution does not require any manual intervention to reroute the traffic or any configuration changes to the CPE. Reroute typically happens within just a few milliseconds, usually faster than when frame relay switches reroute traffic.

FIGURE 7.4

Access protection using SONET rings

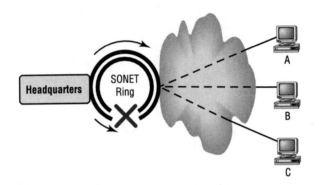

With a SONET ring, unless the frame relay–enabled POP is on the ring itself, the backhaul facility is unprotected.

SONET access has limited availability as of the writing of this book. You can find SONET rings in some high-density areas, such as the downtowns of major metropolitan cities.

Frame Relay Dial-up Access

Many frame relay users use A/B switches or SONET rings as backup for dedicated loops serving large corporate locations. Frame relay dial-up access is the disaster recovery option for small remote locations. If the remote site's local loop fails, the CPE uses an analog dial up or ISDN BRI line to dial in to a RAC (Remote Access Concentrator). The RAC accepts the analog and/or ISDN calls and delivers the information to a frame relay port that has a PVC to the headquarters site. Chapter 4 discusses frame relay dial-up access in detail.

Local Access (and Backhaul), CPE, or Site Protection

This section discusses more ways of protecting your network from local access (and backhaul) failures. It also covers more robust disaster recovery options that reduce the risk of downtime caused by CPE and/or host (site) failures.

DCS-Based Disaster Recovery

Figure 7.5 shows a disaster-recovery configuration slightly similar to the one shown in Figure 7.2. The differences here are that the configuration uses two CPE ports, one primary and one backup, and a DCS (Digital Cross-connect System) to direct (or map) the appropriate local loop to the frame relay port. A DCS is equipment in the service provider's POP that connects two transmission facilities together. During normal conditions, the DCS connects the primary local loop to the frame relay port. If the primary loop fails, the service provider maps the frame relay port to the backup loop.

FIGURE 7.5

Local loop protection using DCS-based local loop redirects

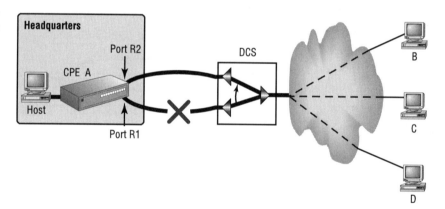

This configuration not only protects you from local loop failures but also from CPE port failures. If for any reason the primary CPE port fails, you can call the service provider to switch to the backup local loop that is connected to the secondary port.

For ease of configuration and management, you can use the same DLCIs for the primary and backup ports on the CPE. During normal conditions, the backup port should be idle and inactive. In case of a disaster, you will activate the backup port, and the distant CPE should learn about the new route to the newly activated port. Most frame relay CPE available in the market today have the intelligence to understand the topology of the network and learn about new routes to various destinations without you having to change the routing tables manually. In the example above, when you activate the backup port—R2—on the CPE A, that port broadcasts its IP address and the route to get to it. The other CPE on the network receive this broadcast message and update their routing tables. The other CPE are also aware that the path to host A via R1 has failed, but the other CPE can now send information to host A via R2. When the other CPE have information destined for location A, they send the traffic to R2 rather than R1.

Figure 7.6 provides a higher level of redundancy because it uses two CPE at the location. It protects your network from not only CPE port failures but total CPE failures. Although you can use only the secondary CPE's port that directly connects to the DCS for backup purposes, you can use other ports on that CPE for other networking application or connections.

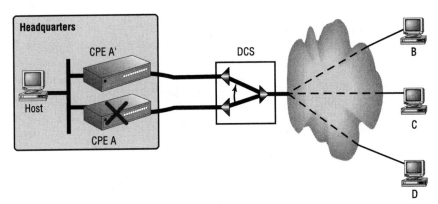

FIGURE 7.6

DCS-based local access and CPE port disaster-recovery option

Figure 7.7 shows the deployment of the backup CPE at a separate, backup host location to protect your network from total site or host disasters. In this case, you can still use the same DLCIs. However, you are now terminating the traffic on a different host with a different IP address. Therefore, the remote sites' CPE routing tables need to be reconfigured to communicate with B using B's IP address instead of A's. If you subscribe to a managed network service, some service providers include CPE software and hardware reconfigurations as part of the service.

FIGURE 7.7

DCS-based site
disaster–recovery
option

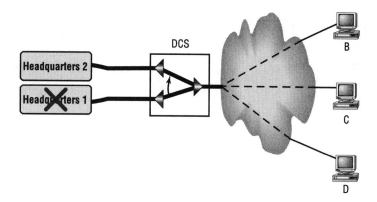

Note that with any of the DCS-based configurations, the primary and backup facilities use the same frame relay port. Therefore, DCS-based solutions cannot recover from failures of the frame relay port, the frame relay switch, or the POP that houses the switch. The DCS itself is a single point of failure.

Also, with any of the DCS-based disaster recovery solutions, most service providers require you to call them to activate a DCS switchover rather than doing the switchover automatically for you. Most service providers can perform a new DCS mapping within 15 to 30 minutes. You also need to call the service provider to switch it back to the original configuration upon problem resolution. This eliminates the possibility of the DCS switching back and forth due to intermittent problems. It also avoids unnecessary switching to the backup facility during a relatively short-term problem (e.g., a power failure for just half a second) when you can afford to wait for resolution. In any case, most service providers require your authorization before switching to or from the backup configuration.

Dual Port-Dual PVC Solution

Other disaster-recovery options similar to the DCS-based solutions use a combination of dual frame relay ports and dual PVCs. In the DCS-based solutions the primary and backup local loops use the same frame relay port. In the dual port–dual PVC option, each local loop connects to a separate port connection. Each remote location that needs to communicate with the host site has two PVCs, one to each of the two local loops (and ports), as shown in Figure 7.8.

FIGURE 7.8

Dual ports and
dual PVCs into
two CPE ports

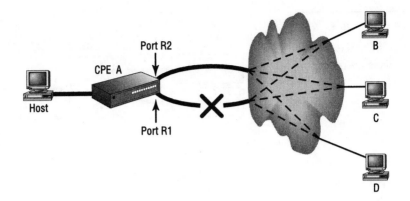

Both sets of PVCs are active at all times. You also have the option to designate one local loop and port as primary and the other local loop and port as backup, or you can use both paths simultaneously in a load-balancing fashion. This means that the CPE distributes the traffic evenly over the two sets of PVCs during normal conditions. In case of a CPE port, local access (and backhaul), or port failure on one path, all traffic can traverse over the PVCs that connect to the other path. Most users use both sets of PVCs during normal conditions rather than reserving one set for backup purposes only. It makes sense because most service providers charge you for both sets of PVCs. However, some service providers might encourage you to set aside one set of backup PVCs by offering significantly reduced prices for those in comparison to the primary PVCs. For the purposes of discussion, assume a load-balancing network.

Because there are two ports and two sets of PVCs, it is recommended to use two different sets of DLCIs for each port for simplicity and to minimize confusion.

When it comes to CIRs, the two sets of PVCs typically mirror each other. You can assign CIRs to the PVCs such that the aggregate of *both* sets of PVC CIRs equate to the average traffic volumes during normal conditions. Given this design, you may need to operate in less than optimal conditions with only half the bandwidth available during disasters. On the other hand, you can assign CIRs to one set of PVCs such that one set can optimally support average traffic volume even during disasters. In this case, you have spare bandwidth available to further boost application performance or support additional applications during normal conditions. For example, you may achieve improved response times for file transfers or e-mail. Alternatively, you can put intracompany voice applications on the frame relay network. If a disaster occurs, you can preempt the voice applications off of the frame relay network and run those over the PSTN.

To protect your network from switch or POP failures using dual ports and PVCs, ask your service provider to terminate the two local loops into two different frame relay switches, preferably in two different POPs.

Figure 7.9 depicts a configuration using two CPE at the host site that are protecting the network from CPE failures.

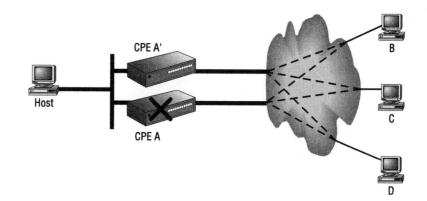

One configuration where you may want to have one set of PVCs as primary and one set as secondary or backup is shown in Figure 7.10 below. Again, you'll have different DLCIs for the PVCs terminating in the primary and backup ports. In a disaster situation, similar to the DCS-based site-recovery option shown in Figure 7.5, the remote locations need to know the IP address of the backup host site.

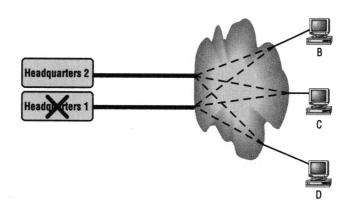

PVC Redirects

PVC redirects work similarly to dual ports and dual PVCs. The biggest difference is that there is only one set of PVCs rather two. In this plan, you obviously cannot load-share or load-balance. Therefore, one frame relay port is designated as primary and the other is secondary or backup.

When a disaster occurs, the service provider typically invokes a script that redirects or remaps the PVCs to the backup port with your authorization. The service provider can redirect the PVCs within a few minutes. The redirection time depends on the number of PVCs to redirect.

The backup port typically uses the same DLCIs as the primary port. It can use the same DLCIs because the redirected PVCs to the backup port are essentially the same PVCs that were on the primary port.

PVC redirects offers a more cost-effective solution compared to dual port–dual PVC designs because you have to pay for only one set of PVCs. However, you lose the advantages of load-balancing and not having to call the service provider to invoke any scripts, except if you rely on the service provider for CPE configuration and management.

The diagrams for PVC redirects look the same as dual port–dual PVCs without the second set of PVCs. The one set of PVCs toggle between the primary and backup ports depending on the situation.

Growable PVCs

Growable PVC configurations look similar to the dual port–dual PVC plan because they also use two ports and two sets of PVCs. In addition, both sets of PVCs are active at all times. The biggest difference with growable PVCs is that the second set of PVCs is primarily used for backup purposes, and you have the ability to increase (or grow) the CIR of these PVCs in disaster situations. You cannot grow the CIR of the primary PVCs. Although the primary use for growable PVCs is backup, you can use both the primary and growable PVCs simultaneously during normal conditions. Because both sets of PVCs are active, the service provider typically assigns two different DLCIs for the primary port and for the backup port that supports the growable PVCs.

The ability to grow the backup PVCs can save you money as you can subscribe to very low CIRs for the backup PVCs and simply grow them if and when required. Some service providers allow you to subscribe to Zero CIR for the backup PVCs. When you grow the backup PVCs, the service provider can charge based on the incremental CIR and minutes of use on a per-PVC basis.

Depending on how quickly you or the service provider can fix the problem, you can assess whether you can run suboptimally on the lower-speed backup PVCs for the duration. However, if you cannot tolerate suboptimal response time for the expected duration of the outage, consider growing the backup PVCs to the CIR level of the primary PVCs. You may need to call your service provider to grow the backup PVCs, or the service provider might offer an online or Web-based network management system that allows authorized personnel in your organization to make the modifications.

Total Network Failures

Although the probability of total frame relay network failures is slim, you can't be too cautious. Total network failures result in the inability to send or receive information between any and all locations on the frame relay network. Total network failures can and have happened and may happen again in the future. Therefore, here are several precautionary implementations to survive this type of catastrophe.

Dial-Around Solution

One solution for smaller remote sites is to have a dial backup solution using either analog dial-up access or ISDN BRI. If the entire frame relay network fails, the remote site can dial around the frame relay network over the PSTN. At the headquarters site, you can use a RAC (Remote Access Concentrator) to receive the analog or ISDN calls. This solution completely bypasses the frame relay network, as shown in Figure 7.11.

FIGURE 7.11

Dial-around solutions completely bypass the frame relay network during an entire network disaster.

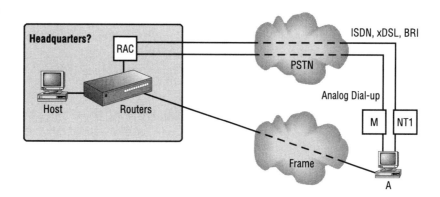

Some service providers have a prepackaged service that includes dial backup. They may provide the analog modems or ISDN NT1 (jack) at the remote sites as well as the RAC at your headquarters.

The dial-around solution also works well when a remote site's local loop fails.

Dual Frame Relay Solution

A dual frame relay solution uses two different frame relay networks from two service providers. Figure 7.12 shows that each location has one connection to one network and another to the other network. The configuration on service provider A's network mirrors the configuration on service provider B's network.

FIGURE 7.12

Dual Frame Relay
Solution

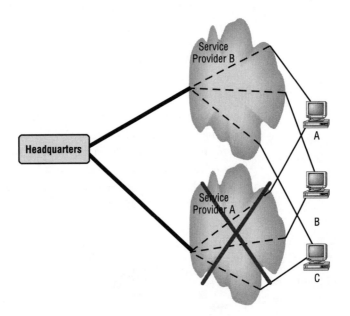

You can load balance between the two networks or use one as primary and the other as backup. Even if one of the service provider's networks completely fail, communications continue to flow over the other service provider's network. Although this provides a very robust disaster-recovery solution, it is often cost-prohibitive for most companies to implement. It also means interfacing, coordinating, and managing two service providers.

Some service providers typically include one or two opportunities for you to test your disaster-recovery plan as part of the service. These are scheduled tests that normally happen during off-hours or on weekends. These tests provide you with some disaster-recovery performance benchmarks to determine whether you need to make changes and further optimize your plan. They also help ensure that if a failure does occur, the plan will work!

Choosing the Best Disaster-Recovery Solution

Choosing the best disaster-recovery solution for your network is not a trivial task. Evaluating the many disaster-recovery solutions with the various options available and determining the differences between the various service provider offerings can drive you crazy. But don't fret yet! If you break-down the decision-making process into bite-sized, chewable chunks, the task becomes more achievable. This section discusses the different parameters you should consider.

Criticality of the Network

First and foremost, assess the level of importance of your network to your business. The network's level of importance increases as

- The number of applications it supports increases.

- The number of locations or users connected increases.

- The network supports more critical business applications, such as order entry, inventory, payroll, billing, collaborative computing, and others.

- The network plays a more significant role in improving overall business efficiency, productivity, competitiveness, and service quality.

- The network helps to generate more revenues and decreases cost, hence improving overall profitability.

- The network provides connectivity to suppliers, partners, and customers.

As the network becomes more important and more integral to your business, losing part or all of this network becomes increasingly painful to your company. This pain generally dictates whether you need to have a disaster-recovery solution. If so, how robust does the plan need to be to minimize or alleviate the pain? In general, more pain equates to the need for a more fault-tolerant disaster-recovery plan.

Business Impact of Failure

Knowing you have pain is only the first step. You now have to quantify your level of pain. To do this, do a "failure" analysis. In this failure analysis, pretend to fail each of the different points of failure on your network and assess the business impact of that failure. As mentioned previously, the typical points of failure are as follows:

- Host
- CPE
- CPE port
- Site
- Local access
- Backhaul
- Frame relay port
- Frame relay switch
- Frame relay–enabled POP or CO
- Entire frame relay network

Consider the likelihood of failure of the different components. Local access and backhaul tend to be the most vulnerable. CPE failures are common, as well. Remember that the service provider already offers some basic level of redundancy for the frame relay equipment and the virtual circuits. Therefore, those components are less likely to fail.

Also assess the different business impacts of failure at various locations on your network, such as headquarters site, regional sales offices, remote sites, and home offices. In an SNA environment where most communications typically happen between the host at the headquarters and the dumb terminals at the remote sites, a failure at the host has a greater business impact than failure at one or more of the remote sites. For example, the local access for a retail-clothing company's headquarters fails. This may result in the remote sales offices not being able to place orders for the duration of the outage because none of the sales offices can access the order-entry system on the mainframe. However, if one of the sales office's local loops fail, the failure will only affect sales from that sales office but not from all of the other sales offices. On the other hand, in networks with distributed hosts or intelligence with any-to-any traffic patterns, failure of any of the locations may affect the business the same way with equal impact.

Doing this exercise will help you prioritize which points of failure you want to protect and which ones you can live with without protection. At some point, most companies have to make a decision about what to protect and what not to protect. Skipping the failure analysis step will make the decision difficult.

Unfortunately, the failure analysis does not cover business impacts not related to network failures or disasters. For example, financial institutions in some countries are mandated by their governments to have a disaster-recovery plan to stay in business. The regulation may or may not specify the level of fault-tolerance required. In this situation, regulation becomes one of the motivations for implementing a plan.

Financial Impact of Failure

You need to quantify your pain by placing a monetary value on it. Using the same list of points of failure, determine the financial impact on your company when each of these components fails. Also estimate the financial impact on your business with prolonged outages. This is a financial analysis.

Again, this step achieves some of the same goals as when you assessed the business impact of failures. However, it gives you additional insight on a possible disaster-recovery budget if you currently don't have one. Many companies have found that as they go through this step, the budget becomes elastic. As the cost of failure increases, the budget seems to increase, as well. For those of you who do not have control over the budget allocations, this financial analysis can help you cost-justify a disaster-recovery plan.

Using the same retail-clothing company example, assume that the company can potentially lose $1 million in sales if the local loop at the headquarters fails for four hours. That estimated loss makes it easy for that company's network manager to buy a geographically diverse local loop terminating into a separate frame relay switch as backup for the primary local loop. The diverse loop may only cost the company about $1,200 per month—a small price to pay, considering the consequences of not having a disaster-recovery plan.

Downtime Tolerance

Determine your threshold or tolerance for downtime. This threshold determines the frequency and length of outage that justifies the implementation of a disaster-recovery plan.

Many service providers offer network availability or reliability ratings for their services. The rating is usually expressed as a percentage, such as 99.5 percent. An availability of 99.5 percent means that the network will be available 99.5 percent of the time. Beware of these ratings, because not all ratings are created equal! Service providers use different measurement methods, calculations, demarcations for the rating (e.g., POP-to-POP or end-to-end, including local access), measurement intervals, and reporting methods for availability.

For discussion purposes, assume that a service provider has a 99.5 percent end-to-end availability objective. That works out to almost two days of downtime over the course of one year. Assume that this is total network availability, meaning that it is the total aggregate downtime of all the locations. Therefore, you can have a total of two days worth of outages at one location, two days of outages spread evenly between all the locations, etc. In the worst case, can you afford two days worth of outages at the headquarters site over a year? Of course, it also depends on the length of each outage incident—two one-day outages, four hours every month, two hours every other week, etc.

Table 7.1 provides an example of the amount of average downtime for some common reliability ratings.

T A B L E 7.1 Average Downtimes for Reliability Ratings	**Network Reliability**	**Annual Downtime**
	99.5%	43.8 hours
	99.9%	8.8 hours
	99.99%	52.6 minutes
	99.999%	5.26 minutes
	99.9999%	32 seconds

If you have very low tolerance for outages and your network needs near–100 percent availability for some network components, you need a backup solution readily available when the disaster happens. Consider SONET rings for local-access protection, dual port–dual PVC into two separate host sites for host-site protection, or even dual frame relay networks for protection against entire network failures. You can design these plans because they require little user or service-provider intervention during the disaster.

Performance Requirements of Backup Solution

When operating in backup mode, determine the level of performance you need from the network. For the different types of failures, estimate the outage time. For example, most service providers quote an MTTR (Mean Time To Repair) of four hours for local loops. Determine whether you can live with less-than-optimal performance while operating in the backup mode for four hours. If you can, consider solutions such as growable PVCs or dual port–dual PVC with the second set of PVCs running at speeds less than the primary PVC. These solutions save you money on the backup PVCs.

You might also consider DCS-based solutions or PVC redirects. However, remember that these solutions require intervention from the service provider and may take a few minutes to set up. If you feel the setup time is acceptable, these solutions usually provide an even more cost-effective solution than growable PVCs or dual port–dual PVC.

Availability and Expertise of In-House Network Personnel

Don't forget to consider the manpower needed to design, implement, maintain, and manage a disaster-recovery plan. Evaluate the network resources available to you internally and their level of expertise. You also need to have the ability to maintain and manage the network $24 \times 7 \times 365$. If you have limited resources, you may want to consider outsourcing or subscribing to a managed network service, in which the service provider is responsible for supporting the entire network and CPE, even during disasters.

However, very few service providers offer services that include the management of the hosts (or the site itself). Some service providers have network integrator partners that can perform that function. Some service providers also partner with a disaster-recovery company to provide the backup host at the disaster-recovery company's location. The service provider may package these partner services or you may need to sign a separate contract with the various partners.

Disaster-Recovery Budget

Do not underestimate the cost of your desired solution. Many companies focus on the transport cost only. Include any cost for CPE, construction for diversity, network design, maintenance and management, test (if the service provider charges for the tests), backup host at a disaster-recovery company's location, and so on. Consider sending an RFP (Request for Proposal) to several service providers not only to evaluate different disaster-recovery plans but also to compare pricing.

After considering the various factors, you will probably want more fault-tolerance, although you may have a limited budget. Prioritization now plays an important part in the decision-making process. Use the list of priorities you developed from the failure analysis and begin filtering the "preferred" and "nice to have" from the "mandatory." If you find that your budget still cannot give you your mandatory requirements, consider a phased implementation. You don't necessarily need to protect everything on day one. You can protect the most important components first, try to get more money, and then implement the other phases once you get additional budget approval. A good failure and financial analysis will give you good ammunition to loosen up the purse strings of the CFO. Remember that budget is often elastic. It expands with increased pain!

Summary

Most frame relay services have some inherent self-healing capabilities, particularly within the frame relay network itself (e.g., the switches and connections between the switches). Although frame relay offers some basic level of fault tolerance, it has unprotected components vulnerable to network failures. You can choose from various disaster-recovery solutions to build a more fault-tolerant network. These solutions protect your network from host, CPE, CPE port, site, local-access, backhaul, frame relay–port, switch, POP, and even entire frame relay network disasters.

In choosing the best disaster-recovery solutions for your company, you need to consider the criticality of your network, business impact of failure, financial impact of failure, downtime tolerance, performance requirement of backup solution, availability and expertise of in-house network personnel, and disaster-recovery budget.

CHAPTER

8

Integrating Voice in a Frame
Relay Network

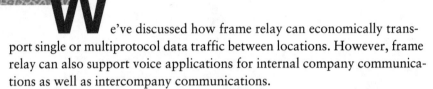

W e've discussed how frame relay can economically transport single or multiprotocol data traffic between locations. However, frame relay can also support voice applications for internal company communications as well as intercompany communications.

For the purposes of this book, *on-net* refers to locations directly connected to the frame relay network, and *off-net* refers to locations not connected to the frame relay network. This chapter primarily focuses on intracompany, on-net voice communications because providers have not yet launched commercially available services that connect off-net locations with on-net locations using PSTN-to–frame relay gateways.

History of Shared Voice and Data Networks

In the 1970s, implementing networks was straightforward. Companies used POTS (Plain Old Telephone Service) over the PSTN for local and long-distance voice communications. Companies deployed private lines as tie lines for connecting Private Branch eXchanges (PBXs) and key systems between locations with high-traffic volumes. Although the hierarchical terminal-to-host data applications ran over multipoint, multidrop circuits, companies typically maintained separate and parallel networks for their voice and data applications.

As DS-1/E-1 circuits became available and affordable, companies gained economies of scale by using channel banks to break down the DS-1/E-1 into 24/30 individual DS-0 channels. Companies allocated some channels to internal voice and others to internal data. Companies also built private networks to aggregate traffic, using intelligent multiplexers capable of rerouting around network failures to increase network survivability. The intelligent multiplexers improved network efficiency and utilization through compression techniques. During this time, companies cost-justified their networks based on voice traffic, and the data used the "free" excess network capacity whenever available.

With the advent of personal computers, LANs, and client-server applications, a more distributed networking environment emerged. This environment placed new stresses on the wide-area network and brought to light many of the disadvantages of private lines. Some of these disadvantages include vulnerability to network outages, inefficient bandwidth allocation, and inflexibilities in accommodating network changes. Packet-switched networks were developed to address the limitations of private lines.

In the meantime, the price and availability of VPNs (Virtual Private Networks) for voice applications improved. Voice applications transitioned to the VPNs, and the data traffic remained on the private backbones.

In the early 1990s, the industry introduced frame relay as a replacement service for private lines and X.25. Frame relay was initially developed to transport LAN internetworking traffic and later used for terminal-to-host applications. Customers immediately saw the cost benefits of integrating multiple applications over a single network infrastructure. It didn't take long for customers to start clamoring for the addition of voice to the frame relay portfolio of supported applications.

Obvious economies-of-scale benefits exist from integrating voice and data applications over frame relay. However, frame relay by nature is less suitable for delay-sensitive and delay variation–sensitive applications, such as voice. Transmission over a public frame relay network can result in artificial, unnatural, and choppy speech transmissions because delay is not constant. Many frame relay networks treat all frames the same regardless of the type of application the frames support, unless the service provider offers frame relay classes of service for different applications. In other words, the network services a delay-sensitive voice frame the same way as a more delay-tolerant data frame.

Therefore, CPE vendors developed innovative solutions to make voice-over frame relay possible. CPE vendors designed FRADs, routers, and access concentrators that can support multiple applications and have the intelligence to ensure end-to-end service quality that meets the unique performance requirements of each application.

Why Voice-Over Frame Relay?

Organizations use frame relay for internal voice traffic for a variety of reasons. The most compelling reasons include cost savings, single-network platform, and improved performance. Each of these reasons are discussed next.

Cost Savings   Saving expenses on internal company calls is the overriding goal of most companies deploying voice-over frame relay. With calls between countries costing many times those of domestic calls (average of 75 cents per minute in the U.S.), many multinational companies look for ways to trim expenses, and some have turned to frame relay for a solution. Most companies deploying voice-over frame relay estimate payback periods of a year or less.

Simplified Network   A single network for voice and data applications offers a solution that's easier to install, maintain, and manage. This frees up some corporate resources and expertise to focus on core business issues rather than on networking. It can also allow the organization to operate with a single IT manager instead of two. On the downside, network failures can affect both the data and voice communications at the same time. But this is not a big issue for two reasons: first, frame relay networks have inherent automatic rerouting; second, companies can use the PSTN for backup purposes.

Better Network Utilization   Most end users design their frame relay networks to meet the bandwidth requirements of their data applications. The virtual circuits have CIRs that provide the ideal application performance during transmissions. However, transmissions are bursty. Rarely would you find sustained and prolonged data transmission that consumes the full bandwidth. When sending a file, you might need the entire CIR or the CIR as well as extra bandwidth (burst). But after the file transfer, other applications can use the bandwidth available. In general, most virtual circuits have low-average utilization levels.

Voice-over frame relay allows you to share a single virtual circuit among your voice and data applications. The network interleaves voice between data bursts or it interleaves data between speech bursts. This results in higher overall network efficiency.

However, you must not always assume that your existing frame relay network design can support voice without increasing the degree of connectivity, CIRs, and port speeds. Voice may not always get a free ride. If you currently have high use on your frame relay network, integrating voice traffic on the network can negatively impact the performance of your data applications.

Quality of Voice-Over Frame Relay

Many end users have questions regarding the quality of voice-over frame relay. Although quality is subjective, the telecommunications industry uses MOS (Mean Opinion Score) to rate relative qualities of voice transmissions. The scale ranges from 0 to 5.0. A mean score of 4.0 to 5.0 is toll quality—the quality of calls over the PSTN. Initially, the quality of voice-over frame relay was relatively poor, but over the years, it has improved.

Some of today's voice-over frame relay implementations using voice-capable frame relay CPE have scored 4.1 to 4.3, scores well within toll-quality range. It is important to note that network design and CPE selection are key ingredients in achieving high-quality voice transmissions over a frame relay network.

Typical Network Designs

Traditionally, organizations deployed separate and parallel data networks to support different data applications and protocols. Many organizations also deployed segregated voice and data networks. These architectures resulted from the lack of viable solutions that integrated both data and voice traffic over the same infrastructure. This leads to many networks that look like the diagram in Figure 8.1.

The sample implementation in Figure 8.1 shows three separate networks. The frame relay network carries the data applications (lines with arrows). The second network consists of connections (dashed lines) to the PSTN for intercompany or external voice communications. Third, all internal company voice communications run over a dedicated private line network (thick black lines). Designing, installing, and managing three separate networks is expensive and

FIGURE 8.1

Separate and parallel
voice and data
networks

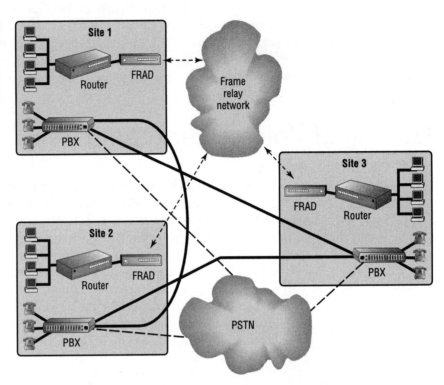

can be labor intensive. Additionally, these network implementations typically result in underutilized network facilities because end users design them to handle peak traffic, not average traffic.

If the same company decides to use a frame relay network to transmit internal company voice traffic in addition to its data traffic, the new design would look similar to the diagram in Figure 8.2.

Notice that the PBX and the router are now connected to the FRAD at each site. The frame relay network now supports the company's intracompany data and voice applications. The connections to the PSTN primarily support inter-company off-net voice calls and overflow internal company calls.

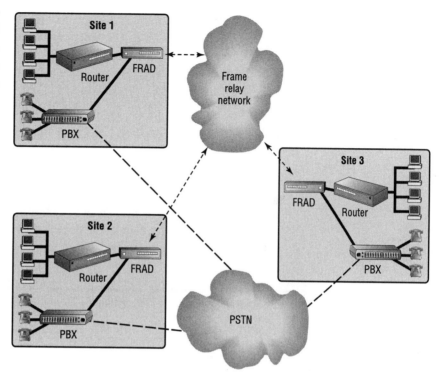

FIGURE 8.2

Frame relay supporting data and intracompany voice

Characteristics of Voice Traffic

Prior to transporting voice over the frame relay network, the transmitting CPE must first convert the analog voice signal to a digital signal. Then the terminating CPE needs to convert the digital signal back to analog. This analog-to-digital and digital-to-analog conversion process is in fact one of the easiest tasks to accomplish. Modems convert signals back and forth for data transmissions across the PSTN, enabling remote LAN access, Internet access, and fax transmissions.

Anyone who has listened to a modem or a fax machine as it sends information can immediately tell the vast difference between the way machines communicate and the way people communicate verbally. Voice communication has characteristics, such as silence, background noise, inflection, tone, a half-duplex traffic pattern (one person speaking at any given time), and time sensitivity, not found in most data protocols. These unique voice characteristics require a set of CPE and network capabilities different from those designed for data transmissions. The next section discusses these capabilities in greater detail.

Voice-Over Frame Relay Transmission Overview

This section provides an overview of voice transmission over frame relay. The following flow diagram (Figure 8.3) depicts the interaction between the caller, the voice-capable CPE and frame relay network, and the called party.

FIGURE 8.3

Voice-over frame relay call flow

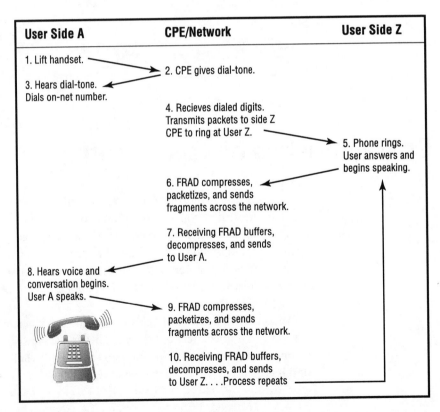

User Side A	CPE/Network	User Side Z
1. Lift handset.	2. CPE gives dial-tone.	
3. Hears dial-tone. Dials on-net number.		
	4. Recieves dialed digits. Transmits packets to side Z CPE to ring at User Z.	5. Phone rings. User answers and begins speaking.
	6. FRAD compresses, packetizes, and sends fragments across the network.	
	7. Receiving FRAD buffers, decompresses, and sends to User A.	
8. Hears voice and conversation begins. User A speaks.	9. FRAD compresses, packetizes, and sends fragments across the network.	
	10. Receiving FRAD buffers, decompresses, and sends to User Z. . . .Process repeats	

Looking at step 3 in Figure 8.3, you can configure the CPE to accept either a complete phone number or an internal company dial plan from the end user dialing the number. You can also configure the CPE to allow end users to choose the PSTN or the frame relay network for voice transmissions on a call-by-call basis. For example, the user may dial 9 to access the PSTN or dial 6 to use the frame relay network before dialing the phone number.

In steps 6 and 9, some FRADs perform additional functions, such as prioritization and echo cancellation, which we'll discuss later in this chapter.

How the CPE Makes It Work

This section discusses the various features CPE vendors implement to support voice-over frame relay network.

Prioritization   The following table shows the various CPE and network functions that contribute to overall one-way delay in a voice-over frame relay implementation. It also indicates some average delay times over a domestic frame relay network.

Input Buffer	15msec
Compression	15msec
FRAD Output Queue	15msec
Network Transmission	25msec
Jitter Buffer	60msec
Decompression	5msec
Total	135msec

The average person can begin to notice degradation in voice quality if one-way delay exceeds more than 225msec. It is therefore important to minimize delay introduced by the network and the CPE as much as possible.

Most voice FRADs employ traffic prioritization schemes to minimize delay on voice traffic. Voice traffic is equally or more sensitive to delay than SNA applications. (Chapter 6 discusses the need to prioritize delay-sensitive SNA traffic over other applications.) Frame relay CPE that do not support voice typically use the first-in, first-out method of handling traffic. However, this method introduces the possibility that a long queue of data frames may delay voice frames, resulting in poor quality voice. The CPE does not necessarily have to send voice before all other traffic in all cases. In fact, if this were to happen, data performance would suffer. Instead, the CPE interleaves data and voice traffic such that the network delivers the voice frames in a timely manner while continuing to transmit data traffic.

During times of network congestion, one of the easiest prioritization methods is to configure the CPE to set the DE bit on all data traffic to 1. By doing so, the frame relay network will discard data traffic first, giving voice a better chance of making it through the network. However, different frame relay networks respond to the DE bit set by the CPE in different ways. Some may not acknowledge or pay attention to DE bits at all. It's best to check with your service provider about how the network responds to DE bits set by the CPE.

Keep in mind that this recommendation of setting the DE bit for data traffic to 1 does not mean that the network will transmit voice more quickly over the network in comparison to data. The setting simply allows you to prioritize which frames get dropped first if the network absolutely has to drop frames. Remember that voice is delay sensitive but not necessarily loss sensitive, while some data applications have the opposite characteristics. Therefore, losing some voice frames may result in some silence, a brief skip somewhere in the conversation, or omission of a word. It may not significantly impact the conversation as the receiver can sometimes still understand the message based on context, or the receiver may simply ask the caller to repeat the message. In some situations, the receiver may not even notice it. You can also use the PSTN as a backup if the network drops an excessive number of voice frames. If you have a significantly higher percentage of voice traffic or if voice is more mission critical to your business, then using the DE bit may offer a viable solution to prioritizing.

Some service providers offer PVC prioritization on the frame relay network. Prioritization features on both the CPE and the frame relay network can result in better voice application performance. The CPE sends higher priority traffic to the network first and PVC prioritization within the network ensures the delivery of higher-priority traffic to its destination first. Refer to Chapter 9 for more details on PVC priorities.

Fragmentation/Segmentation   Most CPE typically use frame prioritization in combination with frame fragmentation. These two features used together can deliver consistent and high-quality data and voice-application performance.

To facilitate efficient transport of both data and voice frames, many voice FRADs divide the outgoing frames into smaller frames, as shown in

Figure 8.4. Fragmentation minimizes or eliminates the possibility of large data frames delaying time-sensitive voice frames. For anyone who has driven down a two-lane road (one lane in each direction) and suddenly found themselves "stuck" behind a big, slow moving truck, the frustration can be overwhelming. You can't pass, and traffic begins to back up. The same is true for voice frames that get stuck behind large data frames. This delays the voice transmission and compromises voice.

FIGURE 8.4

Voice fragmentation/
segmentation

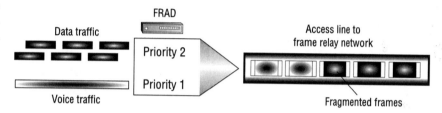

Although the fragmentation of voice and data traffic typically results in reduced delay, less delay variation, and improved voice quality, it can also lead to an increase in overhead. Overhead refers to non-user data necessary for transmission. Each frame has a fixed-length header and trailer regardless of frame size. This results in higher overhead percentage as the frame size decreases—an important consideration when the CPE uses frame fragmentation. The smaller the packets, the higher the overhead percentage. Overhead reduces the usable bandwidth for transporting user data. Therefore, the voice FRADs have to balance providing high-quality voice with using bandwidth efficiently.

Fragmentation not only reduces delay but also helps in reducing the impact of lost frames. You may miss half a word or a word at the most if the frame relay network discards or drops a small voice frame.

Jitter Buffering   Delay variation is caused by network oversubscription and different delay times between consecutive packets sent over the frame relay network. For example, two consecutive voice frames are sent to the frame relay network. If the second frame is delayed at the switch due to congestion for 20 milliseconds, the first packet will arrive at time x and packet 2 at time x + 20ms. If the receiving voice FRAD immediately sends these packets directly to the receiver, then the resulting voice would be jittery if the variation exceeds 25ms. To minimize jitter, voice FRADs have buffers that hold the delivery of incoming frames so slightly delayed frames have a chance to arrive. Jitter buffering controls processing of frames to ensure continuous speech output. Unlike data, late is not necessarily better than never for voice-over frame relay. Jittery voice may sound incomprehensible or muddled. If a frame is delayed a great deal, greater than the jitter buffer can handle, then the network might as well drop it. The CPE must then decide whether to deliver the voice without the missing frame or estimate what the missing frame contained and deliver a reconstructed frame.

The jitter buffer also comes into play when packets arrive at the terminating location out of order. When packets traverse different routes through the network, it's possible they do not arrive in order due to one route having a higher transit delay than another. If this is the case, the jitter buffer allows most of these slightly delayed packets to be inserted in the correct order and therefore re-creates a high-quality voice transmission. If the different route delays the packets significantly, the jitter buffer may have to re-create the voice transmission without the use of these packets—just as though they were dropped.

Voice Interpolation   For some data applications, the higher-layer protocols take responsibility for requesting a retransmission if the network drops a frame. If voice packets are lost/discarded, one method for recovery is for the sender to repeat the message. Fortunately, the sender typically would not need to do this, especially with frame fragmentation. As we mentioned previously, frame fragmentation creates small voice frames. The loss of a small frame is generally not noticeable. The listener may just hear a brief skip.

Some voice FRADs can interpolate the lost information based on the frames before and after the lost frame. The FRAD re-creates the missing frame and delivers it as part of the voice signal.

Route-Through   In star and partially meshed networks, there is not always a direct route between two locations. Frames must tandem through an intermediate site to reach their destination. In Figure 8.5 below, Site 1 needs to talk to Site 3. If the intermediate site's (Site 2) voice FRAD must buffer, decompress, and recompress the voice packets before sending them to the final destination, the delay increases by approximately 100ms. Figure 8.5 illustrates the process.

To avoid voice degradation, some voice FRADs support route-through. With route-through, the FRAD at the intermediate site does not buffer, decompress, and recompress the frames. Instead, it simply redirects the frames to their final destination. Traffic from Site 1 is sent to Site 2. The voice FRAD at Site 2 recognizes that the traffic is intended for Site 3 and immediately redirects the frames. Route-through minimizes the total network delay across the frame relay network.

Compression   Voice traffic takes up a full DS-0 circuit (64Kbps) on traditional voice networks. In order to gain better network utilization, many voice

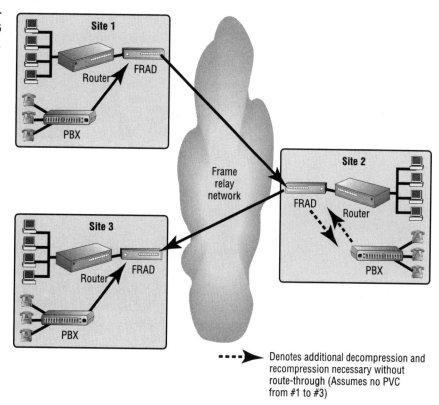

FIGURE 8.5

Voice-over frame relay
without route-through

service providers use compression algorithms that allow the voice to use 32Kbps, doubling the number of voice calls the network can support. Voice FRAD vendors also implement compression algorithms. By compressing the voice traffic, you can send more voice calls and more data across the network. The level of compression typically varies from 32Kbps to 4.8Kbps depending on the compression algorithm used.

There are literally dozens of compression algorithms used by voice FRAD vendors today. Some of the most common ones include ACELP (Algebraic Code Excited Linear Predictive coding), G.727, CELP (Code Excited Linear Predictive coding), G.728, G.726, G.729, etc. The Frame Relay Forum's voice-over frame relay implementation agreement, FRF.11, specifies two compression algorithms: G.727 and G.729. The next section discusses how these compression standards work.

Don't let compression ratings mislead you. A compression algorithm that can compress a voice signal from 64Kbps to 8Kbps may require bandwidth higher or lower than 8Kbps. Other factors, such as frame relay overhead, can increase 8Kbps to perhaps 16Kbps, but silence suppression may bring the bandwidth requirement down to 10Kbps. Your CPE vendors can assist you in determining the effective bandwidth needed.

Figure 8.6 depicts how overhead adds to network bandwidth requirements.

FIGURE 8.6

Voice-over frame relay overheads

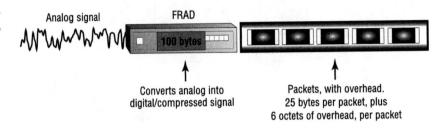

Analog signal — FRAD

Converts analog into digital/compressed signal

Packets, with overhead. 25 bytes per packet, plus 6 octets of overhead, per packet

Silence Detection and Suppression   In combination with compression, it is also possible to filter out silence from voice transmissions. Speech typically has pauses and moments of silence. Silence accounts for about 50 percent of the average voice call. Most voice networks transmit this silence, using as much bandwidth as the actual speech. In order to achieve better network utilization, voice FRADs do not transmit silence, freeing some capacity for other applications or more voice calls. Instead of transmitting the silence, the originating FRAD sends a small packet indicating where the terminating FRAD needs to reinsert the silence and the length of the silent portion back into the speech pattern.

Echo Cancellation   The analog-to-digital hybrid found when analog phones are connected to digital networks typically causes echo. Longer connections are more susceptible to echo because of longer transmission delays. Connections over 500 miles usually need echo cancellers. Most CPE have built-in echo-cancellation capabilities.

The Voice-Over Frame Relay Standard

Early implementations of voice-over frame relay required the deployment of a single-vendor CPE solution to ensure interoperability between locations. Selecting a single vendor was the only way to make sure that the voice FRADs were using the same voice algorithms. The increasing number of voice-over frame relay CPE vendors and end-user implementation drove the development of the standard for voice-over frame relay, allowing you to deploy a multivendor solution. In 1997, the Frame Relay Forum approved a voice-over frame relay standard, Implementation Agreement FRF.11.

The approval of the standard does not change this practice much. Most vendors have enhanced features beyond the scope of the implementation agreement. FRF.11 offers guidelines for compression but does not address silence suppression, fragmentation, and other voice-over frame relay features. This causes substantial ambiguity in FRF.11. The responsibility of ensuring interoperability still largely falls on your shoulders when considering a multivendor solution. But some of the CPE vendors are conducting interoperability tests with each other to minimize end-user interoperability concerns.

The standard accomplishes two main goals. First, it legitimizes the voice-over frame relay market. With standards in place, more vendors and service providers feel comfortable supporting the technology. Second, customers can now more easily deploy multivendor, best-of-breed voice FRAD solutions.

The implementation agreement sets two separate categories of compression that determine whether a vendor is standards compliant. Equipment vendors only need to offer one of the compression options to comply with the standard.

G.727   Vendors are considered Class 1 compliant if they support G.727, a 32Kbps compression algorithm. It uses Adaptive Differential Pulse Code Modulation (ADPCM) speech-coding method. This method calculates the difference between two consecutive voice samples. Rather than transmitting two full voice samples, the FRAD only sends the deviations between the two samples. This decreases the amount of bandwidth required for transmission. At the far end, the receiving FRAD reassembles the voice signals.

G.729   G.729 uses the Conjugate Structure Algebraic Code Explicit Linear Prediction (CS-ACELP) compression algorithm. It compresses a voice signal from 64Kbps to 8Kbps. Vendors who support G.729 are considered Class 2 compliant.

The FRAD analyzes the incoming voice signal and tries to find a similar signal in a "code book." In the code book, each signal is assigned a code number. The FRAD then transmits the code number to the receiving FRAD, which then looks it up in its "code book" and sends that signal. It's similar to stenography: certain symbols represent words and phrases to speed up the note-taking or dictation process. The sending FRAD transmits the code number only over the frame relay network to achieve better bandwidth efficiencies. The receiving FRAD decodes the information and re-creates the voice signal.

Off-net Calling

As mentioned previously, frame relay service providers have not connected their frame relay networks to the PSTN. Therefore, off-net calls are not possible across a frame relay network. But it is possible to dial a local number remotely.

For example, company XYZ has a frame relay network with voice-over frame relay capabilities between its New York and Los Angeles offices. An employee in the New York office wants to call their boss in Los Angeles who happens to be working from home today. The frame relay network does not extend to the boss' home, but instead terminates at the office in Los Angeles. The employee can use the frame relay network to establish a call between the New York office and the Los Angeles office, obtain local dial tone from the Los Angeles PBX, and then place a local call to their boss at home. This saves on long-distance phone charges.

Fax and Modem Traffic over Frame Relay

Frame relay also provides an economical solution to sending faxes. Most equipment vendors that support voice-over frame relay also support faxes. Faxes are much more sensitive to dropped frames compared with voice. Unlike voice frames that can be interpolated or dropped with minimal impact on the voice call, any missing fax frames could result in illegible or incorrect faxes. Imagine a spreadsheet missing a single frame that contained the number one, for example. The spreadsheet would read $ 23,000, when it should have read $123,000. A network design that supports fragmentation, minimizes dropped packets, and prioritizes fax traffic can help solve this problem.

Most CPE vendors use a common implementation for supporting fax over frame relay called *fax relay*. With this implementation, the fax machine sends the fax via an analog modem using the V.29 standard used by most fax machines. V.29 defines the modulation scheme and methods for error-checking and acknowledgments. V.29 enables fax machines to report error messages such as transmission errors.

Similar to SNA applications, excessive network delays can cause the fax to time-out and halt transmission. To avoid time-outs, some FRADs use spoofing. The FRAD connected to the fax machine (at the same location) acts like a fax machine to receive the fax and terminate the V.29 protocol. Because the receiving FRAD makes the transmitting fax machine believe that the fax was successfully received, spoofing minimizes the possibility for time-outs. Because V.29 is terminated, the FRAD does not send any of the error-correction packets over the frame relay network. The FRAD digitizes the fax, encapsulates the fax into frames, and sends it over the frame relay network. Keep in mind that spoofing does not protect the fax from frame losses. You may still receive garbled faxes or faxes with missing information. For this reason, consider assigning the highest priority and highest level of service to fax.

The second method is more of a brute-force method, in which the FRAD transmits the fax with all of the error-checking and using the full 64Kbps bandwidth. Because of the time-out possibilities due to potential delays over a frame relay network, this method is often dismissed.

Voice-Over Frame Relay Services

Only a few service providers offer voice-over frame relay as a standard service or feature today. The service providers that do offer voice-over frame relay typically package the voice FRADs as part of the service. The service provider is responsible for the configuration, installation, maintenance, and management of the voice FRAD and the network. Depending on the service provider, you may or may not have a choice of voice FRAD vendors, but voice-over frame relay services are generally part of the service provider's managed network services family. Refer to Chapter 12 for more information on managed network services.

Some service providers have been reluctant to provide voice-over frame relay because of the limitations of the standards. But the biggest reason is probably that voice-over frame relay poses a threat of cannibalizing the service providers' voice revenues. With most service providers, separate organizations manage the voice and data revenues. Sacrificing voice revenues is not an easy decision for some of the larger service providers. It is often a political issue that may require executive approval to resolve.

The reliance on CPE introduces another issue that contributes to some of the service providers' reluctance to offer voice-over frame relay services. This means that the service provider needs expertise and resources to install, maintain, and manage CPE, which requires remote management capabilities as well as on-site support. Not all service providers can support all these functions effectively. However, some service providers have made strides to answer some of these internal issues. You can anticipate more service providers supporting voice-over frame relay in the future.

Although your service provider of choice may not offer a voice-over frame relay service, this does not mean that you cannot integrate voice on your frame relay network. Most of today's voice-over frame relay implementations run over networks from service providers that do not provide a formal voice-over frame relay service. You can design, build, and manage your own voice-over frame relay solution by buying voice FRADs that can be connected to the public frame relay network. You'll find that most service providers (even though they don't offer the service) and CPE vendors are more than willing to help you design and implement the solution.

Summary

As stated throughout this chapter, reducing voice/fax communications costs continues to drive voice-over frame relay deployments. You may also expect to gain from better overall network utilization and a simplified network; however, without cost savings, voice-over frame relay doesn't make sense.

You should also be aware that voice-over frame relay equipment and networks can deliver toll-quality service, but it takes diligence on your part to ensure you receive this quality. To accomplish this, your equipment will need to prioritize, fragment, buffer, echo cancel, compress, silence-detect, and suppress. In addition, your service provider's network needs to deliver low delay with a high-frame delivery rate. Only by doing all of these things will you be satisfied with a migration to voice-over frame relay.

If your company decides to deploy frame relay to replace your existing data network, it is usually best to migrate your data first; then after the data network is working properly, you should integrate the voice. This will provide you with the highest likelihood of success. When you purchase your "data equipment," make sure it is voice-enabled or can be easily upgraded if voice-over frame relay is in your plans.

CHAPTER

9

Meeting Different Application
Requirements

Virtual circuit priorities and Qualities of Service (QoS) came to the forefront later in the development of frame relay. They were largely non-issues in the early days of frame relay when frame relay services primarily supported LAN applications. Although most frame relay networks were optimized for LAN traffic, end users found ways to integrate other applications, such as SNA, voice, fax, and even some non-real-time video applications, over the same frame relay networks that supported their LAN traffic. Thanks to the evolution and advancements in CPE technologies and implementations, these solutions allow end users to have a single frame relay network that supports multiple applications, resulting in significant cost savings.

The CPE recognizes the different transmission behaviors and required network performance by each application. Some applications, such as e-mail, are more delay tolerant. Other applications, such as fax, are highly intolerant of packet discards or frame loss. Although some CPE service different applications according to their needs, once the frames enter the frame relay network, the network basically treats all frames the same with no regard for varying application performance parameters. CPE-based solutions alone could not guarantee optimal end-to-end application performance.

Frame relay service providers initially launched services designed to solve this problem. Unfortunately, most service providers do not offer this capability today. The service providers have also chosen different implementation schemes, making it difficult to compare apples to apples. This is largely because there were no standards for frame relay priorities or classes of service until recently. The lack of standards also contributed to a myriad of interoperability issues between different switch vendors. Today, service providers primarily rely on the vendor-specific implementations of their frame relay switch vendor(s). Even with the new standards, some vendors have not implemented or do not support the standard yet. Most service providers get around the interoperability issues by deploying a single vendor solution to deliver virtual circuit classes of service offerings. This chapter covers the new standards and some of the more common service implementations currently available.

A Standard Is Born

The ITU (International Telecommunications Union) has two standards that enable frame relay service providers and equipment vendors to support frame relay qualities or classes of service. There are standards for *frame discard priority* and *frame transfer priority*. Frame discard determines the likelihood of frames being dropped, whereas frame transfer determines how quickly a frame passes through the network.

Unlike ATM, the standards for providing frame relay classes of service does not couple class of service as tightly with the technology as does ATM. Rather than making class of service inherent to frame relay technology, the standards ensure interoperability between different CPE vendors by having some industry consensus on implementation.

The current standards also only address discard and transfer priority for SVCs (Switched Virtual Circuits) and not PVCs. Therefore, when an SVC-capable CPE that supports the standards initiates a call with the frame relay network, it requests a certain level of prioritization or class of service by specifying the discard and transfer priority. The frame relay switches in the network then need to provide the appropriate resources to meet the discard and transfer priority requested.

Time-sensitive and loss-sensitive applications such as SNA need high-discard and high-transfer priorities, whereas batch file transfers or FTP (File Transfer Protocol) can have a class of service that has low-discard and low-transfer priorities. Noncompressed video applications, on the other hand, tend to be time sensitive but can tolerate some frame loss. So you can assign a high-transfer priority with a lower-discard priority. Sending a video application using a lower-transfer priority can result in choppy movement as well as breaks and interruptions in the application.

As of the writing of this book, few service providers support SVCs and frame relay classes of service. (See Chapter 10 for more information on SVCs.) Although the standard for SVCs has been around for quite some time now, PVC-based services are more generally available than the SVC-based services. The existence of a standard does not always result in mass deployment of the feature by the service providers. Therefore, this chapter discusses some of the frame relay classes of service or priority services available today—most of which do not use the new standards.

Absolute versus Relative Classes of Service

Frame relay classes of service allow you to more closely align the network performance with the needs of individual applications. Service providers can offer absolute or relative classes of service.

Several parameters typically define a class of service. The parameters may include frame transfer delay and frame discard ratio. A service provider may have three different classes of service, each one with specific values assigned to frame transfer delay and frame discard ratio. Assigning specific values to different parameters that define a class of service creates an *absolute* class of service. Changes in the values of those parameters creates a different class of service. Therefore, any company, application, or source or destination combination that subscribes to a particular absolute Quality of Service gets the same level of service.

Relative class of service simply means that the classes of service assigned to a particular company, application, or source or destination combination are higher or lower compared with another company, application, or source/destination combination's class of service. For example, Company A may want to prioritize its voice applications over its data applications. Therefore, the service provider assigns a "relatively higher" class of service for voice compared with the data for this customer's data applications. Now, let's say that Company B wants to prioritize its applications in the following manner (in a descending order of prioritization): SNA, voice, and file transfers. The values assigned to the parameters that determine the different classes of service for Company B's traffic may be completely different than Company A's. Each company only concerns itself with the relative prioritization of its own traffic.

This chapter discusses two ways service providers currently offer frame relay classes of service by using priority PVCs (relative class of service) and PVC service levels (absolute class of service). Both have different levels of priority or class. Both are assigned on a per-virtual-circuit basis and, ideally, on a per-application basis, as well. With today's services, service providers offer these capabilities for PVCs only. (Capabilities for SVCs are not commercially available yet, but the ITU has created a standard for this, and service provider implementations are likely to follow shortly.)

Although priorities and service levels have some definite similarities, they have little in common. Priority PVCs primarily provide different traffic-management levels. This means that the frame relay network uses an algorithm that determines the rate at which frames for a particular application will be delivered to their destination. This rate depends on the priority level of the PVC/SVC the frames are sent over, relative to other PVC/SVCs destined for the same location.

On the other hand, a PVC service level defines a specific set of service parameters (such as delay and throughput) and values for those parameters. Different values assigned to the parameters create the different classes of service. The service provider typically predefines these values. You most likely have heard of *QoS* (Qualities of Service). For the purposes of this book, QoS and class of service mean the same thing. Having given basic definitions for PVC priorities and classes of service, let's now explore how each functionality works.

Priority PVCs

Priority PVCs are a public frame relay service feature tailored to ensure that mission-critical and delay-sensitive traffic are prioritized over non-mission-critical traffic when these applications compete for network resources at the egress (or exit) of the network. This egress (or termination) port becomes a bottleneck, particularly when multiple locations send information to a single destination, such as with star networks where all remote site traffic converges at the headquarters location. Competition for network resources intensifies at the egress port as the subscription level of that port increases. Imagine what would happen to traffic from four 64Kbps PVCs converging at a single 64Kbps port.

The egress port may be able to support short simultaneous transmissions without dropping frames because of the buffering capability of most frame relay switches. A buffer holds frames in the frame relay switch until the egress port can accommodate more frames for delivery. Unfortunately, the buffer cannot hold an infinite number of frames. Therefore, the buffer may overflow as a result of sustained and prolonged simultaneous transmissions. Buffer overflow translates into dropped frames. The length of time before a buffer drops a frame varies depending on the size of the buffer, speed of the egress port, size of the frames, and subscription level. Without priority PVCs, the buffer indiscriminately drops frames regardless of whether the frame belongs to a frame loss–sensitive fax transmission or a non-mission-critical e-mail, as shown in Figure 9.1.

FIGURE 9.1

Egress port
congestion

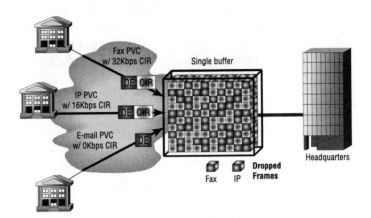

Some service providers give you the option to assign priorities to each of the PVCs on your frame relay network. There are typically three levels of priority: high, medium, and low. Keep in mind that with priority PVCs, the network only prioritizes between different applications on your own network. It does not prioritize your traffic against other end users' traffic.

Let's investigate how priority PVCs work using one implementation. Consider a star network with five remote locations and a headquarters site, each with a 64Kbps frame relay port. Each location has SNA, Telnet, and e-mail traffic. One PVC is assigned between each remote and the headquarters for each of these applications. Therefore, there are three PVCs between each remote and the headquarters. The CIRs are 32Kbps, 16Kbps, and 0Kbps for the SNA, Telnet, and e-mail PVCs, respectively.

Let's assume that during the busy period, there are prolonged and sustained transmissions. This results in some transmissions exceeding CIR and frames marked *discard eligible*. Figure 9.2 depicts the network configuration.

FIGURE 9.2

Frame relay network
with different PVC
priorities

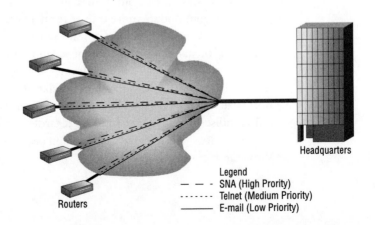

In this network, the SNA, Telnet, and e-mail PVCs are assigned a high, medium, and low priority, respectively. All traffic destined for the headquarters goes through a single buffer at the terminating switch. The buffer has three queues, one for each priority. The algorithm empties the frames of each queue at a specific rate. In this case, the high-priority queue is sampled at four times the rate of the low-priority queue. The medium-priority queue is sampled at two times the rate of the low priority queue. This means that for every four high-priority frames sent, the network sends two medium-priority frames and one low-priority frame, as shown in Figure 9.3. This is true as long as customers are sending traffic in all three priority categories. If there are no high-priority frames being sent to the network, then the network sends all medium-level frames at twice the rate of the low-priority frames. The network does not wait for high-priority frames in order to send the medium- and low-priority frames.

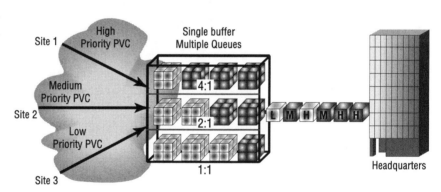

FIGURE 9.3

Queue Sampling

When sampling each queue, the network sends CIR frames before DE frames. This particular algorithm prevents *lock-outs* or *freeze-outs* because it empties each queue in a round-robin fashion. A lock-out is when the network blocks lower-priority frames in queue due to heavy volumes and long transmissions of high-priority frames. Some algorithms can send frames from the lower-priority queues only if the network does not have any high-priority frames to send.

It is best to ask the service provider to explain to you how it plans to prioritize your PVCs. Service providers implement various pricing structures for priority PVCs. Some simply charge an additional flat rate for the capability. Others charge a higher rate for higher-priority PVCs for the same CIR.

PVC Service Levels

Priority PVCs ensure that the network delivers mission-critical traffic at a higher rate or prioritizes it over other traffic types. Although they can help you integrate multiple applications over a single network, priority PVCs alone cannot meet the unique network performance requirements of each application.

For example, voice isn't only delay sensitive, it is also delay *variation* sensitive. Unfortunately, priority PVCs cannot guarantee a specified amount of delay or delay variation. As discussed in Chapter 8, frame fragmentation is one way to reduce end-to-end delay and provides more constant delay variation or delay between frames. Service providers may or may not use frame fragmentation in conjunction with priority PVC.

The limitations of priority PVCs create a need for multiple QoS parameters that can be tailored for each application. Some equipment vendors have, therefore, developed features that allow service providers to offer PVC service level on frame relay.

Some service providers currently offer frame relay services that have LAN and SNA classes of service. The LAN class of service is designed for LAN applications, such as file transfers, Telnet, database sharing, remote database access, e-mail, and others. The SNA class of service is designed for host-to-terminal applications: order entry, inventory, payroll, accounting, and others. The service uses QoS parameters, including average throughput (CIR), maximum throughput rate (port speed), data delivery rate, network availability, PVC priority, and response time (delay). The service providers predefine the acceptable values, or range of values, for each of the parameters.

The SNA class of service has more stringent values, providing shorter delays and higher PVC priorities because SNA is more delay sensitive and typically supports more mission-critical applications than LAN. The service providers define a network-wide delay value and an end-to-end delay value. The network-wide delay value is the delay between frame relay switches; the end-to-end delay includes the local access, with the value varying depending on the port speed.

Data delivery rate is the percentage of frames sent guaranteed by the service provider to be successfully delivered to their destination. Availability is the ratio of the total number of minutes in a 30-day period in which the PVC is available to transport information between two frame relay ports to the total number of minutes in a 30-day period. The service provider publishes a network-wide and an end-to-end availability value. The SNA and LAN classes of service typically have the same data-delivery rate and availability.

With this service, you simply need to specify the port speeds, each PVC's CIR, and the SNA or LAN class for each PVC. Some equipment vendors have developed vendor-specific implementations that provide frame relay classes of service similar to ATMs.

Some of the benefits of implementing frame relay classes of service are that they:

- Allow you to integrate multiple applications over a frame relay network that is optimally tailored to meet the network performance requirements of each application.

- Guarantee a level of network performance for each application.

- Ensure that mission-critical traffic is not impacted by non-mission-critical applications.

- Eliminate the need for multiple, parallel networks to support different applications.

- Provide a simpler network architecture that's easier to maintain and manage.

- Increase equipment and network cost savings.

How Is Frame Relay Different from ATM?

Before we move on, you may be asking yourself, "How is this different from ATM?" Good question indeed!

Asynchronous Transfer Mode (ATM), like frame relay, is a connection-oriented network communications technology. This means that the network relies on predefined and preestablished end-to-end connections to send information. Transmissions between a particular source and destination always take the same route over a set of physical links unless there are situations that warrant rerouting, such as a link failure.

However, unlike frame relay, ATM uses a fixed-length, 53-byte cell rather than variable-length frames to transport information. Fixed-length cells allow ATM to do two things efficiently and effectively: intermingle voice, video, and data applications over a single network, and use high-speed switching and transport of information.

ATM supports a broad range of speeds, starting at 1.5Mbps (DS-1) and up to 622Mbps. ATM also offers different classes of service that provide performance optimized for various applications. ATM supports the following classes of service:

Constant Bit Rate (CBR)   CBR is ideal for applications that require constant and highly predictable bandwidth transmission rates. It maintains the timing relationship between each end during the transmission. Private lines can be transported over ATM using CBR. This is sometimes referred to as *circuit emulation* because it mimics a private-line circuit over a packet network.

Variable Bit Rate (VBR)   Applications that have variable transmission rates can benefit from VBR. The applications normally get a set transmission rate, but transmission can exceed this rate for burst traffic for a specified period of time.

There are two types of VBR service categories: Real Time (RT) and Non-Real Time (NRT). VBR-RT supports real-time applications where each end of the connection maintains a timing relationship. Each end of the connection is waiting for something to happen, for example, videoconferencing.

VBR-NRT supports traffic that does not require a timing relationship and is more tolerant of delays. Some examples of these applications include LAN applications and store-and-forward video.

Available Bit Rate (ABR)   ABR offers a minimum level of transmission bandwidth. This rate can be exceeded if idle capacity is available on the network. The end devices assume there is excess capacity available until the devices receive congestion notification messages or a slow down in traffic received. ABR is optimized for applications that need a high level of performance or low cell loss but can tolerate some variations in transmission speed and network delay. LAN applications that need a guaranteed minimum bandwidth fall in this service category. Currently, most ATM service providers offer only CBR and VBR services. Therefore, most end users use VBR-NRT service for LAN applications that need some guarantees for bandwidth and performance.

Unspecified Bit Rate (UBR)   This is a best-effort service with no service guarantees and no specification for Quality of Service parameters. This is similar to Zero CIR in frame relay. UBR can cost-effectively support non-mission-critical applications. *Cellification* of traffic results in highly efficient and high-speed transport of information.

Why Not Just Use ATM?

For a long time, ATM was the de facto solution if you wanted to run multiple applications over a single network and you wanted the network to cater to the unique requirements of each application. ATM was originally developed for multiprotocol traffic (as was frame relay) but specifically for multiple classes of service. (Frame relay was not.) So why worry about having frame relay classes of service if ATM has a solution? Well, there isn't a cut-and-dry answer. In fact, there are certain situations where each one makes more sense. In the case where you're interconnecting locations that need less than DS-1 access and ports, you can pretty much rule out ATM because the ATM standard specifies speeds starting at DS-1. Also, ATM CPE is not yet as cost effective as frame relay CPE. So, it may be worthwhile to stick with frame relay for as long as you can, unless you think you'll outgrow frame relay soon. Because ATM isn't always the most economical solution for multi-application implementations, frame relay classes of service offer a viable alternative.

Some equipment vendor implementations of classes of service for frame relay look similar to ATM's classes of service. There may be three frame relay classes of service, namely Real Time Variable Frame Rate (rt VFR), Non-Real Time Variable Frame Rate (nrt VFR), and Unspecified/Available Frame Rate (UFR/AFR). They almost look exactly like VBR-RT, VBR-NRT, UBR, and ABR for ATM. Actually, each frame relay class of service has a direct correlation with the corresponding ATM classes of service as far as the applications each class can ideally support. Notice that the list above does not include Constant Frame Rate (CFR) to match ATM's CBR. It's difficult to obtain the very tight specifications and constant performance requirements of CBR with variable-length frames.

The QoS parameters used to define the frame relay classes of service include delay, delay variation, and frame loss. Delay and delay variation were discussed previously. Frame loss guarantees that the network does not exceed a specified number of dropped frames over a specific period of time. The four classes of service are defined in Table 9.1.

Table 9.2 shows some of the applications for which these classes of service were designed.

T A B L E 9.1: Frame Relay Classes of Service and Parameters

Class of Service	Committed Bandwidth	Delay	Delay Variation	Frame Loss
rt VFR	Yes	Low	Medium	Low
nrt VFR	Yes	Higher	Higher	Low
AFR	Some Minimum Level	Not Specified	Not Specified	Not Specified
UFR/AFR	Not Specified	Not Specified	Not Specified	Not Specified

T A B L E 9.2 Applications for Different Frame Relay Classes of Service	Class of Service	Applications
	rt VFR	Packetized Voice and Video, Mission-Critical SNA
	nrt VFR	LAN-to-LAN, Internet Access
	UFR/AFR	E-mail

Like priority PVCs, this implementation also uses a queuing algorithm. There is one queue for each class. The rt VFR and nrt VFR queues are serviced in a round-robin fashion with each other. The UFR/AFR queue is only serviced when the other queues are empty.

Benchmarking Network Performance

The Frame Relay Forum has developed a standard for Service Level Agreements. The standard specifies the parameters that define service quality and a common definition of these terms. The Frame Relay Forum developed this standard to help end users compare the quality of service of different frame relay service providers, measure the quality of different frame relay services, and enforce contractual commitments.

The standard specifies frame transfer delay, frame delivery ratio, data delivery ratio, and service availability as service quality parameters. The standard defines these terms, but it does not specify measurement methodologies or aggregation methodologies for reporting (i.e., per PVC, network-wide, per location, etc.). Therefore, even with the standard, many end users still have a difficult time comparing basic services that provide a single class of service and services that offer multiple classes of service. Please refer to Chapter 13 for more information on service quality and Service Level Agreements.

Summary

Frame relay classes of service allow you to provide a level of service that matches the unique network-performance requirements of various applications, PVCs, or source/destination combinations in your network.

New standards provide frame relay classes of service that do not couple class of service with the technology as tightly as ATM. Rather than making class of service inherent to frame relay technology, the standards ensure interoperability between different CPE vendors by having some industry consensus on implementation. These new standards provide classes of service over SVCs only. The next chapter discusses frame relay SVCs.

Service providers currently use vendor-specific implementations, such as Priority PVCs and PVC service levels, to provide different classes of service. Priority PVCs use traffic-management and queuing schemes, whereas PVC service levels define classes of service using delay, delay variation, and frame loss parameters.

Consider evaluating service providers that offer frame relay classes of service if you have multiple applications, such as voice, SNA, LAN, and others running on your network.

CHAPTER

10

Why and When to Use
Connections-on-Demand

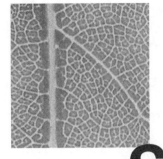

Switched Virtual Circuits (SVCs) offer similar benefits to the different access options we discussed in Chapter 4: they allow more applications, more users, and more locations to take advantage of the frame relay network with its ability to provide connections or bandwidth on demand.

As of the writing of this book, few service providers offer SVCs as a standard option with their frame relay services. The announcement of plans to roll out frame relay SVCs has become a yearly practice for many of the service providers, but the implementation and launch of SVC-based services have consistently slipped year after year. Service providers have cited various reasons for the delays, including lack of SVC-capable Customer Premises Equipment (CPE) and frame relay switches, lack of robust IP to SVC interoperability standards, lack of end-user demand, and billing-system constraints. Recently, the emergence of IP-based and VPN (Virtual Private Network) services have further delayed some service providers' launch of SVC services.

Although there are competing solutions to SVC-based services, in some instances these solutions complement rather than compete directly with SVC services. Chapter 16 discusses VPNs and the impact VPNs will have on frame relay networks.

There are situations in which frame relay SVCs provide the best solution. As with frame relay, demand for SVCs can potentially grow from an understanding of its benefits and applications, regardless of how many service providers launch the service. Unfortunately, end users have traditionally depended on the service providers for education, particularly with frame relay. This chapter will help you obtain a better understanding of SVCs. If you find that you can benefit from the deployment of SVC services, you can then use this knowledge of SVCs to convince service providers to roll out services. At the very least, you can make better implementation decisions when more services become available.

What Are SVCs?

Frame relay requires the definition of a logical path between two locations (frame relay ports) over which to carry information. You can have PVC or SVC logical paths. The biggest difference between PVCs and SVCs is in when the logical paths are established.

Service providers define PVCs within a set installation interval. The installation interval is set by the service provider. It could be a matter of minutes, hours, days, or even months. The service provider defines the path, CIR, and class of service for each PVC within the frame relay switches' switching tables. (Refer to Chapter 9 for more details on and classes of service.) The PVC between two ports always takes the same route as defined by the static switching table, unless the network needs to reroute the PVC because of network failure. You can only transmit information over that PVC after the service provider provisions (defines) it. Once the PVC is established, it is available for your use at all times unless there is a network problem.

With SVCs, your CPE sets up the connection "on demand" when you want to send information to any of your company's locations that have connectivity to the frame relay network. The service provider's frame relay switches need to have the intelligence to quickly establish the entries in the switching tables at the time you request the connection. The exchange of information between two locations traverse the same path for the duration of the session unless there is a reroute situation. Different routes may be chosen for different sessions between the same two locations. The switches tear down the SVC at the end of the session.

Setting up PVCs is like making a long-distance phone call using an operator. The operator manually sets up the call for you before you can talk. Establishing an SVC call is like making a direct dialed (1+) long-distance call. You can talk to anyone connected to the network without manual intervention.

SVC Standards Overview

The Frame Relay Forum completed the SVC specification, called Frame Relay Forum.4 implementation agreement (FRF.4), in 1994. FRF.4 was based on the International Telecommunications Union's (ITU) Q.2931 signaling recommendation for call set up and tear down. The ITU recently passed a standard for frame transfer priority and frame discard priority to provide classes of service over SVCs.

The Internet Engineering Task Force (IETF) is also contributing to the improvement and viability of SVCs with the development of Next Hop Resolution Protocol (NHRP). NHRP will perform automatic address resolution when mapping IP addresses with SVC addresses. NHRP also allows address mappings to change dynamically with changing network configurations. Without NHRP, the SVC address for each of the corresponding IP addresses on your network needs to be manually loaded in the CPE. The next section offers more details about NHRP and CPE support of SVCs.

How Do SVCs Work?

The Frame Relay Forum's implementation agreement specifies the methods and procedures for establishing SVCs. The process involves three stages: call setup, information exchange, and call termination. Figure 10.1 below depicts this process.

FIGURE 10.1

SVC call setup, information exchange, and call termination

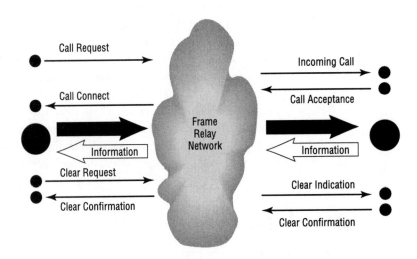

The sender alerts the network that they want to send information to a specified destination. The network then notifies the intended receiver that someone wants to establish a connection. The intended receiver acknowledges the notification and accepts the call. This is considered the call-setup stage.

The network then sets up the SVC and tells the sender that it can begin transferring information. Information flows back and forth between the sender and receiver for the duration of the session. This corresponds to the information-exchange stage.

The call-termination stage begins when there is no more information to send. Either end of the connection sends a request to the network to take down the SVC. The network confirms the request and informs the other end. With an acknowledgement from the other end, the network terminates the call.

FRF.4 also specifies an addressing scheme that allows the frame relay network to determine the destination of the call or the called party. The service provider can either assign an E.164 (ISDN/Telephony Numbering Plan) address, which is just a telephone number, or an X.121 (Data Numbering Plan) number.

Most of today's SVC CPE implementations rely on static tables that map each protocol internetwork address with an SVC address. The entries are loaded manually. This can be time-consuming and prone to human error, particularly in large networks.

The IETF's NHRP standard was designed to resolve address-mapping issues in nonbroadcast networks, such as X.25, frame relay, and ATM. NHRP uses address translation servers to determine unknown address mappings, regardless of the internetwork subnets of the endpoints. The address-translation servers determine the mapping by knowing the next hop to get to the destination. The CPE queries the address-translation server to determine address information. The service provider would typically maintain the entries on the server.

Besides network addresses, the server may also house information on connection priority, class of service, or even security policies for a given connection.

NHRP reduces the amount of traffic between CPE for routing table updates. Information flow is primarily between the CPE and the address-translation server. As long as the server is up-to-date, so is the entire network. This saves considerable bandwidth compared with other broadcast routing protocols, such as Open Shortest Path First (OSPF) and Interior Gateway Routing Protocol (IGRP).

Benefits of SVCs

Depending on your network configuration, traffic patterns, traffic volumes, applications, and CPE capabilities, SVCs can help you achieve application and networking benefits. These benefits ultimately translate to business and financial gains. The following sections will discuss the benefits of SVCs.

Simplified Network Design and Management

Designing an SVC-based network is considerably easier than designing one using PVCs. Your corporate locations simply need access to the frame relay network. Unlike PVCs, you do not need to predefine which locations need to be connected and to assign the CIR for each connection. Furthermore, you don't need to worry about determining the ideal subscription rates for each port connection.

PVC provisioning can be tedious and time consuming, especially with large networks and networks with constantly changing configurations. Adding a new location may necessitate adding PVCs to existing locations and changing existing port speeds. New applications on the network also necessitate reevaluation, which can be difficult if your users are like most and add new applications as they need without any warning. Furthermore, you have to coordinate all changes with your service provider and wait until the service provider has implemented the changes to operate in the new configuration.

SVCs eliminate manual setups. You automatically get a connection when you need it. The ease of connection management becomes increasingly important as more end users demand priorities and classes of service for different applications. Provisioning priorities or classes of service using PVCs increases the complexity in provisioning because each application is assigned a PVC with a specific priority or class.

Although SVCs afford some advantages in provisioning and management, troubleshooting SVCs can present a more complicated task. Service providers need a higher level of debugging and troubleshooting capabilities because it can be difficult to re-create transmissions over dynamically configured connections.

Improved Network Performance

The vast majority of frame relay networks today have hierarchical configurations: typically star, dual star, or hub-and-spoke as illustrated in Figure 10.2.

Unfortunately, these configurations may not be an accurate indication of the networks' underlying traffic patterns. We cannot safely assume that the communication patterns are always one-to-many as is the case with host-to-terminal SNA applications or with client-to-centralized server applications. Some of these networks have sporadic and occasional remote-to-remote communications that cannot cost-justify direct PVCs. Some end users then opt to maintain the hierarchical configurations rather than adding remote-to-remote PVCs to save some money. We will discuss SVC pricing and billing implementations later in this chapter.

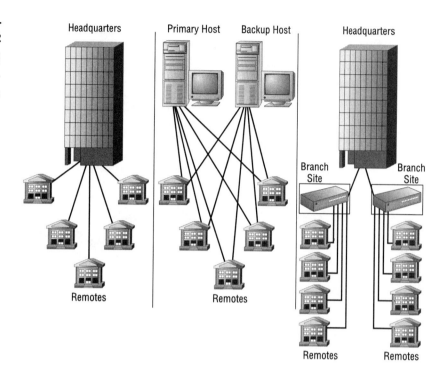

Without a direct path between two remote locations, information exchange between the remotes must traverse over one or more intermediary sites. For example, in the simple 3-node PVC-based network depicted in Figure 10.3, data transfers between Los Angeles and San Francisco must first go through Chicago. This is called *tandeming*. Chicago, in this case, is the *tandem location*. It is an intermediate site that receives information from the network from Los Angeles and sends it back out to the network for delivery to San Francisco.

Tandeming results in additional delay and can impact overall network performance. The intermediate site also becomes a source of congestion and a single point of failure.

SVCs provide more direct connectivity between locations, improving network and application performance. Eliminating tandem traffic reduces the load of the central site CPE. It may then be unnecessary to continue investing in expensive, high-powered CPE at the central site.

Although SVCs can improve performance by providing more direct connections, the length of the call setup can become a performance drawback. Both the CPE and frame relay network contribute to the total call setup time. Fast call setups should be one of your criteria in choosing a CPE vendor and frame relay service provider.

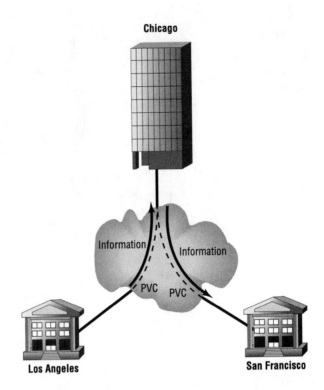

SVCs also allow you to request service levels for different applications. Requesting priorities, for example, ensure that delay-sensitive traffic, such as fax and voice, are serviced before delay-tolerant Internet and LAN applications. Table 10.1 below shows how you may want to prioritize your applications based on sensitivity to delay and frame loss as well as burstiness.

T A B L E 10.1: Example of priority assignments for different applications

Applications	Priority	Delay	Loss	Burstiness
Fax	1	Low	Low	Low
Voice/Video	2	Low	Low	Low
SNA	3	Low	Low	High
Intranet	4	Low	Low	High
Business Internet	5	Low	Low	High

T A B L E 10.1:   Example of priority assignments for different applications *(Continued)*

Applications	Priority	Delay	Loss	Burstiness
Traditional LAN	6	High	Low	High
Casual Internet	7	High	High	High

SVCs offer these service-level advantages at the price of more complex and intelligent CPE. You have to program the intelligence in the CPE. Some CPE allow you to program destination, bandwidths, priorities, security policies, and so on based on TCP/IP socket numbers, applications, etc.

In the future, you can use Winsock II to request bandwidths and priorities for connections. Winsock II is an Applications Programming Interface (API) for Windows. Similarly, Resource Reservation Protocol (RSVP) will allow you to reserve bandwidth and specify priorities for IP applications.

As mentioned previously, NHRP can further simplify this process because specific desired connection features can be stored in the address-translation server. This eases the burden of programming the features in the CPE.

Better Network Utilization

Tandeming consumes more than the required network capacity because information is carried more than once over the network. In the example given previously, the transmission uses bandwidth resources from Los Angeles to Chicago and then again from Chicago to San Francisco.

An SVC from Los Angeles to San Francisco can improve overall network utilization. It frees the other connections to support more traffic and additional applications. Some cost savings can be achieved by reducing the PVCs' CIRs because the PVCs no longer have to support any Los Angeles-to-San Francisco tandem traffic.

A Highly Scalable Solution

The frame relay market has shown very aggressive growth over the past few years. Analysts predict continued growth not only in the number of public frame relay customers but also in the size of customer networks. End users are adding more locations and connectivity on their frame relay networks. Networks are becoming larger and more interconnected or meshed.

To support *N* number of locations in a star network, you would need to define N-1 PVCs. Designing the network as the number of locations increase becomes more complex and time-consuming. Worse yet, fully meshed networks need [N × (N-1)] / 2 PVCs to support any-to-any connectivity. For a 20-location network, you would only need 19 PVCs for a star design but 190 PVCs for a fully meshed configuration. The number of PVCs you need to design and maintain increases exponentially as you add more locations. The addition of just five more locations to this 20 location network increases the number of PVCs required by almost a third, up to 300. If you want to support PVC priorities between each pair of locations, you must further multiply these results by the number of needed priorities.

Fortunately, SVCs allow you to scale your network without worrying about maintaining a large number of logical connections. With SVCs, the network establishes the connections on demand when a particular location has something to send to any other location on the frame relay network.

Call-by-Call Billing

SVCs allow service providers call-by-call billing arrangements rather than the connection-by-connection billing available today with PVCs. Service providers can bill usage based on connection time similar to long-distance telephone calls or the number of transferred frames during the call. Usage based on connect time is ideal for applications used sporadically, such as videoconferencing and file transfers. Usage based on frames transferred might be preferred for applications that have long connect times but little information exchange, such as Web surfing. The service provider may also impose incremental or premium charges for specifying classes of service for the SVCs.

Call-by-call billing allows you to pay for only what you use. However, this might not be an ideal solution for everyone. Some end users consider usage-based billing a risky proposition because of the unpredictability of the monthly bills. Few tools exist for monitoring network traffic, and the amount of transmissions is difficult to predict. You may face the unpleasant reality of a bill that it is three times larger than expected. Furthermore, it is a challenge to budget for expenses that vary widely from month to month.

Service providers are considering several options to solve this dilemma. One way is to charge a fixed rate for having SVCs as a feature, such as an incremental charge per port. Another way is to ensure that the bill will not exceed a set maximum amount, which is called a *cap* or *ceiling*. The cap applies at a certain level of usage. Some service providers may also assess a minimum charge for having the ability to establish SVCs, regardless of usage.

SVC and PVC Zones of Advantage

The differences between SVCs and PVCs create zones of advantages for each of the virtual circuits. Certain applications and network configurations will be more ideally suited for one type versus the other. Given today's fast changing multiprotocol and multiapplication networks, it's nice to know that SVCs and PVCs can coexist. Depending on your networking environment, the most optimal design may involve the coexistence of SVCs and PVCs.

Table 10.2 offers some guidelines for when to choose one over the other in terms of traffic and network attributes. The table below summarizes these guidelines.

T A B L E 10.2 Zones of advantages of PVCs and SVCs	**Traffic/Network Attributes**	**PVCs**	**SVCs**
	Traffic Volumes	Medium to High	Low
	Traffic Patterns	Known and Recurring	Unpredictable and Sporadic
	Degree of Connectivity	Star and Hierarchical	Any-to-Any

Traffic Volumes

Traffic volume refers to the amount of traffic transmitted between two locations within a given time frame. Volume is often measured in number of frames sent or delivered or the amount of bandwidth needed in bits per second (bps). Consider using PVCs for connections that support medium-to-high traffic volumes and SVCs for low-volume connections.

Pricing is a basis for this guideline because there is a crossover between SVCs and PVCs at some level of usage or traffic volume. The exact crossover varies by service provider. But you can anticipate some cost-savings using usage-based SVCs for lower-traffic volumes compared to using a PVC with predefined CIR.

This is similar to how some service providers position usage-based PVCs versus fixed-rate PVCs. Usage-based PVCs are more cost-effective up to a certain level of usage; beyond that level, fixed-rate PVCs are cheaper. However, some service providers have a usage-cap charge equal to the fixed-rate charge for the same amount of PVC CIR. In this case, you can't go wrong by subscribing to the usage-based plan.

Traffic Patterns

Traffic patterns refer to the predictability and frequency of the transmissions. Use PVCs for connectivity between two locations that exchange information on a regular basis. PVCs allow you to predefine the connection and bandwidth while eliminating the need for call setups every time you need to send something.

On the other hand, SVCs offer a good solution if the receiver of the information varies from time to time. It is also well-suited for occasional, highly intermittent, short-duration transmissions. Using PVCs in this environment would require that you predefine connections to every location to which you would "possibly" send information. You end up paying for idle and underutilized connections. With SVCs, you can establish a connection to any location and will pay for only what you use.

Consider the traffic patterns in conjunction with the traffic volumes between two locations. Using the traffic-volume guidelines, you might change your decision once you evaluate the traffic patterns. For example, hourly or even daily low-volume transmissions may benefit more from PVCs, although infrequent high-volume data transfers to varying destinations might be better served by SVCs.

Degree of Connectivity

Degree of connectivity is related to the underlying traffic patterns. For the purposes of these guidelines, let's assume that the connectivity required matches the traffic patterns.

A star network using PVCs is ideal for companies that primarily have remote-to-host communication and very little or no remote-to-remote traffic. This is a typical configuration for most SNA networks. The small volume of remote-to-remote traffic can tandem through the host site if tandeming will not degrade network performance or if there's enough capacity on the network and the host site's CPE. Otherwise, use SVCs between the remotes.

SVCs work well in networks where any location may need to talk to any other location on the network. However, not all fully meshed networks need to be SVC-based. The star network mentioned earlier can become a hybrid, fully meshed network with PVCs and SVCs. The hybrid network is shown in Figure 10.4.

FIGURE 10.4

A hybrid PVC/SVC
network

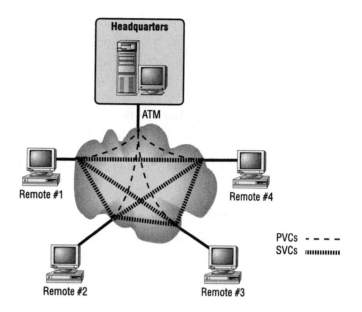

Applications Benefiting from SVCs

The number of applications that can benefit from SVCs increases as corporations grow, as networks become more distributed, and as companies integrate more applications. The following sections discuss some of these applications.

Client-to-Client Communications

The speed and intelligence of today's desktop computers have contributed significantly to the increase in client-to-client communications. The desktops have the horsepower to house and run multiple applications that were traditionally stored in centralized servers. Client-to-client network traffic is growing at a faster rate than client-to-server traffic on the LAN backbone. Sources of client-to-client traffic include personal Web pages and desktop videoconferencing.

Corporations may have employees use personal Web pages on the company's intranet to advertise and share schedules and calendars, current projects, and other relevant information. Collaborative product development, staff meetings, training, and other events can be held using desktop video-conferencing.

Although traffic from these applications are continuing to grow, the traffic patterns are still quite sporadic. SVCs enable direct connectivity between two sites even if traffic is infrequent. Direct connectivity offers the performance required for time-sensitive and time-bound applications, such as videoconferencing. You may only need videoconferencing every Friday morning from 8:30 a.m.–10:00 a.m. or on an as needed basis.

SVCs also offer a viable solution for interconnecting a large number of corporate locations for e-mail and Web page access.

Remote Site Access

Traditionally, remote sites with low-traffic volumes and infrequent transmissions could not cost-justify interconnecting to other corporate locations using frame relay. SVCs offer a viable and more economical solution, particularly when used with dial-up-access methods. You essentially "pay as you transmit/receive" for both access and connectivity.

This is also ideal for work-at-home connectivity requirements after office hours and for telecommuters.

Remote sites and telecommuters can use SVCs not only to access corporate resources but also to access the Internet, as shown in Figure 10.5.

F I G U R E   10.5

Accessing the Internet
using SVCs

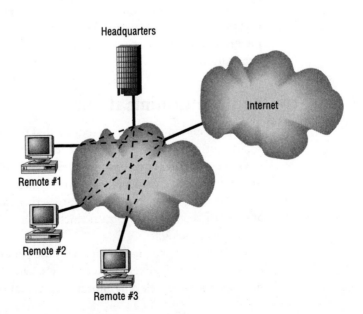

Data Backup and Recovery

Some companies deploy a dual-star PVC-based configuration for disaster-recovery purposes. Information stored at the primary location is typically mirrored or duplicated at the backup host. Each remote site has two PVCs, one terminating at the primary host and the other at the backup host.

In some situations, the PVCs to the backup host are only used when a failure occurs at the host site. This configuration, in effect, doubles the network cost even when only half the network is used most of the time (hopefully, all of the time). Some companies willingly pay the price to ensure a high level of network availability.

However, there are other more cost-effective solutions that also offer high availability. Chapter 7 covers some of these disaster-recovery options in more detail. You can use SVCs instead of PVCs for the backup connections. The remotes access the backup host using SVCs in case of disasters. You can terminate the SVC calls once the primary host is back in operation.

Intracompany Voice Calls

Intracompany voice calls are an excellent application for SVCs. The terminations are unpredictable and transmissions are short and intermittent. The average telephone call is only three minutes. This lends itself well for time-sensitive SVC pricing. Even usage-based pricing based on frames delivered works well with the voice-compression and silence-suppression capabilities of voice Frame Relay Access Devices (FRADs). Refer to Chapter 8 for more information on voice and fax over frame relay.

Enterprise-wide Communications

Enterprise-wide communications refers to communications between a company and its supplier, partners, and customers. You can use PVCs between your company's locations. But SVCs may be a better solution for connections outside the company because of the unpredictability of intercompany communications destinations from one day to the next and low-traffic volumes.

Trader networks enable interenterprise communications. It provides interconnections between companies in the same line of business or companies with common interests. These companies share information, such as medical research findings, patient records, industry news, stock quotes, inventories, calendar of events, schedules, and so on, over the network. The automotive industry in the U.S., for example, implemented its own private trader network called Automotive Network eXchange (ANX).

Extranets are also classified as interenterprise networks. Extranets are primarily designed to support Internet-based applications such as e-mail, Web access, bulletin boards, and other applications shared between corporations. These corporations conduct daily business functions and transactions with each other over the extranet. Extranets with electronic commerce features can support online buy-and-sell transactions.

Overflow Information

SVCs can be used with PVCs to support overflow traffic during peak periods. SVCs are ideal for this situation because, hopefully, traffic overflow doesn't happen on a regular basis, or when it does occur, it only happens for a short time. If you notice more frequent occurrences of traffic overflow, then it might be more economical to increase the CIR of the PVC to accommodate overflow rather than establishing SVCs.

Summary

Unlike PVCs, SVCs provide connections on demand using SVC-capable CPE that signals the network to establish and tear down a connection. This allows more applications, users, and locations to take advantage of the frame relay network.

SVCs simplifies network design and management because you do not need to predefine connections between locations that communicate with each other. It improves network performance by allowing more cost-effective, direct connectivity between locations, eliminating intermediary or tandem connections. Eliminating tandem traffic also improves network utilization because the network carries the traffic once (directly between the two communicating locations) rather than twice (once from the source to the tandem location and again out of the tandem location to the destination). SVCs offer a highly scalable solution providing any-to-any connectivity between locations connected on the network. Finally, service providers can bill SVC usage on a call-by-call basis.

SVCs are ideal for connections with lower-traffic volumes and unpredictable and sporadic traffic patterns. It is ideal for networks that have any-to-any connectivity requirements.

Client-to-client communications, remote-site access, data backup and recovery, intracompany voice, enterprise-wide communications, and overflow information applications can benefit from SVCs.

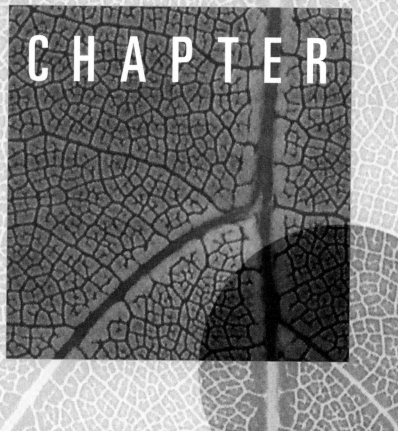

CHAPTER

11

Connecting Frame Relay with ATM

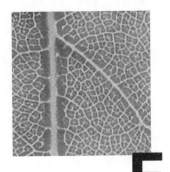

Frame relay–to-ATM service interworking (FRASI) enables frame relay and ATM technologies to coexist and interoperate with each other. This combination provides the best of both worlds, allowing you to choose the most appropriate technology—frame relay or ATM—on a location-by-location basis. Frame relay and ATM complement, rather than compete, with each other in many situations, which allows you to build a highly optimized hybrid network without having to choose one over the other for your entire network.

This chapter offers you insight into the *zones of advantage* of frame relay and ATM—when to use FRASI, the benefits of FRASI, how FRASI works, some alternatives to FRASI, and questions you should ask your service provider when evaluating its FRASI service.

What Is FRASI?

FRASI provides a means to connect a frame relay site and an ATM site. The two locations can communicate seamlessly with each other. You do not need to install special CPE or software or do anything different when sending information between a frame relay location and an ATM site. The translations and protocol conversion happen within the network, transparent to you.

Before you can use FRASI, you need to determine what service to use for each location on your network. The next section provides some guidelines for choosing frame relay or ATM.

Choosing between Frame Relay and ATM

Frame relay and ATM each have their advantages and disadvantages. The area in which each one excels and provides the most optimized solution is its zone of advantage. These zones of advantage are important because your network has different locations with unique networking requirements. A single technology will most likely not meet the requirements of all locations, all at once.

You can take one of two approaches to network design. You can either optimize each location independently or optimize the network as a whole, even if a few sites have slightly suboptimal solutions. Ideally, you want to optimize each location. However, you may begin with the latter approach, choosing a single technology that provides the best overall price and performance. Over time, you can fine-tune each location's solution by choosing the best technology for that location.

Frame relay and ATM have many similarities, including the following:

- Frame relay and ATM are both connection-oriented technologies (see the sidebar "Connection-Oriented versus Connectionless" in Chapter 3 for more details).

- Both transmit packets, with frame relay sending variable-length packets called *frames* and ATM using fixed-length packets (53 bytes long) called *cells*.

- Most frame relay and ATM services have inherent automatic rerouting capabilities.

- Both use statistical multiplexing and share available bandwidth among different applications. Only active applications have access to available resources.

- Logically defined virtual circuits connect locations together.

- The services allow the customers to oversubscribe their ports.

Although frame relay and ATM have many processes in common, each have unique features. In choosing the best technology for each location, consider the bandwidth required, mix of application, availability of services, current CPE installed, and future requirements.

Bandwidth Required

Most frame relay services offer port speeds of 56/64Kbps up to 2Mbps. Some service providers offer high-speed frame relay with greater than 2Mbps ports, up to 45Mbps. Some service providers also offer dial-up access supporting speeds below 56Kbps. On the other hand, ATM services offer port speeds of 1.5Mbps up to 45Mbps. Some service providers also offer SONET speeds: OC-1, OC-3, OC-12, etc. The service providers typically provide the SONET connections on an individual case basis.

Figure 11.1 depicts the different location types, typical speed requirements at these sites, and the technology applicability of frame relay and ATM.

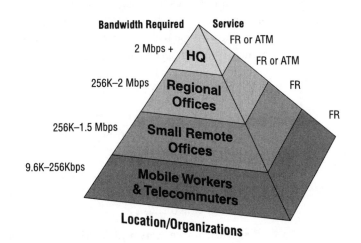

FIGURE 11.1

Corporate location pyramid with bandwidth requirements and technology possibilities

Mobile workers, telecommuters, and small remote offices typically have lower bandwidth requirements due to lower traffic volumes and a lesser number of end users at these locations; therefore, they are better suited for frame relay. Regional offices tend to have higher traffic volumes because they typically process information from multiple remote offices. Some regional sites also concentrate traffic from remotes for delivery to the headquarters. If the regional site needs 1.5Mbps and above, that site can use either frame relay or ATM. The headquarters tends to have large connections because of the number of end users it supports. In an SNA network, most communications happen between the remotes and the host site. This means that the host site supports traffic from all remotes. Similar to the regional offices, connections of 1.5Mbps can use frame relay or ATM.

Mix of Application

ATM offers QoS to meet the unique network performance requirements of different applications. A few service providers also offer frame relay classes of service to accomplish the same goal. However, due to the limited number of service providers that offer frame relay classes of service, you may need to consider ATM for locations that support multiple applications that require different Qualities of Service. Locations that support one traffic type only or that do not require QoS for various applications can use frame relay.

ATM offers CBR (Constant Bit Rate), VBR-NRT (Variable Bit Rate–Non-Real Time), VBR-RT (Variable Bit Rate–Real Time), ABR (Available Bit Rate), and UBR (Unspecified Bit Rate) classes of service. Applications that require constant and highly predictable bandwidth transmission rates can benefit from CBR. VBR-RT is ideal for real-time applications, such as videoconferencing, that require the end devices to maintain a timing relationship. VBR-NRT supports more delay-tolerant applications, such as LAN applications and store-and-forward video. ABR is ideal for LAN applications that need some guaranteed minimum bandwidth. Lastly, UBR is a best-effort service that can cost-effectively support non-mission-critical traffic.

Refer to Chapter 9 for more information on frame relay Priority PVCs, PVC service levels, and ATM QoS.

Availability of Services

Keep in mind that although many service providers offer frame relay services, not all frame relay service providers offer ATM services. Fewer service providers offer frame relay because of the relatively large investment they need to make in network facilities and switches to support the higher bandwidth requirements of ATM services. Additionally, not all service providers target customers with very high bandwidth requirements, which are typically the large companies. If the service provider offers only one service, that service provider most likely offers frame relay. A service provider that offers ATM services but not frame relay is rare.

The service provider may or may not offer both frame relay and ATM services. Therefore, if optimizing your network on a location-by-location basis is critically important to you, choose a service provider that offers both services.

Current CPE Installed

Determine your current CPEs capability to support frame relay or ATM. Most CPE can inherently support frame relay but may require a new interface, new module, software upgrade, or even a completely different CPE to support ATM.

If you currently have frame relay or ATM CPE installed, it makes sense to leverage the existing equipment unless you feel your requirements will change significantly in the near future.

This also becomes a cost consideration if your existing CPE meets your current needs or short-term requirements. Determine whether you can redeploy the current CPE somewhere else or upgrade it to make it work. Otherwise, you may need to invest in brand new CPE.

Future Requirements

When deciding whether to implement frame relay or ATM at a particular location, consider how the location's requirements might change in the near future, perhaps within the next six months to a year. Consider the bandwidth needs, mix of applications, and CPE requirements the location will have. It may be wise to implement the long-term solution rather than go through the hassle of migrating from one service to another.

When to Use FRASI

You can use FRASI to connect lower speed, remote frame relay locations to the high-speed headquarters ATM site. This configuration is typical in star networks, particularly hierarchical SNA networks. Figure 11.2 shows a hierarchical network that uses FRASI.

FRASI can also be used to connect locations that support multiple applications. In Figure 11.3, locations A and B have videoconferencing capabilities. All of the locations in this network, including A and B also have LAN applications. ATM is deployed at A and B whereas the other locations use frame relay. A VBR-RT or CBR virtual circuit connects locations A and B. All other connections to A or B are FRASI PVCs using VBR-NRT on the ATM side of the connection.

F I G U R E   11.2

F I G U R E   11.2

Connecting frame relay remote sites to an ATM headquarters site

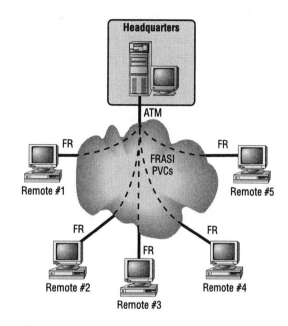

F I G U R E   11.3

Using FRASI for multi-application locations

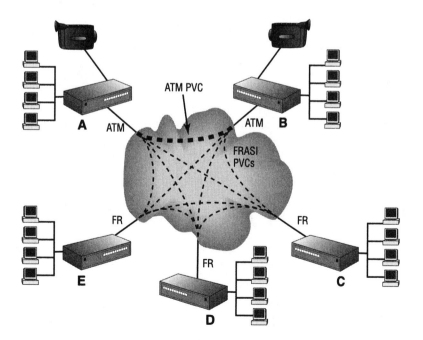

Benefits of FRASI

As mentioned previously, FRASI allows you to choose and optimize your network on a location-by-location basis. Other benefits of implementing FRASI are as follows:

Improves Network Scalability   FRASI allows host sites in SNA networks to support more remote sites. If your network outgrows a 1.5Mbps frame relay port at the host site, you can upgrade to a higher speed ATM port, such as a 3Mbps ATM port, at that location to support more remote sites or higher-speed remote-to-host connections.

Avoids Oversubscription   You do not have to oversubscribe the frame relay port at the host site to support more remote locations because you can upgrade the frame relay port to a higher-speed ATM port. This can improve overall network performance.

Protects Investment in Current CPE   Changing between frame relay and ATM at a particular location does not impact the configuration and current CPE deployments at other locations. FRASI does not require special CPE or software at the premises.

Simplifies the Network   All locations are connected to a single network regardless of the technology used at each location.

Provides a Migration from Frame Relay to ATM   You can easily migrate from frame relay to ATM at a location without affecting the current network design. The location can continue to communicate with other locations with which it has connections. A network can conceivably evolve from a pure frame relay network, to a network that uses FRASI to enable communications between frame relay and ATM site, to a pure ATM network.

How Does FRASI Work?

Frame relay–to-ATM service interworking, as defined in FRF.8, allows a frame relay device to communicate with an ATM device. In this environment neither CPE knows or cares that the technology used at the other end is different. The interworking capability, also known as IWF (InterWorking Function), can reside in a separate piece of equipment between the frame relay

The first version, typically referred to as Scenario 1, of frame relay–to-ATM network interworking enables the transparent transport of frame relay traffic over an ATM network as in the following illustration. All end-user locations use frame relay. The ATM network basically provides a high-speed backbone facility for frame relay traffic. In fact, many service providers use this implementation because ATM gives them a highly scalable backbone to support growing frame relay traffic. The backbone aggregates traffic and provides high-speed trunking.

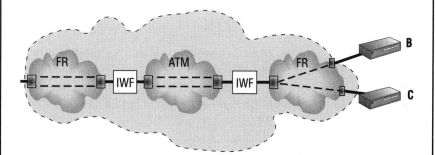

Again, similar to service interworking, the IWF can be external to the frame relay and ATM networks or integrated within a frame relay or ATM switch.

A frame enters the frame relay network for delivery over the ATM network. The ingress ATM switch cellifies the frame and transports the cells across the backbone. The egress ATM switch then reconstructs the frames and delivers them to the final destination via the frame relay network. Unlike FRASI, the ATM network *tunnels* or *encapsulates* the frame relay traffic in ATM. Tunneling means that the ATM network preserves the end user's protocol suite and transports the data unaltered.

To the end user, frame relay–to-ATM network interworking is as transparent as frame relay–to-ATM service interworking. Although network interworking is more geared toward network service providers, there are scenarios in which it is useful for end users also.

A second version of network interworking, called Scenario 2, involves an ATM device communicating with a frame relay device on the other end. The frame relay device does not know nor care about the presence of any ATM transport facilities. In this scenario, the ATM CPE needs special software to emulate some frame relay–specific functions to communicate to the frame relay CPE across the network. This method of network interworking is the least common used because it incurs additional ATM CPE costs for the users.

Alternatives to FRASI

Although FRASI offers many benefits, other frame relay features can help you achieve some of the same benefits FRASI offers depending on the situation. These alternatives include FUNI (Frame-based User Network Interface), DXI (Data eXchange Interface), HSFR (High Speed Frame Relay) services, and hybrid networks. These alternatives have their own set of benefits and drawbacks.

Frame-Based UNI (FUNI)

FUNI provides a solution for locations that want to use their existing frame-based CPE to connect to an ATM network. FUNI provides a cost-effective method of accessing ATM WANs through the use of a frame-based format defined by the ATM Forum. The CPE sends FUNI frames to the service provider's ATM switches with FUNI interfaces. Once in the network, ATM switches the frames into 53-byte ATM cells and transports cells across the backbone. At the terminating ATM switch, the switch reassembles the frame for delivery to the destination CPE. Figure 11.6 shows a FUNI implementation.

FIGURE 11.6

A frame relay location communicating with a FUNI location

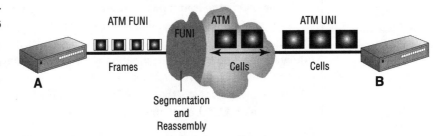

FUNI uses the local access more efficiently as it transports frames that have less overhead compared to ATM cells across the local loop.

Some drawbacks of using FUNI include its limited QoS support (currently supports VBR only), no support for SVCs (Switched Virtual Circuits), limited standards, limited equipment vendor support, and limited availability of commercial services. Although FUNI has a similar frame structure as frame relay, FUNI requires software in the CPE and a FUNI interface and software in the ATM switch in the service provider's network.

DXI

DXI is similar to FUNI, but they differ in where the segmentation and reassembly functions reside. With DXI, these functions reside in an ATM CSU (Channel Service Unit) at the customer premises, as shown in Figure 11.7.

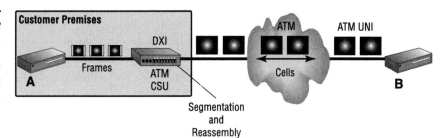

Like FUNI, DXI allows you to use your existing frame-based CPE and simply front-end it with an ATM CSU to connect to an ATM network. Unlike FUNI, the ATM CSU sends cells across the local loop. Therefore, some local loop bandwidth is used for ATM overhead.

High-Speed Frame Relay

Most service providers support up to 1.5Mbps or 2Mbps for frame relay ports. Some service providers can support HSFR ports—speeds beyond 1.5Mbps or 2Mbps. Therefore, HSFR ports overlap with ATM port speeds.

The customer typically needs to subscribe to a DS-3 or E-3 access to take advantage of HSFR. Some service providers offer Fractional DS-3 or Fractional E-3 access. In cases where fractional local loops are available, you can use inverse multiplexers to aggregate multiple DS-1s or E-1s to achieve the higher speed frame relay port. For example, a 6Mbps port requires the inverse multiplexing of four DS-1s or three E-1s. MLFR (MultiLink Frame Relay) provides another alternative to deploying inverse multiplexers. Equipment that supports MLFR have built-in inverse multiplexing capabilities. (See Chapter 4 for more information on inverse multiplexing and MLFR.)

If you deploy HSFR for the headquarters and frame relay for the remotes, FRASI is not necessary. This solution allows you to have a ubiquitous frame relay network, to delay investing in more expensive ATM CPE, and to leverage existing frame relay CPE. However, only a few service providers offer HSFR today.

Figure 11.8 shows an example of a HSFR implementation.

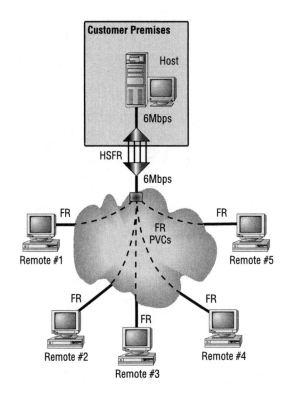

Questions to Ask FRASI Providers

Before implementing FRASI connections in a mission-critical network environment, it is important to do some homework. The following questions provide a good baseline for evaluating network service provider FRASI offerings:

- *What FRASI PVC CIRs does the service provider offer?* The service provider may currently offer a set of PVC CIRs for frame relay different from the CIRs it offers with ATM. For example, its frame relay service may offer CIRs from 64Kbps, up to 1.5Mbps in increments of 64Kbps whereas, its ATM service offers CIRs from 1Mbps up to 45Mbps in 1Mbps increments. If you want to have a FRASI PVC, this means that the only common CIR between the service provider's frame relay and ATM CIRs is 1Mbps. This means that you cannot have any frame relay location with less than a 1Mbps port interwork with an

ATM location. (Remember that each PVC assigned to a port cannot have a CIR larger than the port.) Therefore, you need to ask the service provider whether it will support smaller CIRs for FRASI PVCs.

- *How does the network determine the ATM QoS for the incoming frame relay traffic?* Most service provider typically map the frame relay traffic into VBR-NRT. But do not assume; be sure to ask the service provider whether they offer this service. If the service provider offers frame relay priorities of service or QoS, find out into which ATM QoS each frame relay priority or QoS maps.

- *How does the service provider provision interworking circuits?* Some service providers may need to provision the frame relay PVC separate from the ATM PVC. Other service providers can provision the PVC automatically from end-to-end. The former provisioning process typically occurs more often in networks that use different equipment vendor platforms for the frame relay and ATM. The different methods may or may not make a difference in the time it takes to initially set up your network or to perform moves, adds, and changes to your network's configuration.

- *Can the service provider report on the performance of FRASI PVCs and offer SLA (Service Level Agreements)?* Most service providers can collect and report on the performance of regular frame relay PVCs and ATM PVCs. Because a FRASI PVC traverses two networks, the service provider may or may not be able to provide end-to-end FRASI PVC performance reports. Also, find out whether the service provider offers SLAs or service guarantees for the FRASI PVC. SLAs guarantee you a specific level of performance for various network metrics, including availability, delay or latency, MTTR (Mean Time to Repair), data delivery rate, etc. You typically receive a financial credit or reimbursement if the service provider does not meet the guarantee. Refer to Chapter 13 for more information on SLAs.

- *Are there additional charges for FRASI?* Most service providers charge extra for FRASI. Some service providers may charge for FRASI on a per network, per PVC, or even on a per port basis. The service provider may also charge differently for FRASI PVC CIRs (per unit of bandwidth) compared with the frame relay PVCs and ATM PVCs based on CIR. These charges can have an impact on your decision whether to use FRASI or a FRASI alternative.

Summary

FRASI enables the coexistence of frame relay and ATM in the same network. It allows seamless communications between a frame relay site and an ATM site. This capability resides in the service provider's network and is transparent to the end users.

FRASI allows you to optimize your network on a location-by-location basis. In determining the best technology, consider the bandwidth requirements, mix of applications, availability of service, installed CPE, and future requirements at that location. Other benefits of FRASI include improved network scalability, avoidance of oversubscription, investment protection in current CPE, a simplified network, and a migration path from frame relay to ATM.

You can use FRASI for connecting multiple remote sites to a host location where the remote sites use frame relay and the host site uses ATM. FRASI also enables multi-application locations to use a single network to carry different applications to different locations supporting either frame relay or ATM.

Other features can also provide some of the benefits that FRASI offers. You should consider DXI, FUNI, and HSFR.

The next chapter covers several solutions for managing and operating your frame relay network.

CHAPTER

12

Solutions for Operating and
Managing Your Network

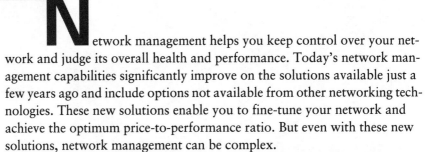

etwork management helps you keep control over your network and judge its overall health and performance. Today's network management capabilities significantly improve on the solutions available just a few years ago and include options not available from other networking technologies. These new solutions enable you to fine-tune your network and achieve the optimum price-to-performance ratio. But even with these new solutions, network management can be complex.

Several factors contribute to the complexity of network management: the number of protocols traversing your network, the size of the network, whether you implement a multivendor network solution or a single vendor solution, and how geographically dispersed are your network locations. There is no "best way" to manage a frame relay network. Your specific network design, business goals, and internal resources will dictate the optimal network-management solution for you.

This chapter discusses network management from the perspective of managing the physical and logical network. It covers the objectives of a network-management system, customer network-management services (CNMS), and what to do if you want someone else to manage your network via a managed-network service (MNS).

Keep in mind that the best management solution in the world, staffed by the most expert problem solvers, cannot make a poorly designed network function well. Network design is a critical element in network management. Before we dive into how to manage your network, a brief discussion of network management objectives is necessary.

The Objectives of Network Management

Network management serves many different purposes within an organization. So many, in fact, that implementing a network management plan can be a daunting task. In Figure 12.1 below, the typical components of network management are shown.

FIGURE 12.1

Typical components
needing management
in a frame relay
network

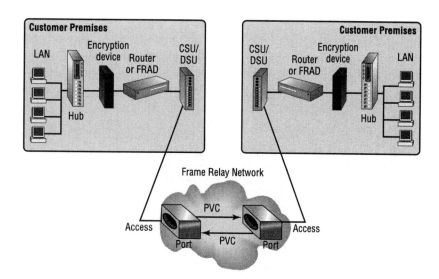

As you can see, there are several components. To make the process of network management a bit more manageable, the ISO (International Standards Organization) model has outlined five distinct network-management categories:

Configuration Management   This includes the management of physical and logical connectivity within your network, such as moves, adds, and changes, as well as ongoing planning and optimization.

Fault Management   This includes the collection and management of and response to network alarms as well as conditions that fail to meet a predefined performance threshold.

Performance Management   This provides information with which to judge the quality of service, performance of individual connections, and the network as a whole.

Security Management   This includes management and control of access to the system and applications.

Accounting/Information Management   This provides information, monitoring, and control over how communications resources are used and allocated.

As you develop you network-management plan, keep these objectives in mind. Make certain all network-management policies and equipment aid in at least one of the areas above. Otherwise, the policy or equipment is probably unnecessary. The following sections discuss each of these five areas in greater detail.

Configuration Management

Configuration management covers both the physical and logical configuration of the network. This area includes everything from your network addressing and DLCI assignments to your port connection and PVC sizing. To manage the configuration, you must have information on the current status and the performance of each network connection as well as a tool to modify the network configuration in response to the information you gather.

You need a tool for remote configuration management of your routers, which may be a proprietary tool from the vendor. You can capture information on the status of the router within an existing SNMP (Simple Network Management Protocol) management system, which will be discussed later in this chapter.

Most service providers offer some sort of customer network-management system for the frame relay service, giving you a graphical depiction of the physical and logical network. In most cases, you will be limited to viewing the current network configuration. Few service providers allow you to change your network configurations through an online system today, but most of them are working on this capability.

A Summary of SNMP

SNMP is an open standard that has been widely accepted and deployed within the LAN internetworking industry. Many things can be accomplished with SNMP, and some cannot—both situations deserve mention.

SNMP stands for Simple Network Management Protocol. Its biggest advantage and its biggest weakness lie in its simplicity. The protocol is a standardized set of messages exchanged between a network-management system supporting SNMP and an SNMP agent within a network device. The agent maintains a database of information (called a Management Information Base, or MIB) about the device's configuration, performance, and status.

MIBs come in standardized, experimental, and proprietary flavors. Many devices support both standardized and proprietary types or a hybrid of the two. For example, the Frame Relay Forum has standardized a MIB for frame relay devices. Most frame relay vendors adhere to this standard MIB, but many also add extensions for their equipment that provide information not specified within the standard MIB. Because there is one MIB per device (e.g., per router, switch, etc.), a large network can mean *lots* of MIBs.

With most frame relay services, the service provider collects information from the SNMP agents in each of the frame relay switches and centrally stores this information in a single MIB to be accessed for data retrieval. This allows the service provider to give you a single source with secure access from which to collect performance statistics on all the port connections and PVCs in your network. This provides you a view of your traffic on the service provider's network—switch-to-switch—and does not typically include access or CPE. However, you can also use SNMP to gather performance statistics and alarms from your own network equipment attached to the frame relay network. This results in many MIBs to manage and the potential for high traffic volumes to be generated as you collect information.

Messages to the MIB take two basic forms: you either get information from the MIB or change a value within the MIB. Getting information from the MIB is called a *GET*. You define what information to GET and how often to GET it.

The second type is a *SET* message in which you set a database entry. With most frame relay services, you can GET information from the service's SNMP agent to determine the performance and status of your port connection and PVCs. You cannot typically SET any values within the MIB to modify your configuration.

Also, an unsolicited message can be sent from the agent to a management system, called a *TRAP*. TRAPs are issued in response to abnormal network conditions when an element of the network falls above or below a predefined performance threshold. Other messages are defined in the standard, but these are the basic ones to be concerned about at this stage.

As you can see, SNMP is a set of rules for exchanging information. It does not help you with interpreting, prioritizing, or viewing that information. It does not provide data in a user-friendly manner, such as with graphs or maps. Applications must be written to take the information from the MIB, or the TRAPS from the agent, and intelligently process it. You can write this application, or you can use the applications written by your service provider, equipment vendor, or a network-management software provider. You will probably do some combination of the three.

SNMP does not provide very good security. Service providers have had to develop security systems for the public frame relay networks that allow each customer access to his network information but not to another customer's information.

SNMP was designed to provide information on the configuration and status of network components. It was not intended to enable complex configuration, command, and control functions. These functions are usually performed using a vendor-specific management tool.

Fault Management

Fault management provides you information regarding the health of the network. Receiving network alarms can be accomplished by using your existing SNMP management system, a system provided by the service provider, or both. Interpreting the alarms and applying intelligent prioritization is another story.

If you are using your own SNMP management system, you configure it to accept unsolicited messages, or SNMP TRAPS, from the service provider's SNMP agent in the frame relay network.

The processing of these alarms depends upon your system and any applications you write or intelligent prioritization and processing you apply. You will probably want to set some intelligent filtering based on alarm types and thresholds, depending upon your preferences and environment. You may also want to prioritize frame relay service alarms with other alarms you are capturing so that when you have several from which to choose, you can prioritize and allocate your own resources to resolve the most critical problems first.

You can also use a service provider network-management tool to gather and report alarms. The service provider has already written applications to filter and interpret the incoming data. The advantage is not having to use your own resources; the disadvantage is an application not customized for your network situation. Many service provider tools allow you to enter and track trouble tickets via this same system.

In the end, if you are managing your own network, you will probably use both approaches. Your own system provides a high-level view of the frame relay service in relation to all the other components in your network. The service provider's management system gives you more detailed information and processing as well as a direct link with the service provider to report and resolve problems. The integration of the two systems on the same workstation can help reduce the number of separate terminals.

Performance Management

Performance management enables you to fine-tune your network PVCs and port speeds. Performance should be judged both at the network level and at the individual component level. You can use several statistics to evaluate the health and performance of your frame relay service. The primary ones include

- Ingress/Egress frame counts and discarded frames for each port connection

- PVC utilization as a percentage of the committed information rate, including average use and peak use in differing time periods

- Discard eligible frames per PVC

- Peak traffic period

- Historical information

You can get this information in at least three different ways. If you are using your own SNMP management system, you can set up a frame relay network MIB in your system that periodically queries the SNMP agent within the service provider's frame relay network and downloads the set of performance parameters you have elected to capture.

You need to predefine the amount and types of information the management system will download from the MIB and the frequency of the downloads. The more information you gather, and the more often you gather it, the better view you have of the network's performance. The trade-off for this real-time information is its impact on network congestion. The more you poll the network devices for statistics, the more traffic congestion you create on your own network, which in turn has an impact on network performance.

You can also use a service provider's customer network-management tool for gathering, interpreting, and displaying the performance information. The service provider has already written applications that provide you with text and graphical depictions of network performance. They may also give you some flexibility for customizing the information and frequency of the report output.

If you use your own tool, you once again have to develop an application to interpret the information and display it in a report. The positive aspect of this is that you can customize your reports and make the frame relay report format consistent with your other network reporting formats. The negative aspect is that you have to dedicate the resources up front for writing the application.

New frame relay network-management packages (CPE and/or software) are available today from several vendors. These packages provide user-friendly, easy-to-interpret, network configuration and performance reports. Some vendors even support an optimization tool, which lets you run "what if" scenarios from past performance information. This enables you to better predict what effects changing PVC sizes will have on network utilization.

Gathering the Data: In-Band versus Out-of-Band Connections

Whether you use your own management system, the service provider's, or both, you need an access mechanism by which to get to the network management data and alarms. You will probably choose between an in-band or out-of-band connection. You can either assign a PVC within the frame relay network to access the service provider's SNMP and other network information, or you can use a stand-alone private line, dial-up connection, or any other access method supported by your service provider.

There are trade-offs in terms of availability versus price. Assigning a PVC makes good financial sense and gives you a very cost-effective mechanism by which to gather network statistics and alarms. Of course, if the local loop fails or there is another outage affecting that PVC, your management system could be without its eyes and ears.

Using a separate private-line connection, however, may not be much more advantageous, even though it is "out-of-band." If a local loop failure is the problem, then a private line into your location would be equally affected unless it was provided over separate entrance facilities.

One solution is to use a PVC, and you should augment this with the ability to dial up into the network and directly into remote routers. For example, you might use a modem and analog line attached to your management system or use the dial-up port connections now available with many routers. This provides the cost-effectiveness of the in-band approach while giving you a path to reestablish monitoring in the case of a failure of that in-band connection.

You may be thinking that network management is a difficult task and wondering whether there are tools or services available to help. Well, there are. The next two sections discuss two such services: customer network management services (CNMS) and managed network services (MNS).

Customer Network Management Services

Customer network-management services have been around almost as long as frame relay service. As frame relay has matured, so have the options for CNMS. A CNMS is simply any report a service provider creates for customer use. In the early days of frame relay, a CNMS always meant a hard-copy report with performance numbers on it. These reports were not easy to read and even harder to make any network decisions based on the information.

Today there are more CNMS options than ever. The most common options include hard-copy, SNMP, and Web-based.

Hard-Copy   Most providers will still provide customers with hard-copy reports if desired. However, few companies like this method except for quarterly or annual reviews with service provider engineers. The hard-copy report format has two distinct disadvantages; you can not create a unique or different report because you do not have access to the data electronically, and the information is non-real-time. For example, if a PVC experiences congestion during a certain period, you will not know about it until the report arrives a week or even a month later.

SNMP   As discussed earlier in this chapter, SNMP is an open standard that has been widely accepted and deployed within the LAN internetworking industry protocol. Because it has been widely deployed and utilized, you may already be familiar with it. With SNMP agents deployed at various locations on the network, information can be gathered and sent to you electronically to be used via a SNMP workstation. This download of information may be possible in as little as 15 minutes after the information is collected. Service providers do not like to give customers direct access to the SNMP information located in the frame relay switches, so instead they download the information to intermediate devices. Once you receive this information, you can either view it via the standard reports the provider supplies or via special views you have created.

Web-based   The next step in CNMS is Web-based reporting. Some providers are already offering this capability today. Web-based reporting allow you to gain network performance information via any Web browser. If you company does not have a SNMP workstation or if you want many people (who don't have workstations) to be able to access information, this is probably the optimal solution. These reports are also delayed and are not real time. They are generally called "near-real-time" and have delays between 30 minutes and 2 hours.

Although no two service provider CNMS reports are identical, most provide basic network performance information. The most common components include the following:

- Network availability
- Network latency (delay)
- Sent packets
- Received packets
- Percentage of discard eligible packets received
- Average PVC utilization
- Average port utilization
- FECN/BECN marked packets

Regardless of what information is measured, most CNMS reports provide you with information solely within the service-provider network. You will likely not be able to see performance information relating to CPE or access-service components. This can be a major issue because these components can have a dramatic impact on overall service satisfaction. For example, you are running a mission-critical and time-sensitive application (such as voice, SNA, or video) across your frame relay network. The report given to you by your provider shows network delay of 75ms—well within the delay tolerances of your time-sensitive application. So why are your users complaining? Well, they are doing so because the CPE or access components are introducing significant delay, perhaps even double or triple that of the network.

As you can see, knowing what is going on from end-to-end and not simply switch-to-switch, can be critical. If your applications are mission critical, you will want to deploy CPE, which can monitor the portions of the network your provider can not. This CPE can be installed and maintained by your company or the service provider as part of a managed network services (discussed in the next section).

If you now think CNMS is a good thing, but it doesn't quite go far enough to provide the level of network-management assistance you require, then you may want to consider ordering an MNS.

Managed Network Services

Most of the major service providers have commercially available MNS. As a matter of fact, many providers offer a MNS as their "standard" service offering. The diagram in Figure 12.2 depicts the different hardware components that can be provided or managed as part of a MNS.

FIGURE 12.2

A comparison of service components for a transport frame relay service versus a managed frame relay service

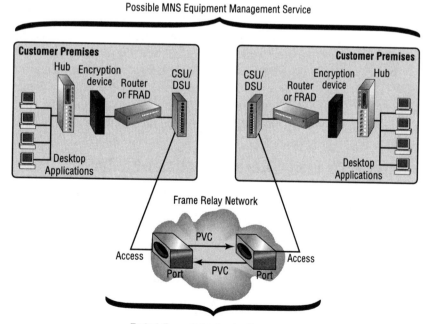

The demand for MNS continues to soar as increasing networking complexity pushes many corporations beyond their traditional comfort zones in networking. Some of the factors that influence your propensity to use a MNS include

- Whether your company adopted a distributed work environment, including a growing number of work-at-home and telecommuter options

- Your desire to integrate client/server LAN applications with legacy host-to-terminal SNA applications

- Your company's plans to use emerging new business applications, such as desktop videoconferencing, remote collaboration and development, Internet telephony, and others

- The speed at which you are growing the number of personal computers and LANs in corporate offices

- Whether your users have a growing demand for high-speed connectivity to increase productivity, shorten product development timeframes, improve sales cycles, and improve competitiveness

- The degree to which you rely on wide-area networking to support daily business practices and communications

These environments, factors, and influences have driven some corporations to develop or acquire in-house networking expertise. Many organizations, however, do not have the luxury of organizing a group solely responsible for designing, implementing, maintaining, and managing the company's network. Furthermore, even if your company has in-house resources, you may find the company resource-constrained and lacking expertise in certain critical areas.

Benefits and Characteristics of MNS

MNS can help address some common issues, such as these:

- Finding time to proactively analyze the network performance, anticipate future problems, and plan for future growth

- The lack of resources and expertise in designing, implementing, maintaining, and managing a network

- Keeping pace with changes in technology and planning for network migrations

- Ensuring that they get the most out of their technology, equipment, and applications investments

- Evaluating different equipment vendors and service providers

- Understanding the components needed and putting the solution together

- Managing and coordinating multiple equipment vendors and service providers

- Managing budget constraints

Perhaps the most important aspect of a MNS has yet to be discussed: the demarcation point. The service demarcation draws the line where your responsibility starts and stops, often determined by the last piece of equipment at the customer's premises that is managed by the service provider. It is very important that you fully understand the demarcation point to avoid finger-pointing, disappointment, or service dissatisfaction.

The following are some common demarcation points for MNS:

CSU/DSU   The most basic MNS goes just a bit beyond transport by integrating the CSU/DSU as part of the package. Although this service may seem to have little added value compared with transport-only services, some CSU/DSUs available today have more sophisticated capabilities in addition to those mentioned previously. The primary purpose of deploying a CSU/DSU as part of a MNS is to perform loop-back testing to determine whether traffic can reach the premises or whether there is a problem elsewhere in the network. Some CSU/DSUs have built-in probes for collecting network-management information. The probes collect SNMP data, store historical information, and enable creation of user-friendly performance reports. These probes enable you and the service provider to have a higher level of network performance visibility and granularity.

Some service providers' basic transport services already package the CSU/DSU device. These service providers use this to differentiate their services from other transport-only services.

WAN Access CPE   WAN access CPE typically refers to the device that directly connects to the CSU/DSU that in turn connects to the WAN. WAN-access CPE may include routers, Frame Relay Access Devices (FRADs), remote-access concentrators, access multiplexers, premise switches, switching routers (layer 3/4 switches), etc.

Some service providers name their MNS based on the type of WAN-access CPE offered, such as Managed Router, Managed FRAD, Managed Access Concentrator, Managed Broadband Switch, and other services.

Local Resource Sharing Media   These devices/media provide a connection between the WAN Access CPE and the computing/storage device. These devices or media enable the sharing of resources among desktops or terminals in a local network. These include LAN connections and cabling (Ethernet, Token Ring, Switched Ethernet, FDDI, etc.), LAN hubs, LAN switches, and others.

Computing/Storage Devices   You may be able to include hardware or software for the desktops, servers, terminals, printers, FEPs (front-end processors), minicomputers, and even mainframes as part of MNS.

But don't think that all MNS are identical or include the same components. There are no standards for MNS, and therefore you must study and compare providers. The next section shows some typical MNS features that are currently offered by several service providers.

Options for an MNS

Today's MNS offerings have evolved to encompass a larger portion of the network-management activities necessary to operate and maintain peak network performance. Where configuration and fault management were at one time the extent of MNS, today's offerings have moved a step beyond to provide you value-added management capabilities. (In the past, you either did without or managed on your own to the best of your abilities and resources.)

When discussing specific individual components, almost every major provider's MNS description includes some or all of the features and capabilities listed below. However, you should be aware that differentiation in these areas is not within the service description but in the actual delivery. The level of service and manner in which it is provided varies greatly from provider to provider. Take for an example, provider performance engineering or network design. The resulting performance from the design recommended by the provider is only as good as the level of expertise of the field and operation-center technicians and engineers making the recommendations.

Typical MNS components include the following:

- Network Design

- Consulting Services

- Networking Equipment

- Implementation Plan
- Support
- Proactive Network Monitoring/Fault Management
- CPE Maintenance
- Configuration Management
- Performance Reporting
- Performance Evaluation and Optimization
- Service Level Agreements
- Multiprotocol Support

Each of these elements is discussed in detail next.

Network Design

In subscribing to a MNS, you will likely find that your provider is much more interested and involved in making recommendations and providing assistance for the design of the network. This is one of the most critical components to network performance and also has an impact on network pricing. If the network is not properly designed, then it will not operate effectively; because the provider is responsible for overall performance under a MNS, they will want to design it correctly the first time.

Network design includes the relationship between issues, such as the routing protocols used, the configuration of the router buffers and prioritization parameters, the configuration of the PVCs, and sizing of CIRs and port connections.

Consulting

The larger providers who support more traditional outsourcing services (e.g., desktops) and are therefore staffed in this area are typically the only ones to offer consulting services. Consulting charges are based on time and materials and are often purchased for capabilities, such as routing protocol determination and more strategic network planning or migration.

Networking Equipment

Choice of equipment is usually a combination of your preference and service provider engineering input as to the CPE most suited to your application. You will have some level of flexibility as most of the carriers support at least two or three of the primary router/FRAD vendors' products. Most support equipment vendors as customer demand warrants or will handle equipment outside the standards on a case-by-case basis. Having options allows you to select the equipment that best fits your environment, protocols, and requirements. It could also mean that if you have already set your standards on a specific manufacturer and it is one the carrier supports, then you could continue using this vendor within the managed network service.

Prior to delivering the equipment to your site for installation, it should be pretested and preconfigured. The configuration at this stage would ensure that the correct number and type of LAN interfaces is included, all cabling is included, etc.

Implementation Plan

You will typically work with the carrier to develop a complete, written implementation plan for the network. This includes site-by-site planning of equipment and network installation within the context of the complete installation process. The document should specify those areas, such as site preparation and internal cabling, for which you are responsible. It should also specify what constitutes complete and satisfactory installation at each site.

Support

Dedicated support teams or individuals are typically assigned to you upon purchasing the service. A lead engineer is assigned to manage the entire implementation process and ongoing management of the network as your single point of contact. Support teams are located in the management service center or network control center closest to the your headquarters location. Depending on the provider and service coverage, these centers can be located throughout the U.S. and abroad. Smaller providers typically have one major support center where all management, maintenance, and operation of the network take place.

Proactive Network Monitoring

Proactive means monitoring in real time and reacting to service degradation without the impetus of a call from you. It also means not only telling you something is wrong after it happens but helping you plan for future events to avoid problems before they occur.

Your carrier will keep a record of your complete network configuration and a real-time view of the status of physical and logical connections. Alarms on the network will trigger a proactive response in which the carrier will open a trouble ticket and will begin to isolate and resolve the problem. If you call in to report trouble, you may find that a ticket is already open and a technician is at work on the resolution.

You are also able to pen a trouble ticket yourself. Keep in mind that there are certain things for which the carrier is responsible and other things over which you maintain control. LAN-to-LAN traffic within the same building and application-level issues are in your domain.

Some carriers offer different grades of service for network monitoring and proactive trouble correction. For example, the standard monitoring package is usually seven days a week, 24 hours a day, including all holidays and weekends. Some carriers offer different service levels, so that you can choose 24 hours a day all week long, or just 8 A.M. to 5 P.M. business-day monitoring.

CPE Maintenance

Most providers offer two or more levels of hardware-maintenance agreements. Some may provide support from 8 A.M. to 5 P.M., Monday through Friday, with next business day replacement of equipment. The same provider may also offer, for an additional fee, 24 hours a day by seven days per week support with guaranteed two hour replacement. Availability of the higher service levels is also often dependent on site location. Most service providers do not have local maintenance resources (in-house or third-party) deployed everywhere throughout the country. Whichever level of support you elect, make sure you choose a carrier that will provide onsite sparing (i.e., onsite spare parts) with a maintenance technician, in case the entire unit must be removed and repaired.

Configuration Management

Configuration management is the management of the router address tables, including moves, adds, and changes of attached device addresses and the addition/deletion of network protocols. You can typically submit your requests for moves/adds/changes over the phone, via fax, or over the Web.

Configuration management also includes management and use of the router options for protocol prioritization, buffer queues, and issues for managing routing protocols and broadcasts over the WAN. You should quiz prospective carriers on their knowledge of these issues and their plans to handle your protocols. If they are not prepared to discuss these issues with you, they may not have the expertise needed to manage and maintain your network.

The following are some of the logical configurations that require management:

- IP Addressing Scheme and Subnet Masks
- Encapsulation Type (HDLC, Frame Relay, Ethernet, etc.)
- Passwords
- Access Lists/Filters
- Routing Protocols
- LMI Type
- SNMP Community String
- System Log Machine

Performance Reporting

Although you are outsourcing the management of your network to the carrier, you will want to have a way to evaluate and judge the carrier performance. One method to accomplish this is through the performance reporting packages supplied by your carrier. These reports are typically available either from an online system or in hardcopy format. Some services charge extra for these reports while others do not. Keep in mind that interpretation of the reports is not the same thing as production and delivery of reports, and the interpretation is critical.

Reports will typically include outage and trouble-ticket summaries, including reason codes and resolution times, and utilization reports for port connections and individual PVCs. Trend reports are also available for the ports and PVCs showing a historical summary of performance over time.

There are many variations of performance reports. They vary in the delivery method, delivery frequency, timeliness of updates, reported parameters, information granularity, and interpretations and recommendations.

Delivery Method   You will likely prefer to obtain performance reports through a Web interface as compared with hard copy, FTP, or SNMP feeds to an online network management station.

Delivery Frequency   Most service providers offer performance reports on a monthly basis at the very least. More frequent delivery of reports (e.g., real time, every 15 minutes, hourly, daily, etc.) are often accomplished electronically using the Web.

Timeliness of Updates   Information freshness is particularly important if you run mission-critical and revenue-impacting applications on the network. Availability of real-time or near real-time updates may have an impact on your choice of service provider.

Reported Parameters   Some of the most common parameters reported include utilization, availability, data delivery rate, throughput, and delay. You should also ask about application and protocol performance parameters that can be reported.

Information Granularity   The granularity of information provided may be tied to the timeliness of updates. More comprehensive and more granular information may only be available with more frequent updates. You will also want to see statistics offered on a network-wide and per-component basis to allow you to drill down to the level of detail needed.

Interpretations and Recommendations   Although many service providers offer very comprehensive performance reports, including information on a wide variety of parameters with a high degree of granularity, many do not currently offer suggestions for how to use these reports, interpretations, and recommendations for action. If this is not a standard part of the provider's reporting package, you will want to ensure that this level of support occurs through regular interaction with your dedicated support team or individual.

Performance Evaluation and Optimization

Performance evaluation and optimization is accomplished in several ways and via several groups dependent on the provider. Although outlined as a specific component within the MNS service, for many providers this is a very loose process whereby field sales representatives simply make note of any out of the ordinary statistics within the reports. Within other organizations, formal monthly review processes take place with trained engineering staff to analyze the information being provided to you.

You should insist that a single, knowledgeable individual be in charge of evaluating your monthly performance report. This means they should review the network in its entirety and make sure that the overall configuration continues to be properly designed as traffic patterns, applications, and business environments undergo changes.

At least once a year you should have a formal evaluation with your carrier. This should be a planning session where you discuss both the past performance and the future network requirements.

On evaluating past performance, make sure that escalation procedures have worked properly and that problems have been addressed and resolved in a timely fashion. Also look for indications that the network design has remained consistent with the changing needs of the network and that your carrier has proactively suggested changes.

Future planning should include a site-by-site evaluation of expected business changes, new applications, new sites, sites being moved or deleted, personnel growth, planned protocols to be added/deleted, etc. This will allow you and the carrier to proactively plan how you will accommodate these changes as they occur. If you have a highly dynamic business, you may need a semiannual or even quarterly review.

Service Level Agreements

Service guarantees offer you financial reimbursements and/or contractual waivers if the provider fails to meet the terms of the guarantee. Most providers today have standardized SLAs that are automatically given to you as a MNS customer. However, your networking environment may require that you negotiate certain aspects or additional SLAs outside of what the carrier is offering. SLAs are closely tied to performance reporting, as this is typically the only method you have for determining whether the level of service guaranteed has actually been delivered. Very few providers proactively inform you or apply credits to your invoice when they miss an item on the SLA.

Typical SLAs address the following areas:

- Mean Time to Repair
- Installation Intervals
- Availability
- Throughput
- Delay
- Data Delivery Rate

Multiprotocol Support

Providers offer varying degrees of protocol support and expertise. TCP/IP and IPX protocols are the most commonly supported by today's MNS offerings.

Other protocols supported include SNA SDLC, DECnet, and AppleTalk. You will want to ensure that service provider operations personnel have knowledge and experience in managing networks running the protocols you are likely to employ on your frame relay network.

Provider Packaging

MNS offerings continue to become more specific in the applications they are targeting. What was originally a service to address basic LAN-to-LAN connectivity via frame relay has evolved to cover much more in the way of protocols, and for certain providers, transport delivery. At the most basic level, most providers today offer a managed router and managed FRAD solution, with the router solution addressing LAN connectivity and the FRAD solution primarily targeting SNA applications.

In addition to router and FRAD options, most providers also offer various packages to address individual needs and levels of expertise. Traditionally, packages revolve around a basic, enhanced, and premium theme where the number and type of components included differs between the packages. Some providers will allow you to pick and choose different packages for different locations based on the needs of that location. Most often, you will require more assistance and support with remote locations than at headquarters where your IT staff traditionally resides. Some examples of the components that will vary between the packages are network monitoring coverage, onsite CPE maintenance response time, detail and frequency of performance reporting, and help desk–access availability.

As the MNS market matures, providers are finding more unique ways to package their solutions to make them generally more attractive to you in addressing your specific needs or hot buttons.

Transport

Some providers may offer you a "technology transparent" MNS service. This is ideal if you have little to no knowledge of the particular WAN technology used in your solution. The various transport and CPE parameters are all predefined to some degree, reducing the number of decisions required by you in implementing the MNS.

Application or Protocol

MNS can also be based on targeting certain applications or protocols. For example, many providers focus on the SNA marketplace with specialized

MNS packages addressing the needs of these enterprises. From network design and configuration, to prioritization, to the CPE utilized, the service is totally SNA-centric. There are even Central Office–based solutions targeted at SNA networks that allow you to transparently migrate to frame relay with no physical impact on your individual sites. All the required CPE functionality resides in the providers Central Office.

Demarcation Point

The service demarcation draws the line where you and your provider's responsibility starts and stops. Most often this is determined by the last piece of equipment at your premise that you are responsible for managing.

Some MNS packages are based on the service demarcation, in which all the service components for each level of service have predefined defaults or options.

For example, a provider may offer a MNS with basic, enhanced, and premium levels of service. The basic, enhanced, and premium services may differ by including the CSU/DSU, the WAN-access CPE, and the LAN hub, respectively within the packages. You may be able to subscribe to a particular service level for all of your locations or choose the appropriate service level on a location-by-location basis.

A La Carte

A la carte MNS is when the provider offers a laundry list or menu of components and allows you to pick and choose the features you require for your environment. This kind of packaging allows you to create a customized solution to some degree. For example, you might be able to choose from one of three router vendors and one of two maintenance packages on a location-by-location basis.

Pricing Structures

Pricing structures will vary by the packaging employed by the provider. In general, MNS services will add an additional recurring and installation charge to each of your site locations. Again, packaging will have an impact on the manner in which you are charged (e.g., all-inclusive package per site with local loop, Port, PVC, CPE, and management), but it will increase the overall price to your service provider over a basic frame relay service. The pro-MNS business case justifying your purchase is the result of the internal cost savings from a staffing and tools perspective along with the soft cost benefits of allocating your resources to more core business functions.

Specifically from a CPE perspective, service providers offer lease, rent, or purchase options. Pricing is dependent on the type or brand of CPE installed, the number of devices in the network, the software configuration installed on the equipment, and the number of WAN and LAN ports.

Installation fees are also a standard part of MNS, and they may or may not be waived with a term agreement. Some providers will also offer volume and term discounts that may be applicable to the CPE.

Choosing a Provider

Each carrier defines its service a little differently from the next, but overall, you will find similarity in the descriptions of these services. The real key, however, is not in how these services are described but how they are provided. Ask a lot of questions. Use the issues brought up throughout this book to guide your questions and judge the answers you receive. Also, look for a carrier that can provide the right level of service and type of equipment for your network. Some carriers offer ancillary services and equipment, such as intelligent hubs, LAN installation, and other inside wiring, which could sway your decision.

Most notably, choose a carrier with whom you are comfortable working. You are in essence taking on a new employee or business partner, and the chemistry must be right.

Summary

Network management represents one of the most important aspects of deploying a frame relay network. Without someone—you, your service provider, or a third party performing network management duties—you will never be able to ensure you are receiving the optimum price to performance ratio. A complete network management plan must include all components of the network from end to end and usually includes CNMS and/or MNS. Your goal must always be to have a network capable of delivering the performance your applications require. You should negotiate a Service Level Agreement (SLA). In the next chapter, we address setting your network performance expectations via SLAs.

CHAPTER

13

Managing Your Service Provider
with Service Level Agreements

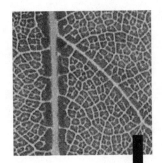

In the previous couple of chapters, we covered managed network services and disaster recovery options. We also learned about options for network management. These services, and the concerns they mean to address, often lead network managers to seek one additional service feature: Service Level Agreements (SLAs), or guarantees.

When discussing public data services such as frame relay, it is common practice to denote the provider network as a cloud (as we have done in this book). Although drawing a cloud can be helpful when discussing services and the network in general, it is important to realize the cloud comprises physical circuits and equipment. As with any network, there are times when these circuits are fully utilized, the equipment fails, or other issues impact the performance of your service. Before the days of shared networks, you would address this by deciding how mission-critical the traffic you send is and then deploy your own equipment and additional circuits to ensure the network performed to your required levels. In a shared public network, you can only control these same issues outside the network. The service provider takes control of the cloud performance, meaning you must rely on the service provider to deploy and maintain a network capable of meeting your performance requirements. To ensure the service provider supplies the promised network performance, an SLA should be negotiated.

In this chapter, you will learn about typical frame relay SLA components, measurement calculations, exclusions, and credits. There is no such thing as a "perfect" or standard SLA. Keep in mind as you read through this chapter that the best SLA for you is the one tailored to meet your specific network goals and performance requirements while staying within your budget constraints.

History of SLAs

Although the term *SLA* is relatively new, the concept is quite old. If you have ever bought a car, electronics equipment, or almost anything else of value, you are usually offered a guarantee or warranty on the item. An SLA is the same thing: a guarantee or warranty offered by frame relay service providers.

SLAs have been around the telecommunications industry for years and have been a part of frame relay since the first customer-ordered service. In the early days of frame relay (1991 through about 1994), potential customers were uncertain about how a shared network would perform and whether frame relay services would give them the performance they needed. In an effort to make potential customers feel more comfortable regarding migrating to frame relay, many service providers offered "switchback" guarantees. If customers were unhappy with frame relay service, they were allowed to switch back to their original service with no penalty. This represented the birth of frame relay SLAs. Since then, SLAs have been one of the most dynamic areas within frame relay services.

The evolution of frame relay SLAs to include more metrics (the variables being measured as part of the SLA) means more opportunity for you to negotiate a better contract and receive better service than in previous years—assuming you know what to ask for and what to watch out for. The following sections provide you with the information necessary to negotiate a strong and effective SLA.

Beware of service providers that offer "Service Level Objectives." These are *not* the same as SLAs. The difference is that an "objective" is simply a target the provider hopes to meet. Service Level Objectives do not offer benefits to customers for missed objectives; however, an SLA offers customers a benefit, such as a credit on monthly bills, if the SLA is not met.

FRF.13—The Service Level Definition Implementation Agreement

In 1998, the Frame Relay Forum approved an implementation agreement specifically for SLAs, called *FRF.13*. It addresses the following issues:

- Delay

- Frame Delivery Ratio

- Data Delivery

- Service Availability

In addition to the metrics, the agreement provides terms used to name the components of a frame relay connection in an SLA. Due to all the effort necessary to create the document, it is clear that the Frame Relay Forum and the rest of the industry believe SLAs are important to the success of frame relay services. But little incentive exists for service providers to follow the guidelines outlined in FRF.13. Most service providers already offer SLAs that include metrics not addressed in the implementation agreement and do not wish to modify their SLAs and systems to follow the Forum's outline. Because few, if any, providers follow FRF.13, it is not addressed in detail in this chapter. If you want more information on FRF.13, check out the Frame Relay Forum Web site at www.frforum.com.

What Part of Your Network Do SLAs Cover?

As we discussed throughout this book, frame relay services can be transport only, transport and access, or a fully managed offering, which includes CPE (either CSU/DSU to CSU/DSU or router to router). The options you have for SLAs include all of these services, as well. Figure 13.1 depicts the different network components that can be covered by a frame relay SLA.

FIGURE 13.1

Possible frame relay
service components
included in an SLA

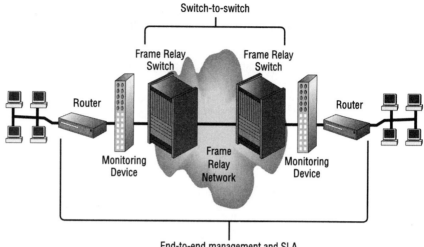

FIGURE 13.1

Possible frame relay
service components
included in an SLA

In addition to the portions of the network an SLA is intended to cover, there are specific metrics common to many service provider frame relay SLAs. The most common metrics are the following:

- Network availability
- PVC availability
- PVC delay (packet delay)
- Frame/data delivery rate
- Mean time to repair

Many others will be briefly discussed, but the metrics just mentioned are included in most standard and custom SLAs and are discussed in detail in the following sections.

Network Availability

By far the most commonly offered frame relay SLA relates to network availability. It provides the foundation upon which all other SLAs must rely. The SLA measures the percentage of time the network is available for use.

This SLA generally provides network availability in the 99.95 percent to 100 percent range and is typically measured over the course of a month. A commonly used formula for this measurement is as follows:

```
(24 Hours × Days in Month × Number of Sites) – Network
Outage Time - Excluded Time
(24 Hours × Days in Month × Number of Sites) - Excluded Time
```

An outage is defined as the following:

- Service interruptions

- Data loss exceeding committed levels

- Network latency exceeding committed levels

Outage duration is measured from when either the service provider or customer detects the problem (whichever is earlier) to when service is restored to the original performance specifications.

Table 13.1 shows the typical included and excluded items for calculating network availability.

T A B L E   13.1:   Included and Excluded Network Availability Components

Included Components	Excluded Components
All components of the frame relay service provided and managed by the service provider	The failure of any components beyond your side of either the access provider demarcation or the CPE if not provided by the service provider
Service provider-provided local-access facilities used to access the service provider frame relay network	Network downtime during the service providers scheduled maintenance window
Service provider-provided CPE	Causes beyond the reasonable control of the service provider

PVC Availability

In addition to overall network availability, many customers are concerned with specific PVC availability. By negotiating a PVC availability component as part of your overall frame relay SLA, you can ensure each PVC delivers the performance necessary between sites and as your applications demand.

End-to-end PVC availability is calculated as the percentage of time a frame relay PVC is capable of accepting and delivering frames to the total time in the measurement period. The calculation for end-to-end PVC availability for a given month is as follows:

```
(24 Hours x Days in Month) - PVC Outage Time - Excluded Time
(24 Hours x Days in Month) - Excluded Time
```

Table 13.2 shows typical PVC included and excluded components.

T A B L E 13.2: Included and Excluded PVC Components

Included	Excluded
All PVCs (individually)	The failure of any components beyond the demarcation point
	Network downtime during the service provider's scheduled maintenance window
	The failure of any components, which cannot be corrected due to causes beyond the reasonable control of the service provider

The PVC availability component's real benefit is it allows you to specify higher availability for mission-critical PVCs and specify lower availability for less critical PVCs (if appropriate). This can lead to lower cost connections for less critical PVCs, which may mean a lower total bill for your company.

Packet Delay

You should be concerned with not only the availability of your network and network components but also with the speed at which your traffic is delivered. Most frame relay SLAs include a metric for network delay. For businesses running time-sensitive applications or protocols, minimizing delay represents an important issue.

End-to-end PVC delay is generally calculated as the measurement of time taken for a frame to go from one end of a frame relay PVC to the other and back again. (This is also known as *round-trip* delay.) It can be measured end-to-end, from customer demarcation to customer demarcation, including the local-access facility. It can also be measured simply switch-to-switch within the provider's network. Some providers average the delay over the course of a day, week, or month, which results in minimizing the value of the SLA.

A sample packet delay component is shown in Table 13.3.

T A B L E 13.3: A Sample Packet Delay Component

Samples	Switch-to-Switch	End-to-End
In Country	64Kb Port = 130ms DS-1 Port =130ms	64Kb Port = 200ms DS-1 Port =140ms
International	64Kb Port = 160ms DS-1 Port =160m	64Kb Port = 250ms DS-1 Port =200ms

The components are shown in Table 13.4.

T A B L E 13.4: A Sample Packet Delay Component

Included	Excluded
All components of the service provider frame relay network	Equipment beyond the demarcation or the CSU/DSU/Channel Bank, if provided by the carrier
Service provider-provided local access facilities used to access the frame relay network	Frames larger than x bytes (excludes atypical frame sizes)
Service provider-provided CPE	

Frame/Packet Delivery Rate

As we discussed in earlier chapters, frame relay networks can drop packets during times of severe network congestion, so you will want to ensure the arrival of packets you send to their destination. If you negotiate an SLA that includes this option, it is called *Frame/Packet Delivery Ratio* (FDR).(In this category, service providers typically differentiate between packets sent within CIR and those sent in excess of CIR [DE].) Expect service providers to offer a 99.9x percent FDR for CIR traffic and 9x percent FDR for DE traffic.

The typical formula for calculating FDR is as follows:

```
CIR FDR = CIR Frames Delivered - Exclusions/CIR Frames
Sent - Exclusions
DE FDR = DE Frames Delivered - Exclusions/DE Frames
Sent - Exclusions
```

The typically excluded items for FDR components are data loss due to failures of local-access facilities, frames lost due to customer oversubscription of CIR at the egress port and data loss during a service provider's scheduled maintenance window.

Mean Time to Repair

Mean time to *repair,* or MTTR, is the final common SLA metric we will discuss. However, it is important to note what MTTR is *not.* Many providers use the acronym MTTR to denote "Mean time to *respond,*" which means they will respond to an issue within x hours but may not repair it for x additional hours. Be certain that when you get an MTTR SLA metric, it denotes what you want it to.

The typical MTTR states that a service provider will restore service within x hours. This time frame may vary based on where your sites are located and whether the problem is CPE-based or inside the frame relay network.

Generally, service providers commit to maintain a 4-hour repair time for non-CPE-related trouble tickets, which are reports from customers about an problems with their services. This includes access and network components. For CPE-related trouble tickets, a 4-hour to 8-hour MTTR is common.

This metric is calculated by measuring the elapsed time from when the trouble call was placed until the time service is restored to normal operating performance.

Other SLA Metrics

In addition to the standard SLA metrics outlined above, others exist that some service providers offer today or plan to offer in the near future. These include the following:

Protocol Performance   Instead of simply guaranteeing an overall performance target for your traffic, some providers allow you to designate different levels of service for different PVCs or protocols. For example, SNA and voice traffic are extremely time sensitive. You may want to have an SLA that includes lower delay for these and higher delay for applications such as e-mail. Obviously, you should expect to pay more for better delay characteristics.

Installation Timeframe   A large part of your initial satisfaction with frame relay may hinge on how smoothly the initial implementation goes. Some providers guarantee that your access, ports, PVCs, and perhaps even your CPE will be installed within x days or by an agreed upon date.

Billing Accuracy   Anyone who has ordered telecommunications service has probably experienced an incorrect bill at some point. It can be a major drain on internal resources trying to get bills corrected. To establish customer confidence in their billing systems, some providers will guarantee correct bills or at least that a bill is $99.x$ percent correct.

Business Outage   The business-outage metric is new, and you probably shouldn't expect many providers to offer this metric unless your network is extremely strategic to the provider. For example, assume your annual revenue is $365,000. If your network goes down for 24 hours during the course of a year, that means it will probably cost you 1/365 of your revenue. Therefore, the provider will credit you $1,000. This is in addition to any other SLAs and credits you may have negotiated. The larger your revenue, the more attractive this metric is to your company.

Each metric discussed in this chapter provides basic SLA information and benchmarks. But if SLAs were this simple, we wouldn't devote an entire chapter to them, and it wouldn't have taken over a year for the Frame Relay Forum to approve FRF.13. The next sections address areas where you need to pay attention to the detail of the SLAs you negotiate.

Common Exclusions for SLAs

In each of the standard SLA metrics discussed previously, some typical "exclusions" were shown. These exclusions can dramatically impact the value of a given SLA. Service providers have become very creative in defining their SLAs, and you need to be at least as clever in evaluating them.

The goal of negotiating SLAs is not simply to find the highest network-availability percentage, the lowest delay in milliseconds, and the shortest MTTR. It may seem logical to do this, but you must keep in mind any exclusions the provider may place on the SLAs. For example, Provider A may offer network availability of 100 percent, which appears better than Provider B, which only supports network availability of 98 percent. Upon studying the SLA contract, you discover Provider A has over 15 different "exclusions," and Provider B has only three. In that case, Provider B may actually offer a better network-availability metric, even though the percentage is lower.

Here are some common examples of exclusions or areas that can have an impact on the attractiveness of a provider's SLA:

Force Majeure (Acts of God)   Many SLAs, such as network availability, do not apply if failure to meet the target was due to an "Act of God." Generally, this means any natural disaster, such as earthquake, tornado, hurricane, flood, etc. It can also include terrorism and other intentional acts of sabotage.

Planned Outages/Upgrades   Frame relay networks are "living" networks, meaning your provider must upgrade switches, trunks, etc., to offer high-quality, feature-rich services. Therefore, the provider will need to interrupt your service occasionally to upgrade the network. During these planned upgrades, metrics, such as availability and delivery, are temporarily "turned off" and not included in the calculations. Be sure these planned upgrades cannot occur during critical times for your business and are always known to you *in advance.*

Day/Time Restrictions   Some providers measure metrics, such as delay and frame delivery rate, over each 24 hours. If delay is 250ms during your business day (8 hours) but 100ms after hours, then the service provider would not be in violation of the SLA if the average delay was targeted at 150ms—even though you are not receiving the performance you require during the critical time for your business. Be sure to check for which period SLAs are measured and how they are calculated.

Discard Eligible Packets   Some providers exclude DE packets from the calculations completely. If you are ordering a Zero CIR service or expect to be bursting often, make certain DE packets are included in the SLA.

As you can tell, SLAs are much more complicated than they originally appeared to be. But if you think negotiating a good SLA seems challenging, the policing or monitoring of the SLA can be an even greater challenge.

Monitoring the SLA—Proving It

Negotiating the SLA is only the first step in the process. During the negotiations and throughout the life of the frame relay network, you must have a way to monitor the network and determine whether the SLA is being met. There are two primary ways to do this: CNMS reports and monitoring CPE.

CNMS Reports   Today, most providers that offer CNMS reports have incorporated SLA reporting. Regardless of the method of delivery—hardcopy, SNMP, or Web—you can view these reports to determine whether the provider is meeting the SLA.

Monitoring CPE   This CPE can be a CSU/DSU (or NTU), router, or separate probe. These devices have been enhanced to provide you with online reports for the most common SLA metrics (as well as a lot of other information used to troubleshoot problems quickly when they occur).

Using CNMS reports is the default for networks because these reports come directly from the provider and, therefore, will not be questioned if an SLA is not met. But in many cases, the SLA includes metrics not solely within the cloud (the domain of most CNMS reports). Therefore, for end-to-end SLAs and for SLAs not covered by CNMS, a CPE monitoring device is the only option.

Regardless of the reporting method, you should realize that few providers "self police." Even though your provider may manage the network and provide CNMS reports, it is often the customer's responsibility to notify the provider that an SLA has been missed. This requires additional resources with your organization to review network performance and compare the performance to the negotiated SLA. Before you sign the contract for service, ask your provider who is responsible for this duty and what CNMS reports or CPE reports are considered "valid" for showing actual network performance and possible SLA violations.

Benefits—What's in It for You?

As stated at the beginning of the chapter, if an SLA does not include some customer benefit, it is simply an objective and not worth much to you as a frame relay customer. The benefits represent the "teeth" of any SLA. Without these, the service provider has little incentive (other than keeping you satisfied as a customer) for meeting an SLA.

Many different types of benefits are possible. The major ones are outlined below.

Money Credits   The most common form of SLA benefit is a service credit. This usually takes the form of either cash back or a credit for future months' service. Examples include a percent discount off your port recurring fee, free installation, free reports, or credits paid to your company following poor performance.

Increased Service/Performance   This is a little-known but useful SLA benefit. For customers, particularly Zero CIR customers who may be told they will get a certain level of performance and then do not, the service provider may increase your CIR or port or some other service component at no charge. This is attractive if the service increase is permanent, but watch out for providers who can change the service back to the original levels without your approval.

Change of Service   Some providers allow you to change to another service or even service provider if you are unsatisfied. In some cases, they may even pay for your change fees and installation charges on the new network, although this is rare.

Summary

As you can see from the above discussion, SLAs may appear simple on the surface, but you must understand the details to determine whether the SLA is truly providing the apparent benefit. Gaining a detailed understanding of items and areas included, and especially those excluded, can mean the difference between a valuable and worthless SLA.

Service providers continue to enhance SLAs in an effort to attract customers in competitive markets. If your network is medium to large, be sure to negotiate nonstandard SLAs. The standard SLAs are typically for small networks and represent a starting point for better SLAs for customers with larger networks.

Your standard SLA should include the following metrics:

- Network availability
- PVC availability
- Packet delay
- Frame delivery rate
- Mean time to repair

Some providers require your network design to be "approved" by their internal design team for SLAs to be valid. This ensures the design is appropriate and capable of supporting the applications when performing normally. The next chapter discusses the design process in detail.

CHAPTER

14

Designing the Network

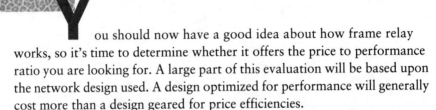

You should now have a good idea about how frame relay works, so it's time to determine whether it offers the price to performance ratio you are looking for. A large part of this evaluation will be based upon the network design used. A design optimized for performance will generally cost more than a design geared for price efficiencies.

The process of designing a frame relay network can be different than designing a private-line network. The traffic-profile information you must consider is largely the same as for a private network, but the ultimate network design that information suggests will probably be very different. Your underlying, site-to-site traffic pattern can be more closely matched by a frame relay network than by a private-line network because establishing PVCs is usually more economical than establishing private-line connections.

Many companies do not have a good feel for the underlying traffic patterns, the average and peak use of individual network connections or individual applications. This means this initial network design may be based significantly on indirect indicators and will need to be fine-tuned over time as more direct traffic-pattern information is gathered.

This chapter provides guidelines and suggestions for what to look at when designing your network and how to use the information that you do have available to determine your port connection speeds, your connectivity requirements (e.g., PVCs or SVCs), and the required speed for each connection (e.g., the PVC/SVC CIR).

Determining Your Network Objectives

Although it may sound too academic and theoretical to say that the place to begin is by understanding your network objectives, this is in fact the case. These high-level objectives may provide guidance when choosing between alternative topologies, determining CIRs, deciding upon oversubscription allowances and burst assignments, etc.

For example, you may want to set a goal that any user accessing the network anytime from anywhere will experience a consistent look, feel, and network performance. Another goal may be that you want the network to manage itself with as little human intervention as possible and that MNS options are used for daily management instead of your internal resources. Although many network managers might say they want these characteristics, they might not follow through on the network design to ensure them, especially if it means increased network costs. You need to determine, up front, what objectives will guide your design. Goals, such as minimizing cost and maximizing performance, work against each other and force compromise. If you can put hard numbers around your objectives, such as "no more than one-second response time for the interactive applications from any network point," so much the better.

For example, realistic numbers you might want to consider are

- 1 second for block-oriented applications, such as SNA

- 80ms at the outside for interactive TCP/IP applications

- 100ms for screen update–oriented client/server

- 60ms for general interactive, character-based applications

- Availability of 99.99 percent

Be certain you determine your objectives for different sites because they could have a big impact on network design and cost at a given location. For example, you may determine that no amount of network downtime is acceptable for the business at the primary data-processing location. In this case, you may be willing to spend more money for geographically diverse local loops into geographically diverse frame relay port connections. This same requirement and the added expense that goes with it may not hold true for your remote sales offices.

Taking Inventory of Your Network

To begin your network design process, there are two main steps. First, you must understand your current network topology and do a detailed site inventory. Second, you must collect information about the underlying traffic patterns of the applications being supported.

The inventory helps you to know which network elements are under design consideration. You do not want to overlook a necessary part of the network design, such as hardware or access, at any location. In addition to the frame relay network elements, each site must have access, a router (or some other type of frame relay equipment), and a CSU/DSU (NTU). The point is to inventory each location separately to determine which elements are already in place and which are not. The inventory should also include a review of the existing network topology.

It is helpful to keep a specification sheet on each site, so you can record information about that site that might affect the network design. This information can include whether the site is critical enough to warrant the evaluation of access diversity for network protection, whether the site will operate as a backup data center during a disaster scenario, whether the site needs to change its network configuration during a disaster scenario, etc. Other information that can be helpful in designing the network into each site is discussed next.

The specification sheet should include any information you have on the following topics:

- Network applications, including average file size, transaction frequency, time-of-day utilization pattern, number of users, and relative priority level of the application.

- Protocols.

- Other existing equipment, such as SNA devices that might be under lease (and amortization and cost status if applicable).

- Existing network facilities serving the site or application and average performance: For example, are you seeing congestion problems, such as slow response times, with the current network? When?

Although frame relay is designed to help cost-effectively flatten network architectures, you may find that not every site cost-justifies a direct connection. This is especially true for low-volume sites that are geographically close to larger locations that can cost-justify a direct connection. The branch location inherits all the connectivity of the hub site by connecting directly to that hub site and using the hub location's PVCs. You want to evaluate the economic trade-offs of different network topologies before making a final decision.

Many frame relay users find that the paperwork created during this design process serves as historical reference in the documentation package that supports the network. Archive notes, saved simulations, charts and graphs, and assumptions used to design the network can be used later to validate the assumptions and answer questions about process or calculation. They can also be used in the future for network modification.

The next step in the network design process is to determine PVC information. Many people try to determine port speed before the PVCs, but this is not wise. You need to know the PVC requirements to determine the port speed.

Creating a PVC Map

Begin the design process by plotting all your locations on a map so that you have a general idea of the relative proximity of each location and the geographic coverage necessary. These are the sites requiring connectivity. Next, design paths from one edge location to a related location, as defined by a need to exchange information. This graphical representation can form the basis of a PVC map developed at later stages.

When you design your frame relay network, design each site individually and then take a step back to make sure the final design makes sense.

In putting together the PVC map, look at each network location (e.g., each edge site on the network) separately. You need to determine the other remote locations to which a *direct* frame relay connection (PVC) is probably required. Notice that we said "direct connection." You may need the ability to communicate with a lot of other remote sites, but the volume of traffic may not justify a direct connection.

As with other network architectures, frame relay allows you to create a logical mesh of connectivity without creating a physical mesh. This is cost effective when a very small amount of traffic volume exists between two locations, such as two remote sales offices. It's also possible that SVCs would be a good solution to consider (see Chapter 10).

Some traffic between some locations, such as e-mail between remote sales sites, may first be routed through one or more intermediate locations before reaching the final destination.

Determining PVC CIR

With the PVC map created, you should now start to focus on PVC CIR. When deciding on the size and speed (i.e., the committed information rate) of the PVCs at a network location, you may want to treat PVCs as one-way, or *simplex*, connections. This means you look at each direction of the traffic separately. This approach is warranted if you suspect that you have one or more applications in which the volume of traffic in one direction is substantially different from the volume of traffic in the other direction. Looking at each direction of a connection separately is fairly easy and can be done systematically throughout the network by looking at the *outbound* connectivity requirements from one site to each of the other sites to which it has a direct PVC connection. *Outbound* means the traffic volume *from* that site *to* other sites. The return connectivity requirements are actually outbound PVCs from the other locations back to the first site and would be designed when you set up the outbound network requirements from each of those locations.

Although PVCs are logical, full-duplex connections, some carriers allow you to purchase a different CIR in each direction of the PVC to more cost-effectively support asymmetric traffic patterns.

Initially, you may not have enough information about your traffic pattern to tell whether you need more or less capacity in a single direction. Once you are up and running in a frame relay environment, the network can provide you with this information. You can then go back and fine-tune the frame relay network design.

After estimating applications and connectivity needs, you must determine the actual CIR for the PVCs/SVCs. You decision on the committed information rate can be easy or hard, depending on how much information you already have about traffic patterns and average and peak volume as well as how much guesstimating you are comfortable with doing for the initial design.

Again, if you do not have hard numbers, do not be alarmed. Common sense and some basic mathematics can take you a long way in this process. You may need to make working assumptions about file size and frequency if you do not have specific numbers to go by. Record any assumptions on the specification sheet. Keeping track of your working assumptions helps you to communicate your needs when working with different service providers.

Guidelines can be helpful as you design the CIR. These guidelines are typically company-specific and based on previous networking experience. For example, you may have already developed a guideline that says "no more than five order-entry users per 56Kbps of available network capacity."

Look at each PVC out of a site individually, and choose a CIR that supports the expected average traffic volume from the first site to the second. The burst capability of the PVC should not be counted on for transmissions when designing the network. The burst should simply be looked upon as a way to more quickly clear congestion from the port connection, handle busy periods for a given application or PVC, and get large files through the network more quickly.

The burst capability has a "smoothing" effect on application performance and protocol errors at the application level. Sometimes this effect is also achieved at the transport level and the frame relay level. More advanced designers should be aware of the effects of serialization delay, packetization and queuing delay, and the effect of the burst capability on the network and the application.

There is still one last vital piece of the puzzle still needs to be discussed, the one we suggested to not do first: determining the port connection.

Determining Port Connection Speed

The port-connection speed at a network location should be determined after you know the total of the CIRs out of and into that site. Once all of the PVCs have been determined and a CIR for each PVC chosen, then go back to each location and determine what port-connection speed makes sense, balancing performance and financial considerations.

This may now sound strange, but as a general rule in determining the port-connection speed, you should look at the inbound CIR total for that site and begin your design with the minimum port-connection speed needed to support the traffic volume. The reason is the outbound PVCs can rely on buffers at the router and port-connection site when contention for network capacity is occurring. The inbound PVCs are not afforded this luxury. Therefore, when too many inbound PVCs are simultaneously contending for the same port-connection space in an oversubscribed environment, some data may be discarded and require a retransmission.

If the inbound and outbound CIR totals are different, and the outbound total is significantly higher than the inbound's, you may want to adjust the port-connection speed upward until you reach a point where the oversubscription level for the outbound traffic is at a level with which you are comfortable. In most networks, the traffic patterns are symmetrical enough that the total inbound versus outbound CIR will not be much different. Only in the case of highly asymmetrical traffic patterns do you need to double-check the port's ability to meet the needs of traffic in both directions.

Do not total both the inbound CIRs and the outbound CIRs to determine your port speed. If you do, you will choose a speed that is much greater than what you need. Look at each direction of traffic separately, and make sure that the port-connection speed you choose can handle each direction.

It is difficult to conceptualize, but *the inbound and outbound traffic streams do not contend for the same port capacity.* Think of it as being two separate port connections—one that is dynamically allocated for the inbound traffic and one that is dynamically allocated for the outbound traffic. You pay for only one port connection, and you choose only one port-connection speed for both the inbound and outbound traffic, but the traffic itself does not mix on the same port connection.

In determining the port's speed, consider a 100 to 200 percent subscription level, depending upon how intermittent the applications are and the likelihood of every PVC being simultaneously active. If you remember, oversubscribing a port connection means assigning more total CIR, across all of the PVCs supported by the port connection, than what the port connection could actually handle at any given point in time. For example, you could assign eight PVCs to a 256Kbps port connection, each with a CIR of 64Kbps, for a total of 512Kbps. Oversubscribing a port connection saves you money at the site because it means a lower port-connection speed can be used. In this example, if a 256Kbps port connection is used for all eight PVCs, the price could be about 25 percent less at that site than if a 512Kbps port speed were used.

Setting Up a Pilot Network

P*iloting* is a technique you may find very useful as you launch into your first frame relay network experience. In setting up a pilot network, choose a few sample network locations for initial frame relay installation, and then proceed to install and benchmark test the network before installing frame relay to other locations.

During the pilot stage, you can test some of the assumptions you may have brought from the private-line network to determine whether they are still appropriate in a frame relay environment. Experiments on the pilot network serve as reference for building the real network or as feedback for network design.

The pilot network does not have to be a time-consuming or costly project. It can simply be the first phase of your overall network implementation. If you run the pilot network in parallel to your existing network for a short time—say, 30 days—you can benchmark the two networks initially to determine any change in application performance.

You can then use the parallel configuration as a safety net by rolling existing applications onto the frame relay network before the leased line is disconnected. This allows you to quickly switch the application back to the previous network should any performance-affecting problems arise.

This can also be an excellent time to view CNMS reports or see how the order-entry and trouble-resolution processes work. If you are not satisfied during the pilot, you probably won't be with the live network.

A Network Example

Looking at a frame relay example illustrates some of the different design principles and guidelines we covered earlier in the chapter. In your initial network design, you want to begin as simply as possible and then enhance the network once you have more experience.

Designing a Simple Network

The most simple frame relay network is one in which every site is similar to other sites and in which either a star or a full-mesh network configuration is needed. A good example is a large law firm with several locations nationwide, with partners and researchers at each site. We will use a firm with six locations, Ethernet LANs already installed at each site, and the need to share documents of cases and research material over the network.

Given that these files are large, the lawyers' time is expensive, and clients are billed for expenses incurred on their cases, this law firm does not need to be overly concerned with network costs. What it needs is a very reliable service that supports any-to-any connectivity.

A situation like this is a bit unusual because in this example, every network site may actually need a direct connection to every other site. The organization is fairly flat, and the number of lawyers and amount of traffic at each site are about the same.

Determining CIR

Determining CIR is a matter of deciding how big the average file or data set is, how often files are transmitted, and how rapid a response time is needed.

The specifications for each site look about the same.

- Each location has five to eight lawyers as well as five to eight research assistants, a secretary, and some interns.

- Ethernet LANs are already in place.

- There are no routers or CSU/DSUs installed because the company has been using dial-up connectivity with modems.

- The response times are several minutes or more per file transfer, and it is costing the firm money in lost time.

- TCP/IP is the only protocol. E-mail is used extensively within an office, and sometimes large files are attached. The firm wants company-wide e-mail.

- No technical network expertise exists at any of the sites.

- The documents range from a single page up to several hundred pages. The average size is 10 to 40 pages.

- Each lawyer sends five to eight large documents across the network on an average day. There is no specific pattern for traffic between certain offices; it is very homogeneous.

- The research assistants use the network much more frequently, but the files tend to be smaller. They average 10 to 20 document exchanges per day.

Port Connection Speed and Access

Any of these transfer times are acceptable, so the firm could make a choice based on cost. For example, the firm could choose to use a single DS-0 local loop from each site into the network, with a 56/64Kbps port connection. The firm could oversubscribe this line by 500 percent, by giving each of the five PVCs a CIR of 56/64Kbps. The downside to this solution is that if more than one PVC is active at any one time, they will be contending for the same port-connection space and will operate at less than the 56/64Kbps CIR.

Because cost is not the most important issue but response time is, an alternative would be to use a DS-1 local loop and a higher port-connection speed. Some level of oversubscription is acceptable, because not all the PVCs will be active at the same time.

If a 192Kbps PVC was used from each site to every other site, then the total inbound (and outbound) CIR from each site would be 960Kbps (192K times five PVCs). If a 128Kbps PVC is used, the total inbound and outbound CIR would be 640Kbps.

E-mail: Designing Your Network to Handle It

E-mail is such a growing network application that a quick word on the topic is in order. E-mail in the Novell Netware environment or in the Internet environment is usually demand-based, with file sizes less than 4KB except when large files are attached. Unless special application software is used, e-mail messages are queued up and dispatched one at a time over the network until the queue is empty. The queue service interval (i.e., run interval) determines the busy percentage of the channel more than the size of the e-mail message does.

Because cost is not the primary issue for our law firm and response time is, we will assume for this example that each site has a PVC to the other five locations. The CIR for each PVC would probably be between 64K and 192Kbps. Here's why:

- If the average document is 10 to 40 pages, then this equates to about 15,000 to 60,000 bytes (1,500 characters per page). There are eight bits in every byte, so multiplying this number by eight will give the total number of bits in the average small file. In this example, the files are 120,000 to 480,000 bits. At 64,000 bits per second, the file would transfer in 1.875 to 7.5 seconds, assuming no propagation delay by the network.

- If a 192Kbps PVC were used, the response times would decrease by two thirds, to .63 and 2.5. If a 128Kbps PVC were used, response times would decrease by half, to .94 and 3.75.

- If the application is a store-and-forward design, then this difference in transfer time may not matter much. If the applications include real-time desktop collaboration or if someone is likely to be waiting on the files as they are transferred, then there could be a business impact from the additional transfer time.

If the firm chose to use 192Kbps PVCs, a 384K or 512Kbps port connection would make the most sense. Because the CIRs would be relatively high and the likelihood of the PVCs all being active at once relatively low, a higher level of oversubscription would not be a problem.

The 384Kbps port connection, with the PVCs, would equate to 250 percent subscription and about $1,200 to $1,500 per month per site, before local access. If the access is about $300 per DS-1 loop, the entire network would cost about $10,000 per month, before term and volume discounts are applied.

Of course, if the DS-0 loops with the 56/64Kbps port connection were used instead, the entire network would be less than half that amount per month.

Carrier-Provided Equipment and Management Options

This law firm is not in the network business and has little expertise with routers, so using the frame relay carrier to provide all of the equipment and possibly a managed network service should be strongly considered. With a managed network service, the provider monitors the network around the clock and takes responsibility for fixing any problems with the wide-area network addressing. They provide a much higher level of technical support than if the standard frame relay service were purchased without this option. Of course, this option costs more. However, in the case of the law firm, the option would make sense.

Summary

After reading this chapter, you should be able to step through the phases of designing a frame relay network: determining your objectives, taking a site inventory, creating a PVC map, determining PVC CIR, determining port-connection speeds, and perhaps installing a pilot network. As you move through the process, it will be much easier if you have information of historic traffic patterns and applications to help you create a more appropriate first design. If you don't have this information, don't worry. You can also rely on help from a service provider—but be careful because its designs tend to be tailored to its network solution. If you don't have good historical information, simply design an initial configuration that seems logical given your current network facilities and performance and your near-term growth forecasts. Then, if the design is not optimal once you have traffic statistics to examine, change it. One of the major advantages to frame relay is that it is relatively easy to modify in comparison to dedicated network solutions.

Once you've designed the network, it's time to decide which provider to select for your frame relay service. This is discussed in the next chapter, Chapter 15.

CHAPTER

15

Developing a Request for Proposal

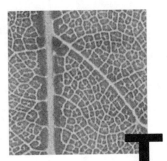

his chapter discusses the process of service-provider selection and outlines a proven methodology for managing this process from the requirements-gathering phase through the Request for Proposal (RFP) to the actual selection of a service provider. Specifically, we will walk you through the overall RFP process and discuss the contents of a typical RFP and the chronology of the vendor-selection process.

The important thing to remember in this exercise is that your end goal is probably not simply to discover the low-cost vendor. Although cost is always a major factor in any decision, it is vital to use the process to further your own education regarding available service features so that you come out with the overall best solution. You should view the entire proposal process as an opportunity to have service-provider personnel (who probably have a lot more experience with the technology than you do) examine your company's environment and provide guidance on everything from topology and network-management strategies to whether or not you actually have an application for frame relay. This means sharing as much as possible about your network requirements as well as requiring the potential providers to make a thorough and intelligent response to your request.

The RFP Process

At the outset of the RFP process, you need to know what you would like to get accomplished and your time frame for completion. It is difficult to begin the vendor-selection process without a clearly defined timeline. This timeline puts you in control of the order of events. Making this timeline known to all involved parties is one component of effective vendor management.

As an example, some service providers will request the option of rebidding services should other service providers undercut their prices. If you do not allow for this rebid in your timeline, the service provider will likely be a bit more careful in its initial price calculations. By establishing and managing a timetable, you are making firm the ground rules for negotiation. As with any good guideline, you can also decide when to bend or break it.

Following is a proposed chronology for the RFP process.

Getting Organized

First, you should organize and develop a guideline. Here are some steps to help you get started.

1. Identify and contact potential bidders.

2. Appropriate the staff to support the process.

3. Meet to clarify and record objectives.

4. Set up project timeline.

5. Assign RFP writing responsibilities for each RFP section to your staff.

The first task consists of producing a letter expressing your interest in a frame relay network and asking the service provider to supply a package of information on its offerings. This letter, usually referred to as a *Request for Information* (RFI), should go out to any service provider you might consider. Later, you can make a preliminary evaluation, narrowing the process down to three to five service providers, if possible. If you have equipment vendors submit separate bids, then there might be another three to five vendors to consider. The more players involved, the more difficult the project is to manage.

You may want different experts within your own group to write different components of the RFP. Make sure that a common format is followed by all writers. It may be tempting to have junior members of the staff put together the base information, but it is crucial to have a few expert individuals who are responsible for the actual content of the document. This way, meetings with the service providers can be held in small groups with only these key people.

You may want to design your own frame relay network and insist that each service provider give a price for the design *without modification*. You might also specify a very strict format for this response, including a site-by-site pricing matrix you design and the service provider fills out. In addition, you can give each service provider the option of including up to two (or some other number) alternative network designs or proposals. You may choose to require a specific format for these alternatives, or you can let the service provider choose the response format.

Remember that the more flexibility you give your service provider, the more difficult it can be to figure it out and compare alternatives.

Drafting the RFP

The next set of steps will help you draft the Request for Proposal.

1. Produce and review the draft copy of the RFP.

2. Review materials from service providers.

3. Decide on the recipients of the RFP.

4. Plan any site visits.

Once the process begins, your goal should be to make the service providers start working for you, instead of vice versa, as soon as possible. Set definitive time limits on discussions of who should receive the RFP and other issues that might slow down the process of delivering the document.

You also want to make any plans for travel related to the bid during this week. Sometimes service providers offer to take customers to the network control center, to a network lab, or to a current customer site for a reference visit. Time these visits so that the findings can have an impact on your decision.

If you get the opportunity to speak directly with a service provider's operations staff, ask lots of questions about how they manage and monitor the network, the level of proactive trouble monitoring and correction, their knowledge about different protocols, troubleshooting and escalation procedures, and so on. Some service providers also have network design centers or test laboratories in which engineers can model a potential network.

It is important to schedule any such visit as soon as is viable. So you need to decide whether this will be part of your objectives, whether it will be specifically required in the RFP, and how many such visits you will have the time to accomplish.

You should come out of this step with a clear idea of RFP recipients, a general plan for the travel schedule, and the changes required to produce a final document. The specific issues and steps associated with creating an RFP are discussed in the section "Objectives of Creating an RFP" later in this chapter.

Sending the RFP

Here's what to do when sending the Request for Proposal.

1. Send the RFP to selected service providers.

2. Make site visits or contact references.

3. Field initial questions from service providers.

If you have constructed your RFP properly and included all necessary information, service-provider questions should be limited to important issues and areas in which you have asked them to provide suggestions for alternate approaches. Having denoted contacts on your RFP, you should make sure these people are available and are providing the required answers.

It is standard practice to give service providers two to three weeks to respond to the RFP (longer for larger or complex networks). Although it is possible to make them move faster, it does not really benefit anyone, as the proposals will reflect the haste with which they were prepared. If questions come in, it is customary to send out the answers in written form to everyone involved, again to make sure everyone is getting the same picture.

You do not necessarily need to visit a reference customer's site. You can gather plenty of information over the phone. Just make sure you have a complete list of the issues you want to cover. At the end of the conversation, ask the person you are contacting what they would do differently, so you can benefit from their experience.

Evaluating Responses

When evaluating the responses you have received, follow these steps.

1. Review the service-provider proposals.

2. Develop a short list, if appropriate.

3. Develop a list of questions and areas of clarification for each service provider.

4. Conduct service-provider meetings.

5. Begin assigning evaluation ratings.

As proposals are delivered, you and your colleagues should immediately begin reading them. You are looking for areas in which the service provider or vendor did not directly respond to the request and areas in which they have provided responses not meeting your requirements. The aim is to quickly develop a list of these issues, which is then sent back to the service provider on the understanding that you will be expecting the bidder to address them in your scheduled meeting.

At some point, you should make a determination on the feasibility of going through with each meeting. There are times in which service-provider proposals are so far "off the mark" that the potential customer has simply told them they are no longer under consideration at this point. This usually sparks a rapid response from the service provider, and it is at your discretion whether or not to allow them to amend the proposal. Historically, customers generally allow the service provider to make a recovery only to decide against them in the final analysis. If the service provider is really out of contention, it is a waste of everyone's time to allow them back into the process.

The next step is to have each service provider present its case in a face-to-face meeting. Service providers often see this as an opportunity to impress you with their multimedia slide shows. Service providers will also attempt to jockey for position so they are the first or last to present. For this reason, you should be proactive in setting up these appointments. Do not tell the service provider when the other meetings are. Also, make it clear you will be sending them a list of issues to be covered in the meeting.

Have your salesperson notify you prior to the meeting of the number of persons, including titles, attending. Do not allow more than two to five people, or the meeting will become too difficult to manage. Make sure the technical support person or the field engineer, who will be supporting your account on an ongoing basis, is present at this meeting. If this person has been instrumental in designing your network and will continue to provide ongoing technical support, you deserve the chance to judge this person's competency.

Make sure the service provider knows the agenda ahead of time and the objectives to be accomplished in the meeting. Simple questions and answers should take up most or all of the agenda.

Use the meeting as an opportunity to understand what issues the service provider has considered in the network design and the implications of each on the final configuration. After the meeting you should begin to populate your evaluation matrix.

Trimming It Down

Now that you've hashed out what you're looking for, it's time to choose the ones who make the cut. Here are the steps for trimming down your selection.

1. Complete the evaluation of service providers.

2. Select the winner, or select the finalists (no more than two).

3. Compile a list of remaining issues with each service provider.

Once the meetings with each service provider have been completed, each person involved in the evaluation process needs to develop a list of strengths and weaknesses for each service provider. Have each person independently fill in the evaluation matrix and identify any deal "killers" that would prohibit the selection of a particular provider.

Once each person has formed his or her own impressions, you should consolidate all matrix information and present it in a single form. Develop a final rating for each service provider on each of the criteria, based on the average of all of the individual ratings. In a group meeting, you can discuss each service provider one by one. You may find a clear winner at this point, in which case you can begin focusing on implementation with that provider. However, in most cases, a few providers will be rated highly, necessitating a final meeting with the service providers on this short list.

Picking the Winner

Making the final decision is simplified with these steps.

1. Select your service provider.

2. Notify other service providers of your choice, and begin implementation.

Do whatever is necessary to bring the decision to closure. It is possible that you will be so torn between two providers that the best way to make a final decision will be to provide each service provider with a network site at which to activate service. This parallel implementation could provide you with the final puzzle piece that allows you to choose the business partner that will provide the highest quality service and support. You can judge each service provider's ability to manage the implementation process on your behalf, solve implementation problems, and test and establish your service.

The process of parallel implementation is guaranteed to drag out the RFP and network-implementation process, so look before you leap. If you can establish a clear winner without this step, do it.

Once you have made your choice, the service providers not selected may make last-ditch efforts to win the business. Generally, it is not constructive to open up the process to these providers. Only after all the above steps have been taken is it time to get on with the full implementation of your frame relay network.

Now that you know the entire RFP process, it is important to step back and discuss drafting the RFP in greater detail.

Objectives of Creating an RFP

The first step in the RFP process is figuring out what you want. After all, you cannot know whether you are satisfied unless you know what you are asking for.

Each company considering a frame relay network has a slightly different set of objectives. It is crucial to develop and record your specific objectives, not only to include in your RFP but also to use as a guide throughout the process.

Here are some objectives to consider:

Business Objectives   These objectives relate to your organization's core business. If you make shoes, then you should clearly state how you hope this proposed network will help your company make or market shoes more efficiently, more effectively, or less expensively. You may want to specifically outline your tactical, as well as strategic, objectives.

Performance Objectives   Specify your performance objectives, including any existing benchmarks. You should provide this detail on an application-by-application basis. Many companies use metrics such as throughput, measured in packets or kilobits per second, and screen response time.

Cost/Value Objectives   Although cost is seemingly clear-cut, the low-cost vendor may also be proposing the lowest-value network. Cost should be considered in both capital expenditures and annual service costs. If your organization has a preference or requirement for low capital costs, then this should be clearly stated.

Training Objectives   As mentioned, this process provides an excellent opportunity for you and your staff to learn more about the technology and how to design and manage a network. Determine what your goals are in this area, including which people you want to be educated and what you want them to learn. These goals might include sending your technical people to a service provider's network management center to discuss and learn about monitoring, having your engineers and designers work with the service provider's designers to understand the effects of different protocols, and visiting a testing laboratory to learn about simulations.

Scope Objectives   How much of the network is under consideration? Do you need routers and CSU/DSUs only, or do you also need inside wiring, LANs, or smart hubs? Do you want a single provider for both the equipment and the network, or will you consider separate providers?

Implementation Objectives   How quickly must the new network be implemented? Do you want a phased approach, or do you want to bring the new network up at all sites within a few weeks? Are there any special implementation issues the service provider or equipment provider should be aware of that might have an impact on network design or implementation planning? Will you be planning on-site inventories of your sites? Who will conduct these and when?

Expected Deliverables   Clearly outline the output you expect from the process. Do you want each bidder to submit several different network designs from which to choose? Do you want each provider to outline several different support alternatives, ranging from just network to a "plug and play" package? Do you expect an implementation plan developed as part of the design process? Will you expect the proposals to be submitted in a specific format? Will you require a formal presentation from all providers or from only those that make your short list?

Future Positioning Objectives   Lastly, it is useful to take a look forward to where your business and network will be throughout the possible life cycle of this network. Which applications do you hope to migrate to the frame relay network in the future? Which networks do you hope to consolidate? Are there new applications or business processes you hope to enable? Do you foresee locations where other protocols, such as ISDN, SMDS, or ATM, will be needed, and will the ability to interwork protocols be important in your future network? Once you can outline your future vision for the network, you can look for business partners that share that vision.

During the proposal and implementation process, you will find it useful to refer back to this listing and compare your actual performance against these objectives.

RFP Evaluation Criteria

Many customers embarking on this process find themselves in the middle of the RFP process without any formal methodology for evaluating the potential network providers. You must structure your process up front because it is difficult to do this in retrospect.

Although it is nearly impossible to make the evaluation process into a completely objective exercise, it is possible to develop a list of evaluation criteria to be used as a common, agreed-upon guide for the evaluation of the vendors. Following is a listing of criteria commonly used to differentiate service providers:

- Price
- Reliability
- Customer service
- Operations support
- Technical field support
- Performance
- Network management alternatives
- Implementation support
- Equipment choices/support
- Number and location of switches
- Speed of backbone network
- Cell relay or frame switching
- Proactive monitoring and trouble ticketing
- Protocol interworking
- Billing alternatives
- Flexible pricing schemes
- Internet access
- Disaster recovery
- Access recovery
- Integrated access
- Managed network service offering
- Flexible contract terms
- Service Level Agreements
- International service availability
- Future service plans

The list provides a good start, but it is vital to uncover the specific criteria important to your organization.

Your evaluation criteria should be rated on a numerical scale and put into a spreadsheet. Rating the criteria refers to the development of a system for weighting each criterion in terms of importance and for numerically judging each provider on each criterion. In the end, you can total each service provider's score across all elements and use this information in your final decision.

No RFP is awarded based solely on calculated numbers from weightings. However, numbers are usually used to back up what ends up being a good gut feeling about the way to go. If the process is set up correctly and you stay true to your goals, then the numbers and your gut feelings should line up. If not, then this serves to highlight some things to revisit to validate the results and your choice.

Again, it is not advisable to make a decision based solely on this kind of data, but it is an excellent way to narrow down the competition and gain some peace of mind over final decisions. Now that you have a good idea of what's important to your company, it's time to create the RFP.

Writing the RFP

Overall, the RFP should provide enough detail for the service provider to make a complete bid, and it should be organized in such a way that the service provider does not have to wade through a mass of information to get to the key points. For this reason, it is advisable to use bullets and tabular formats as much as possible and to provide a clear table of contents.

A sample table of contents for an RFP is provided below. This is just a suggested format and, although it has proven effective for several organizations, rarely can it be used without some modifications. A discussion in detail about the outline follows.

1. Overview

    A. Summary of Business

    B. Listing of Objectives

2. Background

   A. Project Brief

   B. Ground Rules

   C. Timeline

   D. Corporate and/or Network Organization Summary

3. Current Network

   A. Overview (with diagram)

   B. Applications

   C. Site Information

   D. Limitations

4. Proposed Network

   A. Overview (with design, if available)

   B. New Applications or Changes to Existing Applications

   C. Pertinent Business Factors (e.g., downsizing)

   D. General Requirements

   E. Benchmarks

   F. Contract Provisions

5. Outline for Response

   A. Proposed Network Design

   B. Alternative Designs and/or Ancillary Services

   C. Response to General Requirements

   D. Costs

   E. Implementation Plan

6. Attachments

7. Glossary

Overview

This section should be only a few paragraphs in length. It provides a summary of your business, the service you anticipate purchasing, and a listing of the key reasons and objectives for issuing the request. If you are considering the option of a managed network service, state it clearly in this section as well as any other requirements that significantly affect the type of service you wish to purchase.

Depending upon what you are including in this proposal, some vendors may only be bidding on certain sections (such as equipment only or the frame relay network only). It is important that everyone bidding have a clear idea of "the big picture."

Background

This section provides a more in-depth brief of the requests with a summary of the number of locations, applications, and users to be served. It will also lay out the ground rules for the entire process. Examples of essential components include

- Service providers are expected to include final "best price" in the proposal. Rebids will not be accepted.

- Service providers unable to complete a bid in the allotted time frame will not be considered.

- Bids will remain confidential throughout the process.

- Service providers are expected to use given contacts throughout the evaluation process. (Salespeople often try to speak only to the decision-maker.)

- Service providers will be expected to have the required technical experts at meetings.

- Presentations will be scheduled in the order of the arrival of the proposals.

- Proposals not meeting the format guidelines will not be accepted.

Your intended timeline for the RFP process and then for network implementation should be clearly defined in this section.

This section should also include a description of your network-management and support organization, including number of employees and levels of expertise. It is better to let the service provider know up front whether you will need extensive assistance during the implementation. The service provider may choose to propose some outsourcing options based on this information.

You may want to provide specific detail on the management system(s) you currently use, the network analysis tools you have available, the staff's level of experience with routers and internetworks, and so on. After reading this section, the bidders should have a good idea of the organization that will be supporting the network once it is in place.

Current Network

This section familiarizes the service provider with your current network environment. The service provider needs to know and understand how you are using your current network and how it is performing. This tells the service provider your past priorities and the shape of your solutions. It also provides indications of the current network's failure to meet performance objectives.

A map of the existing network is critical. Most organizations have maps of their physical networks and many have made logical maps, as well. All of this information, as long as it is accurate, is useful.

Assemble any or all of this information and provide it as part of the RFP. If you want the service providers to help you design your frame relay network, they need every scrap of relevant information you can provide.

For each existing circuit in your network, provide a matrix that lists the

- Service provider
- Applications being supported
- Access type
- CPE
- Average circuit-utilization estimate
- Current performance or benchmark information
- Disaster-recovery provisions
- Network/circuit-recovery provisions, including diversity

This provides a good "snapshot" of the current network. Following the summary of the entire network, it is advisable to list each application separately. For each application include

- Summary of application
- Platform (hardware, software, network, protocol)
- Number of users with location distribution
- Patterns of traffic by time of day or day of week
- Average size and frequency of transactions
- Availability requirements

You want to have a similar overview for each site. The following is a listing of proposed information to include. Some of the items are identical to those in the preceding lists because for certain applications, it might be more appropriate to provide the information on a network level, whereas in other situations, it may be more useful to provide a site-by-site analysis. You need to decide what is best for your network.

- Location

- Applications used at that site

- Number of users for each application and in total

- CPE (including smart hubs, controllers, etc.)

- LANs

- Other network services used (e.g., voice, dial-up data)

- Special disaster-recovery requirements

- Traffic patterns to and from other locations

You need to include information on any new application that is not currently supported but will be once the frame relay network is in place. Provide any projections for traffic patterns and utilization you can as well as the number of users for the applications, projections for implementation, etc.

Proposed Network

In this section, you want to spell out exactly what it is you are planning on purchasing and what you expect from the new network. Your objectives for the new network are an important component of this section.

You should have some idea of what the new network will consist of and provide as much detail as possible regarding your initial designs. Service providers should actively question your design to see whether it is the best option. Be wary of the service provider that simply copies your specification and tags it with a price. You may simply have done a superb job at design, or the service provider may not be allocating appropriate expertise to your bid.

Note, in bullet form, your specific requirements for each site and application. Each chapter in this book gives you information on requirements in specific areas, such as the network, backhauling, loop recovery, site recovery, network management, and so on.

Provide a site-by-site and application-by-application comparison of the current network requirements with your new network requirements. For example, if a site does not have loop-recovery provisions in the current network but you want them in the new network, you would specifically point out this fact.

You may want to specify certain design alternatives that you will or will not accept, such as oversubscription of a port connection or use of Zero CIR PVCs. This can also include accepting equipment bids from service providers and other proposals for ancillary services, such as network management packages and Internet access.

Outline for Response

The service providers should be advised on exactly how to respond to your request. Although it is not necessary to provide the service provider with a fill-in-the-blanks form, it is advisable to request specific point-by-point answers to each requirement and an overall format for the final proposal.

This is critical to the success of the RFP. The service providers have their own boilerplate proposal responses for frame relay, in which they tell you how great they are and how no one else compares. You need to structure your request for a response in such a way that breaks them out of that mold, or you will have to spend a lot of time sifting through sales pitches looking for answers to your questions. Some of the most successful RFPs ask for specific summary pages on simple things, including the following:

- Total installation expense—services
- Total installation expense—equipment
- Total installation expense—other
- Total monthly expense—services
- Total monthly expense—equipment
- Total monthly expense—other
- Total time to install

By forcing the service providers to specifically address your questions, you can better compare the final bids. Let them put all the sales fluff up front, but when it comes to specific answers, make them follow format.

Your RFP can include a format outline, such as a section-by-section breakdown, including:

1. Executive overview of your proposal
2. Service provider overview/information

3. Pricing of *your* network design

4. Pricing for the ancillary services you specifically request in the RFP

5. Alternative designs, ancillary services, and pricing

6. Implementation of the plan

You may want to provide detail on your objectives within each section or to provide specific section requirements.

When pricing your network design, you should provide information on the format of this pricing, as discussed below. You may specify that each service provider should provide pricing on certain ancillary services, such as network management or managed network support. If this is the case, also specify the format, such as pricing on a per-site basis and not a network-level price. You may want to provide an open, or "other," category, in which the service provider can propose alternatives, such as equipment or Internet access, in conjunction with pricing for your network design.

Section 5 of this RFP encourages the service provider to challenge any of your design points or requirements and develop a new network design. There have been more than a few cases in which a customer puts out a request for a frame relay network, and one (or more) of the service providers proposes a private line or hybrid network solution. Give the service providers a chance to optimize your network, and then you be the judge of whether or not the modified solution meets your needs better than the one you proposed.

You should specify a format for the presentation of pricing. You should be able to get a complete breakdown of charges on a site-by-site basis. Each service provider prices the frame relay service component of the network very differently, so trying to fit them all into a rigorous format will just be frustrating for you and the bidder. However, you can specify a general format, such as site-by-site price breakdowns that include the price for equipment, maintenance, management, access, and IXC detailed separately. You can also request a specific format for summarizing the network totals. For example, do you want IXC, access, and equipment totaled separately, or do you want each site totaled separately for all elements?

Require the service provider to provide a discount matrix based on different term contracts and volume levels. This should be separate from the base pricing.

Although it is largely unfair to the service providers, few customers these days pay for installation charges. You should be able to negotiate a waiver of these in exchange for a term contract.

If there is a possibility of moving voice traffic to the service provider, ask for bids that reflect cross-product discounts or concessions.

Request an implementation plan, a description of the progression of events, and information about the exact individuals who will be supporting each area or component of the installation.

Attachments

This section includes any detailed performance and/or traffic data you have collected, simulation results you have run, and possibly the worksheets you used in developing your own design. The RFP process isn't intended to be a mystery game in which service providers have to dig up clues, and the best digger wins. You want the best possible network design, so provide as much information to all participants as possible.

Glossary

This may sound like you are writing a book, but many firms fall quickly into their own lingo, making it hard for service providers to fully understand what you are talking about. If you refer to sites in a particular way or if you call your routers by particular names that are nonstandard, then this is the place to put some of that information. Because you have to respond in written format to all bidders for each question, you really want to minimize the problems up front, and confusion over terms is always a big issue.

Summary

Certainly, writing an RFP is an involved process, but with frame relay, it is a necessary one. In general, the more time spent up front with an RFP, the more successful your process will be. By defining and refining your descriptions, explanations, and structures in the RFP, you will provide the best guidance to the service providers. And that means the best output for your solution.

Best of luck writing your RFP and implementing your frame relay network.

CHAPTER

16

How Frame Relay Plays
in an IP World

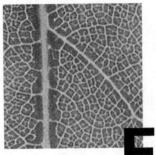

Frame relay has gained popularity for many reasons, as we have discussed throughout this book. One of the major reasons for frame relay's success is that businesses needed a way to economically transport multi-protocol traffic. Prior to frame relay's introduction, companies were forced to deploy multiple parallel networks, one for each protocol. Now, all your traffic can be sent across a single access line via a single frame relay network. If you continue to run multiprotocol traffic, then frame relay will continue to offer an opportunity for economical transport while delivering the performance your applications require.

Since the introduction of frame relay, there has been a major change in the business communications market: business migration to IP. With many businesses migrating to IP, the multiprotocol benefit of frame relay is reduced. In this chapter, you will see how VPNs have evolved and what impact IP VPNs are likely to have on frame relay services.

History of VPNs

When frame relay was first marketed in the U.S., it was described as a *Virtual Private Network,* or VPN solution. It was given this label because, unlike dedicated private-line networks, frame relay services did not require customers to set up dedicated circuits between each pair of communicating locations. The network handled site-to-site connectivity logically by subdividing one large network into PVCs. So while each subscriber does not have individual dedicated circuits, the circuits are at least *virtually* private.

Since frame relay's introduction, the term VPN has taken on a new meaning. Rather than virtualizing networks at layer two (as in frame relay or ATM), the popularity of the Internet and the IP protocol has led to the desire to build VPNs based on a shared layer three (IP) network. This arrangement can allow you to take advantage of the economics of the Internet or other shared IP platforms to save on networking costs when compared to traditional data services. Much as frame relay virtualized data networks by replacing dedicated circuits with logical connections, IP networks and VPNs are further virtualizing networks by replacing logical connections, or PVCs, with fully meshed routing tables.

Aside from simple cost savings, IP VPNs may offer a number of other advantages:

- A standards-based solution for integrating partners, customers, and suppliers into an enterprise network

- Ubiquitous, global network access for traveling and remote employees

- A single network protocol to manage

Despite these advantages, today's VPN solutions have a number of limitations. The current crop of VPN products and services require complex setup and configuration procedures. They also require that you possess some level of knowledge regarding Internet security and encryption—skills that are not easily acquired. Most importantly, VPNs are reliant upon IP networks for transport, and IP networks are designed to provide "best effort" handling of all packets. In other words, IP networks treat all packets exactly the same and do not provide for precedence or Quality of Service (QoS) controls.

A Quick VPN Tutorial

V*irtual Private Networking* is defined in this book as a private communications network existing within a shared or public network platform, which may be the Internet.

The *V* in VPN stands for *virtual,* which means that VPN subscribers are sharing a common infrastructure with other users. In other words, users do not have private, dedicated point-to-point connections. This is very similar to the concept of PVCs and SVCs.

Private implies that we are securing these networks in some way. Because the Internet protocol was designed to be open, anyone connected to the network would have the ability to intercept, read, or change our data in transit. Other users may also be able to gain access to systems or networks that contain confidential data. For these reasons, IP communications require special security-technology treatments in order to meet your enterprise security requirements.

VPNs are being used by businesses to accomplish one or more of the following goals:

- Remote access for telecommuters and traveling employees to corporate computer resources

- Site-to-site connections or communications between enterprise locations

- Extranets, or the extension intranets that include partners, suppliers, and customers

- Electronic commerce, or the ability to conduct financial transactions with other organizations or customers

Several of the above goals sound similar to frame relay goals. To date, the most common application is for enabling remote access. Other networking solutions compare favorably with the flexibility and cost savings promised by Internet-based Virtual Private Networks. Although many frame relay providers offer remote-access solutions to their customers, few of these solutions have the global reach of an Internet VPN. Internet VPNs are not tied to a single provider's network and are accessible from anywhere that Internet access is available.

VPNs are implemented in one of two ways. They are either developed "in house" by IT managers who combine Internet connectivity with VPN equipment, or they are offered as a fully managed service by Internet service providers (ISPs) or other IP Network Providers.

As already mentioned, the IP protocol was intended to be open, and therefore, much of the initial work on IP VPNs was in the field of network security. IP VPN users must take special steps to guarantee the safety and confidentiality of their data. These issues are not major hurdles for frame relay, which inherently addresses these issues. Specifically, IP VPN enterprises must ensure

Confidentiality   Messages can only be read by sender and receiver.

Authentication   Messages are indeed from the expected originator.

Access control   Users can only utilize those resources that they are approved to utilize.

Integrity   Messages have not been altered in transit.

Nonrepudiation   Strong authentication that ensures contracting parties cannot "back out" of agreements or claim ignorance.

In order to make VPNs secure and in order to meet the needs described already, a number of tools have been developed. The VPN security tool that receives the most attention from the press and media is encryption. Encryption is simply a process of "scrambling" data based on some set of rules. Encryption provides confidentiality because only those with knowledge of the scrambling process or the encryption keys used can decode encrypted messages. Once the realm of spy novels and military uses, encryption is becoming more and more available and viable as a networking tool for the masses. By comparison, a low percentage of frame relay customers require encryption devices because the network and traffic are viewed as more secure.

VPNs also make use of a variety of strong authentication tools, such as

- Smart cards
- One-time passwords
- Digital certificates
- Biometric authentication

Authentication may be based on something that the user *possesses,* such as a smart card; something the user *knows,* such as a password; or something the user *is,* such as a finger, voice, or retinal print. The strongest of the authentication processes are based on some combination of two or more of the above, requiring, for example, a password (something you know) with a hardware token (something you have) challenge.

In order to ensure that security could be applied in a unified manner by all enterprises and that VPNs built with different vendor equipment would be able to interoperate, the Internet Engineering Task Force (IETF) has worked to develop a standard for IP VPN security. The standard, known as Internet Protocol Security (IPSec), makes use of both authentication and encryption technologies to ensure all of the security goals listed above. IPSec provides a strong measure of security for companies that wish to make use of the Internet and other low-cost public IP networks. Although this protocol is under constant development and will be for some time, it has become *the* standard for VPN security due to the following:

Flexibility   IPSec is designed to accommodate new encryption and authentication technologies as they are developed in the future. The protocol also provides a number of options to provide varying levels of security as necessary.

Adaptability   IPSec may be implemented in client computers or in networking equipment, which means that users do not have to make changes to applications in order to implement strong security.

Open Standards   IPSec was developed by the IETF, the group responsible for setting the technical direction for the Internet. In the past, security solutions came from individual vendors, resulting in a noninteroperable environment. IPSec is a standard that ensures that solutions based on this protocol will interoperate and that users will be able to create extranets or use equipment from multiple vendors.

The IPSec protocol suite also includes a comprehensive means of managing and exchanging encryption keys. The protocol has gained near-universal acceptance as the security solution of choice for IP-based VPNs and is enjoying widespread support in the industry. Vendors of IPSec gear are working to ensure interoperability between their products in order to guarantee that customers deploying IPSec equipment will be capable of constructing extranets with others, regardless of which vendors their partners are using.

Although Internet security has been the primary focus of the VPN efforts to date, the attentions of users, vendors, and service providers are beginning to turn to network performance. In fact, due in part to the widespread acceptance of IPSec, network performance has replaced network security as the number-one concern for VPN implementers. Why the focus on performance? Because the IP protocol was designed to treat all traffic equally, it has not been deployed in a way that allows for different qualities or "classes" of service. This is acceptable in Internet access networks, in which all traffic *should* be treated exactly the same. In mission-critical business networks, however, users may wish to prioritize traffic based on one or more of the following:

- User (source or destination)

- Application type

- Time and date

In order for VPNs to achieve widespread acceptance on a scale similar to frame relay, granular traffic-classification schemes are needed. Users must have a means of prioritizing their own traffic (type 1) relative to their own traffic (type 2), and service providers must deploy the tools to prioritize a customer's traffic relative to the traffic of other customers. Many frame relay equipment vendors and service providers already support methods of prioritizing applications, protocols, and PVCs.

The VPN Business Case

IP VPNs offer a number of benefits beyond simple month-to-month cost savings; however, the early hype surrounding IP VPNs has focused on the monetary aspects of the services. Just as frame relay offered tremendous savings over traditional private-line solutions, IP VPNs now promise savings over frame relay networks in many situations. How much can IP VPNs save over frame relay? That depends on a number of factors, particularly network size and the level of site-to-site meshing that is required. Generally speaking, the larger the network and the greater the amount of meshing needed, the more significant the savings achieved with a VPN.

VPNs may deliver savings over frame relay in a number of areas. VPN services are typically offered as managed services, which means that the VPN service provider plays some role in the configuration and ongoing management of the network. By combining low-cost access and transport with high-value services, such as network management and support, VPN providers allow customers to save on network and internal support costs. If instead you are simply interested in a transport service, frame relay may be more economical in some situations.

Although the month-to-month savings offered by IP VPNs may be compelling to some, the true value of these services lies in other benefits that may not be delivered via frame relay or other services. These "soft" benefits are difficult to quantify but may greatly outweigh the simple cost savings for your organization. IP VPN business benefits may include

Network Simplification   From a user perspective, VPNs are based on a single protocol. This fact may reduce long-term network support costs.

Network Ubiquity   Frame relay and other data network services are confined to the boundaries of a service provider's network. Internet-based VPNs are confined only to the limits of the global Internet.

Application Convergence   One of the primary goals for VPN vendors and service providers is to enable VPNs to support all types of communications traffic. Most applications can now operate over an IP network, including application data, e-mail, voice, video, fax, etc. These applications can achieve mission-critical performance on an IP platform, so user organizations will be able to maintain a single network platform for all forms of communications. Even SNA can now be transported across IP. If everything can be efficiently converted and transported across IP, then the multiprotocol advantage of frame relay becomes a less significant issue.

Summary

All the vendor and media hype surrounding VPNs has caused some to speculate as to whether or not frame relay is still needed. Although the potential benefits of VPNs are compelling, a great deal still must be accomplished before VPNs achieve the acceptance of frame relay. As described previously, these networks currently have no standardized means of guaranteeing the performance of user traffic. For many, this may be simply unacceptable. Because applications, such as voice, video, and even terminal sessions, are not tolerant of poor network performance, VPNs may not be an option for you until they are deployed with mission-critical Service Level Agreements, and Class of Service options.

There are also many network managers who will never believe Internet VPNs can be secure. There have been many well-publicized instances of malicious hackers gaining entry to Internet-connected networks as well as instances of data being intercepted, altered, or forged while traversing the Internet. These threats are all very real, and they remain a concern even when encryption and authentication measures are employed.

Finally, many of the networks used by service providers to offer VPN services are actually built upon frame relay or a combination of ATM and frame relay. IP is a layer three protocol and is typically (although not always) implemented on top of a layer two link protocol, such as frame relay or ATM. In this sense, VPNs are actually *driving* the deployment of frame relay, as service providers expand their backbones to support this new service. Due to these issues, frame relay will continue to thrive as both an underlying transport technology and as an end-user service.

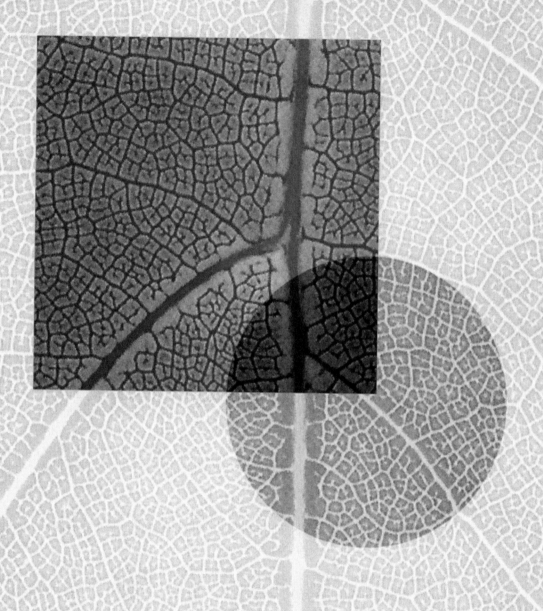

Glossary

3174 controller   IBM's cluster controller. It connects to terminals and other I/O devices on one end and a mainframe channel on the other.

3172 controller   IBM's network controller. It connects to the mainframe channel on one end, and the LAN media (Ethernet, Token Ring, FDDI) on the other.

3270 terminals   IBM class of terminals (or printers) used in SNA networks, often called *dumb* terminals when compared with their more intelligent cousin, the personal computer.

3745 front-end processor   IBM's communications controllers, often called front-end processors. 3745 devices channel-attach to the mainframe and support connections to LANs and other FEPs.

ABR (Available Bit Rate)   An ATM (Asynchronous Transfer Mode) class of service used to support various bursty applications.

Access link   The local access connection between a customer's premises and a carrier's POP.

Access protection   *Access protection* refers to the process of protecting a local loop from network outages and failures. Access protection can take many forms, such as purchasing two geographically diverse local facilities, adding protection switches to the ends of geographically diverse local loops, or buying service from a local-access provider that offers a survivable ring-based architecture to automatically route around network failures.

Analog   Comes from the word *analogous,* which means *similar to.* In telephone transmission, the signal being transmitted—voice, video, or image—is analogous to the original signal. In telecommunications, analog means telephone transmission or switching that is not digital.

Analog transmission   A way of sending signals—voice, video, or data—in which the transmitted signal is analogous to the original signal. For example, if you spoke into a microphone and saw your voice on an oscilloscope and then you took the same voice as it was transmitted on the phone line and threw that signal onto the oscilloscope, the two signals would look essentially the same. The only difference would be that the electrically transmitted signal would be at a higher frequency.

Annex A The first of the frame relay standard extensions, *Annex A* outlines provisions for a local-management interface (LMI) between customer premises equipment and the frame relay network for the purpose of querying network-status information.

Annex D The second frame relay standard extension, *Annex D* deals with the communication and signaling between customer premises equipment and frame relay network equipment for the purpose of querying network-status information.

Apple Talk Apple Computer's proprietary networking protocol for linking Macintosh computers and peripherals, especially printers. This protocol is independent of what network it is layered on.

APPN (Advanced Peer-to-Peer Network Protocol) *APPN* is a distributed networking feature IBM has added to its Systems Network Architecture (SNA). It provides optimized routing of communications between devices and simplifies the process of adding workstations and systems to a network. In addition to enabling users to send data and messages to each other faster, APPN is designed to support efficient and transparent sharing of applications in a distributed computing environment.

ARPAnet (Advanced Research Projects Agency Network) A Department of Defense data network, developed by ARPA, which tied together many users and computers in universities, government, and businesses. *ARPAnet* has been the forerunner of many developments in commercial data communications, including packet switching, which was first tested on a large scale on this network.

AS/400 IBM's midrange minicomputer. *AS/400* stands for Application System/400.

Asymmetrical PVC This term refers to a PVC that supports simplex, or asymmetrical, assignments of committed information rates in each direction of transmission. A PVC transmission path is *duplex,* which means there must be a communications path in each direction between two points being connected. However, with an *asymmetrical PVC,* the network capacity in each direction does not necessarily have to be equal.

Asynchronous Transfer Mode (ATM)   A high-speed networking technology that uses packets of a fixed size (or cells). *ATM* uses logical connections to provide Quality of Service guarantees. These guarantees enable disparate traffic, such as voice, data, and video, to be carried over the same local- or wide-area network.

Automatic rerouting   This refers to the process by which an intelligent voice or data network can automatically route a call or virtual circuit around a network failure. With frame relay, PVCs represent a fixed path through the network. However, in the event of a network failure along the primary path over which the PVC is routed, the PVC will be automatically routed to a secondary network path until the primary path is physically restored.

Bandwidth   The range from highest to lowest frequencies transmitted on a network. *Bandwidth* measures network capacity. If you have sufficient bandwidth, your applications will perform as necessary. If you do not have enough bandwidth, you will drop packets or traffic will be delayed more than desired.

BECN (Backward Explicit Congestion Notification)   *BECN* notifies the user that congestion-avoidance procedures should be initiated for traffic in the opposite direction of the received frame. It indicates that the frames the user transmits on this logical connection may encounter congested resources. In other words, slow down, you are moving too fast; your bits may not get through or the bits may be delayed.

Bit   *Bit* is a contraction of the term *Binary digiT*. It is the smallest unit of information (data) a computer can process, representing high or low, yes or no, or 1 or 0. It is the basic unit in data communications. A bit can have a value of zero (a mark) or one (a space).

Bridge   A network device that connects two networks that use the same protocols. A *bridge* can forward frames or packets between the connected networks.

Bursting   *Bursting* is temporarily using more bandwidth than is allocated to a particular connection (PVC). A customer may have a 16Kbps PVC but burst to the access speed of 64Kbps. The result is often a lower-cost, faster delivery service. Not all providers support bursting.

Byte   A *byte* is typically eight bits of information composed of zeros or ones, one of which may include a parity bit. Most character sets, e.g., ASCII or EBCDIC, use one byte per character of information (such as a letter, number, or digit), a punctuation mark, or a symbol (such as $). A byte is to a bit what a word is to a character. In some circles, a byte is called an *octet*.

CBR (Constant Bit Rate)   *CBR* supports a constant or guaranteed rate to transport information. It is used for services, such as traditional video or voice, that require rigid bandwidth requirements.

Cell relay   A form of packet switching using fixed-length packets, which results in lower processing and higher speeds. *Cell relay* is a generic term for a protocol based on small fixed packet sizes capable of supporting voice video and data at very high speeds. ATM is perhaps the most common form of cell relay service. In ATM, information is handled in fixed-length cells of 53 octets (bytes). A cell has 48 bytes of information and 5 bytes of address.

Centralized environment   Refers to a network environment, or topology, in which decision making, file storage and other network functions are performed at a single, or centralized, location instead of being distributed through the network. This type of environment is common to hierarchical architectures, such as IBM's System Network Architecture, and to mainframe-based applications.

Channel bank   A *channel bank* is also multiplexer, which is a device that puts many lower-speed connections onto one higher-speed link.

Channel Service Unit (CSU/DSU)   A device used to connect a digital line coming in from the service provider. A CSU performs some line-conditioning and equalization functions, and it responds to loopback commands sent from the central office. It is called *CSU/DSU* because it contains a built-in DSU (Digital Service Unit) device that terminates a digital channel at the customers' premises. In many cases the CSU/DSU capabilities are integrated in the FRAD or Router.

CIR (Committed Information Rate)   A performance measurement of minimum "guaranteed" throughput on a user's PVC circuit for frame relay service—the throughput customers order and providers define in the frame relay network. The *CIR* is often viewed as the "average" amount of bandwidth required by a customer.

Circuit-switched   The process of setting up and keeping a circuit open between two or more users, such that the users have exclusive and full use of the circuit until the connection is released, in contrast to a packet-switched environment, where there is no "open" circuit end-to-end for transport of traffic.

Client/server   A *client* is a device on a network that receives some "service" from another device, the server. In general terms, *client/server* refers to a computing system that splits the workload between PCs and one or more larger computers on a network.

Cluster controller   A device that can control the input/output operations of more than one device connected to it (e.g., a terminal). It is also an interface between several bisynchronous devices and a PAD, NC, or communication facility. The *cluster controller* handles remote communications processing for its attached devices. The most common types are the IBM 327X.

Concentrator   This telecommunications device allows a number of circuits (typically slow-speed ones) to be connected to a smaller number of lines for transmission under the assumption that not all of the larger group of lines will be used at the same time. The *concentrator* allows a shared transmission medium to accommodate more data sources than there are channels currently available within the transmission medium.

Configuration management   One of five categories of network management defined by the ISO (International Standards Organization), *configuration* management is the process of adding, deleting, and modifying connections, addresses, and topologies within a network.

Congestion management   The ability of a network to effectively deal with heavy traffic volumes; solutions include traffic scheduling and enabling output ports to control the traffic flow.

Connectivity   Property of a network that allows remote network sites to communicate with each other.

CPE (Customer-Provided Equipment or Customer Premise Equipment)
Originally *CPE* referred to equipment on the customer's premises that had been bought from a vendor that was not the local phone company. Now it simply refers to telephone equipment—routers, CSUs, key systems, PBXs, answering machines, etc.—that resides on the customer's premises. "Premises" might be anything from an office to a factory to a home.

CPU (Central Processing Unit)   *CPU* is the computing part, or the "brain" of the computer. It manipulates data and processes instructions coming from software or a human operator.

Data   A representation of facts, concepts, or instructions in a formalized manner, suitable for communication, interpretation, or processing. *Data* are usually anything other than voice.

Data link   *Data link* describes the communications link used for data transmission from a source to a destination, such as a phone line for data transmission or a fiber optic transmitter, cable, and receiver that transmits digital data between two points.

Data Link Connection Identifier (DLCI)   The frame relay virtual-circuit number corresponding to a particular destination that is part of the frame relay header and is usually ten bits long. The *DLCI* is typically associated with a particular PVC on the network.

DE (Discard Eligible)   The frame relay standard specifies that data sent across a virtual connection in excess of that connection's committed information rate (CIR) will be marked by the network as being eligible for discard in the event of network congestion. *DE* data is the first to be discarded by the network when congestion occurs, thus providing protection for data sent within the parameters of the CIR. It is the responsibility of the intelligent end equipment or protocol to recognize the discard and respond by resending the information.

Distributed environment   Refers to a network environment, or topology, in which decision-making, file storage, and other network functions are not centralized but, instead, are found through the network. This type of environment is typical for client/server applications and peer-to-peer architectures.

DLSw (Data Link Switching)   IBM's method for carrying SNA and NetBIOS over TCP/IP operating at the Data Link layer. *DLSw*, an open Internet spec, can be used with OSPF or PPP.

DLUR/DLUS   A dependent LU requestor/server.

DS-0 (Digital Service, level 0)   *DS-0* is 64,000bps, the worldwide standard speed for digitizing one voice conversation using pulse code modulation (PCM).

DS-1 (Digital Service, level 1) *DS-1* is 1.544Mbps in North America, and 2.048Mbps elsewhere. Why there's no consistency is one of those wonderful, unanswered questions. The 1.544 standard is an old Bell System standard. The 2.048 standard is an ITU-T standard. The standard for 1.544Mbps is 24 voice conversations, each encoded at 64Kbps. The standard for 2.048MBPS is 30 conversations.

DS-3 (Digital Service, level 3) *DS-3* is equivalent to 28 T-1 channels, and it operates at 44.736Mbps. DS-3 is also incorrectly referred to as T-3.

DSU See *Channel Service Unit*.

Dual homing *Dual homing* is the process of using two geographically diverse frame relay port connections, each with its own set of virtual circuits, to support a network location running critical business applications that cannot afford network downtime.

Dumb terminal A computer terminal with no processing or no programming capabilities. It derives all its power from the computer it is attached to—usually over a local hardwire or a phone line. A *dumb terminal* does not employ a data transmission protocol and only sends or receives data one character at a time, sequentially.

EA (Extended Addressing) In many bit-oriented protocols, *extended addressing* is a facility that allows larger addresses than normal to be used. In IBM's SNA, it is the addition of two high-order bits to the basic addressing scheme. The frame relay standard also includes extended addressing bits.

Edge site A remote network site; a site at the edge of the network.

Egress The exit point. *Egress* refers to information being sent out of, as opposed to being sent into, a frame relay port connection or other network element.

Emulate *Emulate* means to duplicate one system with another. It also means to imitate a computer or computer system by a combination of hardware and software that allows programs written for one computer or terminal to run on another.

EN (End Node) A node that can only send and receive information for its own use, such as a PC. It cannot route and forward information to another node.

Encapsulation   *Encapsulation* means to encase. Because frame relay is a transport technology, it was designed to transport multiple protocols (IP, SNA, IPX, etc.). These other protocols are encapsulated in a frame relay packet to be transmitted across a frame relay network.

Error-checking and correction   *Error-checking* is the process of checking a "packet" being transmitted over a network to determine whether the package or the data content within the package has been damaged. Damaged packets are discarded. Error correction is the process of correcting the damage by resending a copy of the original packet. In public frame relay services, the network performs the function of error-checking but not error correction. That function is left to the intelligent end equipment.

Ethernet   A local-area network protocol used for connecting computers, printers, workstations, terminals, etc. *Ethernet* operates over twisted wire and over coaxial cable at speeds up to 10Mbps. Recent advances have seen the introduction of Fast Ethernet at 100Mbps and Gigabit Ethernet that operates at 1000Mbps or 1Gbps.

Fast-packet multiplexing   *Multiplexing* is putting more than one "conversation" onto one circuit. You can do this in either of two ways: by splitting the channels sideways into subchannels of narrower frequency, which is called *Frequency Division Multiplexing,* or by splitting the channels by time, like a railroad train. The first car carries "Conversation 1." The second carries "Conversation 2." They are split apart at the other end.

Fault management   Detects, isolates, and corrects network faults. It is one of five categories of network management defined by the ISO (International Standards Organization).

FECN (Forward Congestion Notification Bits)   This bit notifies the user that congestion-avoidance procedures should be initiated where applicable for traffic in the same direction as the received frame. It indicates that this frame, on this logical connection, has encountered congested resources.

Fiber optics   A technology in which light is used to transport information from one point to another. More specifically, *fiber optics* are thin filaments of glass through which light beams carrying enormous amounts of data are transmitted over long distances. Modulating light on thin strands of glass produces major benefits in high bandwidth, relatively low-cost, low-power consumption, small space needs, total insensitivity to electromagnetic interference, and great insensitivity to being bugged. All of these benefits have great attraction to anyone who needs vast, clean transmission capacity.

Flag A *flag* is a variable in a program that informs the program later on that a condition has been met. In synchronous transmission, a flag is a pattern of six consecutive "1" bits used to mark the beginning and end of a *frame*. (IBM jargon for a packet.) The character representation of the six consecutive "1" bits is 01111110.

Flow control *Flow control* is the hardware, software, and procedure for controlling the transfer of messages or characters between two points in a data network—such as between a protocol converter and a printer—to prevent loss of data when the receiving device's buffer begins to reach its capacity. Flow control is also the process of protecting network service by denying access to additional traffic that would further add to congestion.

FRADs (Frame Relay Assembler/Disassembler) *Frame relay access devices*.

Frame *Frame* is a group of data bits in a specific format with a flag at each end to indicate the beginning and end of the frame. The defined format enables network equipment to recognize the meaning and purpose of specific bits. The group of bits are sent serially (one after another). A frame is also a logical transmission unit. A frame usually contains its own control information for addressing and error-checking, and it is the basic data transmission unit employed in bit-oriented protocols.

Frame-check sequence (FCS) *Frame-check sequences* are the bits added to a frame for error detection. If the FCS bit is marked in a frame relay packet, the switches know the frame has an error and immediately discards that frame.

Frame multiplexing The process of handling traffic from multiple simultaneous inputs by sending the frames out one at a time in accordance with a specific set of rules. Instead of multiplexing traffic from a lower-speed connection into a higher-speed connection based on a specific time duration for each low-speed channel, frame multiplexing using the length of a given frame as the measurement.

Frame relay Wide-area networking interface protocol that statistically shares bandwidth by transporting variable-length packets over virtual connections.

Frame Relay Forum Organization of frame relay equipment vendors and service providers, working to speed the development and deployment of frame relay products and interfaces with other broadband technologies, such as ATM.

FRND (Frame Relay Network Device) A frame relay access device or frame relay network switch.

Front-end processor (FEP) A *FEP* is a computer under the control of another, larger computer (such as a mainframe) in a network. The FEP does simple, basic "housekeeping" operations on the data streams as they arrive to be processed by the bigger computer. The FEP acts as a sort of intelligent traffic cop. It relieves the bigger, host computer of some of its telecommunications input/output burden, so that the host computer can concentrate on handling the processing burden.

Full-duplex Transmission in two directions simultaneously or, more technically, bidirectional, simultaneous 2-way communications. The best 2-way phone conversations take place on 4-wire circuits, two for transmission in one direction and two for transmission in the other. All long-distance circuits are 4-wire. Most local lines are 2-wire, which means they're a compromise.

HDLC (High-Level Data Link Control) A standard bit-oriented protocol developed by the International Standards Organization (ISO). In *HDLC*, control information is always placed in the same position. Specific bit patterns used for control differ dramatically from those used in representing data, so errors are less likely to occur.

Host An intelligent device attached to a network.

HPR (High Performance Routing) A local-area networking term. *HPR* is the next-generation APPN—referred to in the past as APPN+—that adds IP-like dynamic networking features —(e.g., dynamic alternate routing in the event of path failure) to APPN, and uses a routing mechanism that works at layer two, using a RIF concept similar to that found in SRB.

Hub The point on a network where a bunch of circuits are connected. Generally, *hub* is the "central" site in a network. There can be multiple hubs or a single hub for each network.

Hybrid network *Hybrid network* is a communications network that has some links capable of sending and receiving only analog signals and other links capable of handling only digital signals. The current public-switched telephone network is Hybrid. It is a network with a combination of dissimilar network services, such as frame relay, private lines, and/or X.25. Hybrid network is also an amalgam of public and private network transmission facilities.

Ingress   The incoming traffic, or incoming direction to a network device.

Integrated access   *Integrated access* a term for the provision of access for multiple services, such as voice and data.

Intelligent hub   A hub that functions both as a bridge and multiprotocol router.

Interface   An *interface* is defined as a mechanical or electrical link connecting two or more pieces of equipment together. It also refers to a shared boundary or physical point of demarcation between two devices where the electrical signals, connectors, timing, and handshaking are defined. The procedures, codes, and protocols that enable two entities to interact for a meaningful exchange of information. Interface also means to bring two things or people together to allow them to talk.

Internetworking   *Internetworking* means communication between two networks or two types of networks or end equipment. This communication may or may not involve a difference in the signaling or protocol elements supported. Internetworking also means joining local-area networks together. This way users can get access to other files, databases, and applications. Bridges and routers are the devices, which accomplish the task of joining LANs. Internetworking may be done with cables, for example, joining LANs together in the same building, or it may be done with telecommunications circuits, such as joining LANs together across the globe.

Interoperability   The ability to operate software and exchange information in a heterogeneous network, such as one large network made up of several different local-area networks.

Interswitch trunk   A circuit between two switching machines.

Interworking   The ability to seamlessly communicate between devices supporting dissimilar protocols, such as frame relay and ATM, by translating between the protocols, not through encapsulation. Many carriers are planning to implement the necessary equipment and conversion algorithms to allow the network itself to transparently convert from frame relay to ATM and vice versa.

IP (Internet Protocol)   A connectionless networking protocol. *IP* is the protocol of the Internet and other connectionless networks, including many corporate LANs and wide-area data networks.

IPX (Internet Packet eXchange)   Novell NetWare's native LAN communications protocol, used to move data between server or workstation programs running on different network nodes. *IPX* packets are encapsulated and carried by the packets used in Ethernet and the similar frames used in Token-Ring networks.

ISDN (Integrated Services Digital Network)   International digital network supporting voice, video, and data over multiples of 64Kbps circuits.

ISO (International Organization for Standardization)   Founded in 1946, *ISO* is a worldwide federation of national standards bodies from more than 100 countries, with one representative from each country. Among the standards it fosters is Open Systems Interconnection (OSI), a universal reference model for communication protocols. Many countries have national standards organizations, such as the American National Standards Institute (ANSI), that participate in and contribute to ISO standards making.

ITU (International Telecommunication Union)   A UN sanctioned international organization of member states that creates standards for international telecommunications systems.

IXC (IntereXchange Channel, or IntereXchange Carrier)   As contrasted to the LEC, the Local Exchange Carrier. InterExchange Carriers used to be called "Other Common Carriers," but that grouping didn't include AT&T. Now AT&T, MCI WorldCom, Sprint, and all the long-distance carriers are called InterExchange Carriers.

Kbps (Kilobits Per Second)   One thousand bits per second.

LAN (Local-Area Network)   A short-distance data-communications network (usually within a building or campus) used to link together computers and peripheral devices, such as printers, under some form of standard control.

LATA (Local Access and Transport Area)   One of many local geographical areas in the U.S. within which a local telephone company may offer telecommunications services—local or long distance. The traditional limitations of LATA boundaries are becoming less significant as the FCC passes new regulations.

Leased lines   Same as a leased or dedicated circuit, private-line, leased channel.

LEN (Low-End Node)   An IBM term for a specific category of network devices. Also see *EN (End Node)*.

LLC (Logical Link Control)   A protocol developed by the IEEE 802.2 committee for data-link-level transmission control. It is the upper sublayer of the IEEE layer two (OSI) protocol that complements the MAC protocol. IEEE standard 802.2 includes end-system addressing and error-checking. It also provides a common access control standard and governs the assembly of data packets and their exchange between data stations, independent of how the packets are transmitted on the LAN.

LMI (Local Management Interface)   A specification for the use of frame-relay products that define a method of exchanging status information between devices, such as routers.

Local loop   The physical wires that run from the subscriber's telephone set, PBX, or key telephone system to the telephone company central office. Increasingly, the *local loop* now goes from the main distribution frame in the basement to the phone company. And the subscriber is responsible for getting the wires from the box in the basement to the phone, PBX, or key system.

LU   *LU* means *line unit*. It is also defined as *logical unit,* which is an access port for users in SNA, or in a bisync network, a port through which the user gains access to the network services. A LU can support sessions with the host-based System Services Control Point (SSCP) and other LUs. The final definition is *Local Use flag* and it is occasionally used to initialize approval for local cellular calls. The cellular carrier insures that local users are registered with a local system.

Mbps (Megabits Per Second)   Million bits per second.

MAC   *MAC* stands for Moves, Adds, and Changes. It also stands for Media Access Control. A media-specific access control protocol within IEEE 802 specifications. Currently it includes variations for the Token Ring, token bus, and CSMA/CD. The lower sublayer of the IEEE's link layer (OSI) that complements the Logical Link Control (LLC).

Mainframe   A powerful computer, a mainframe is almost always linked to a large set of peripheral devices (disk storage, printers, and so forth), and used in a multipurpose environment at the corporate or major divisional level. The term *mainframe* derives from the racks that typically hold a large computer and its memory.

MIB (Management Information Base)   A directory listing the logical names of all information resources residing in a network and pertinent to the network's management. Within the Internet *MIB* employed for SNMP (Simple Network Management Protocol)-based management, ASN.1 (Abstract Syntax Notation One) is used to describe network management variables. These variables, which include such information as error counts or on/off status of a device, are assigned a place on a tree data structure. MIB is used in X.400 electronic mail.

Modem   Acronym for MOdulator/DEModulator. A *modem* is a piece of equipment that converts digital signals to analog signals and vice versa. Modems are used to send data signals (digital) over the telephone network, which usually is analog. The modem modulates the "1s" and "0s" into tones that can be carried by the phone network. At the other end, the demodulator part of the modem converts the tones back into digital 1s and 0s.

Multiplexer   A *multiplexer* is a piece of electronic equipment that allows two or more signals to pass over one communications circuit. That circuit may be a phone line, a microwave circuit, or a through-the-air TV signal, or that circuit may be analog or digital. Many multiplexing techniques are available to accommodate both.

Multipoint   A configuration or topology designed to transmit data between a central site and a number of remote terminals on the same circuit. Individual terminals will generally be able to transmit to the central site but not to each other.

Multipoint circuits   A circuit connecting three or more locations. It is often called a *multidrop* circuit. See also *multipoint*.

NCP   In IBM language, *NCP* means Network Control Program, which is a program that controls the operations of the communication controllers—3704 and 3705—in an IBM SNA network.

NetBIOS (Network Basic Input/Output System)   A layer of software originally developed by IBM and Sytek to link a network operating system with specific hardware. Originally designed as the network controller for IBM's PC Network LAN, *NetBIOS* has now been extended to allow programs written using the NetBIOS interface to operate on the IBM Token Ring.

Netview   An IBM product for management of heterogeneous networks that integrates the functions of three formerly separate communications network management programs.

Network *Networks* are common in our lives—think about trains and phones. A network ties things together. Computer networks connect all types of computers and computer related things: terminals, printers, modems, door-entry sensors, temperature monitors, etc. The networks we're most familiar with are long-distance ones, such as phones and trains. But there are also local-area networks (LANs), which exist within a limited geographic area, such as the few hundred feet of a small office, an entire building, or even a "campus," such as a university or industrial park.

Network management A set of procedures, software, equipment, and operations designed to keep a network operating near maximum efficiency.

Network redundancy *Network redundancy* means that the network topology has been constructed so that a failure of a network component can be automatically and rapidly recovered by using identical components engineered into the network for recovery purposes.

NN (Network Node) In frame relay, a *network node* is typically the frame relay service port connection and its associated virtual circuits.

NNI (Network-to-Network Interface) There are two types of network interfaces specified by the frame relay standards. The first is a user-to-network *(UNI)* interface, and the second is a *network-to-network interface (NNI)*. The NNI describes the connection between two public frame relay services and includes elements, such as bidirectional polling, to assist the network services providers with gaining information on the status of the public networks being interconnected.

Nodes A point of connection into a network. In multipoint networks, a *node* means a unit that is polled. In LANs, it's a device on the ring. In packet-switched networks, it's one of the many packet switches that form the network's backbone.

NTU (Network Termination Unit) A device that is placed at the final interconnect point between the PSTN and the customer-owned equipment. NTUs allow the carrier to isolate their equipment from the customers for various testing procedures.

OpenView Hewlett-Packard's suite of a network management application, a server platform, and support services. Used primarily for monitoring and managing a customer's network.

OSI (Open System Interconnect) An ISO publication that defines seven independent layers of communication protocols. Each layer enhances the communication services of the layer just below it and shields the layer above it from the implementation details of the lower layer. In theory, this allows communication systems to be built from independently developed layers.

OSI Model The ISO-defined, seven-layer network model for network protocols. From the bottom up, the layers are physical, data link, network, transport, session, presentation, and application.

Oversubscription In frame relay, *oversubscription* refers to a port connection state where the sum total of the committed information rates for the permanent virtual circuits supported by that port is greater than the port connection speed. While the port connection cannot simultaneously support transmissions at greater than its connection speed, its ability to dynamically allocate traffic makes oversubscription a cost-effective way to gain a high level of direct network interconnectivity.

Packet A bundle of data, usually in binary form, organized in a specific way for transmission. Three principal elements are included in the *packet*: control information (destination, origin, length of packet, etc.); the data to be transmitted; and error-detection and -correction bits. See also *Frame*.

Packet-interleaving Refers to the process of multiplexing multiple incoming packets from multiple channels onto a single outgoing channel by sampling one or more packets from the first channel, then the next, and so on.

Packet-switching Sending data in packets through a network to a remote location. The data to be sent is subdivided into individual packets of data, each packet having a unique identification and carrying its own destination address. This way each packet can go by a different route. The packets may also arrive in a different order than how they were shipped. The packet ID lets the data be reassembled in proper sequence.

Parallel networks *Parallel networks,* or segregated networks, exist when a single network location supports more than one physical wide-area network connection for the purpose of supporting one or more applications.

PC *Personal computer.*

Performance management Measures and records resource utilization. It is one of the categories of network management defined by the ISO (International Standards Organization).

Pilot   In networking, *pilot* refers to a trial network in which a small subset of locations are interconnected for the purpose of testing network, protocol, and application performance.

Platform   The hardware and/or software that makes up the underlying infrastructure for a service.

Polling   Connecting to another system to check for things such as mail or news. A form of data or fax network arrangement whereby a central computer or fax machine asks each remote location in turn (and very quickly) whether it wants to send some information. The purpose is to give each user or each remote data terminal an opportunity to transmit and receive information on a circuit, using facilities that are being shared. *Polling* is typically used on a multipoint or multidrop line.

Port   *Port* is an entrance to or exit from a network; the physical or electrical interface through which one gains access; a point in the computer or telephone system where data may be accessed.

Port connection   The point of entry into a public frame relay network service.

Prioritization parameters   The hierarchical rules that a network device, such as a router, applies to incoming traffic to determine which traffic should be handled first, next, and so on.

Private line   A *private line* is a direct channel specifically dedicated to a customer's use between specified points; a line leased from a carrier, local or long distance; or a nonswitched circuit, where one end of the line is directly connected to the other end. AT&T's definition of a private line is "a dedicated, nonswitchable link from one or more customer-specified locations to one or more customer-specified locations."

Private network   A series of offices connected together by leased and non-leased lines with switching facilities and transmission equipment owned and operated by the user or by the carrier and leased to the user.

Protocol   A *protocol* is a specific set of rules, procedures, or conventions relating to format and timing of data transmission between two devices as well as a procedure for adding order to the exchange of data. A protocol is also a standard procedure that two data devices must accept and use to be able to understand each other, much like to two people both speaking English to communicate. The protocols for data communications cover such things as framing, error handling, transparency, and line control.

Protocol conversion   A data communications procedure that permits computers operating with different protocols to communicate with each other.

Protocol stack   A group of drivers that work together to span the layers in the network protocol hierarchy.

PSTN (Public Switched Telephone Network)   An abbreviation used to refer to the worldwide voice network.

Public network   A network operated by common carriers or telecommunications administrations for the provision of circuit-switched, packet-switched, and leased-line circuits to the public. See also *Private network*.

PVC (Permanent Virtual Circuits)   A virtual circuit that provides the equivalent of a dedicated private-line service over a packet-switching network. The network maintains the logical connection at all times. See also *SVC*.

QoS (Quality of Service)   *QoS* parameters ensure minimum levels of network performance for carried traffic.

Queue   A stream of tasks waiting to be executed. A series of calls or messages waiting for connection to a line. See also *Queuing*.

Queue service interval   The maximum length of time a queue will go unsampled.

Queuing   The act of "stacking" or holding calls to be handled by a specific person, trunk, or trunk group.

RBOC (Regional Bell Operating Company)   One of the seven Bell operating companies set up after AT&T's divestiture. The *RBOCs* were carved out of the old AT&T/Bell System by Judge Harold Greene when he signed off on the divestiture of the Bell operating companies from AT&T at the end of 1984. The structure is changing again due to recent mergers and acquisitions.

RFC (Request for Comment)   An Internet term. The contents of an *RFC* may range from an official standardized protocol specification to research results or proposals. A set of papers in which the Internet's standards, proposed standards, and generally agreed-upon ideas are documented and published.

RFC 1144   This RFC will provide overhead compression for the TCP/IP protocol down to five octets. It does this by anticipating that the next packet in a file transfer sequence will have the same address and the same sequence number plus one as the previous packet.

RFC 1490   *RFC 1490*, formerly known as RFC 1294, is for multiprotocol encapsulation. The bottom line benefits are to increase interoperability between frame relay devices from different vendors. This means that you can use one vendor's routers (or other equipment type) at some locations and a different vendor's equipment at other locations.

Ring network configuration   A network that links PBXs, computers, terminals, printers, and other devices in a circular communications link.

Router   A computer that forwards packets through a network using information contained in the packet header. A *router* maintains routing tables that enable it to select the best outgoing link for forwarding the packet to the next router.

SDLC (Synchronous Data Link Control)   A bit-oriented synchronous communications protocol developed by IBM, where the message may contain any collection or sequence of bits without being mistaken for a control character. SDLC is used in IBM's SNA (System Network Architecture).

Security Management   Protects a network from invalid accesses. It is one of the management categories defined by the ISO (International Standards Organization).

Serialization   To change from parallel-by-byte to serial-by-bit. This is necessary when routers prepare traffic to be transmitted across frame relay networks and can add a delay component called *serialization delay*.

Server   A *server* is a shared computer on the local-area network that can be as simple as a regular PC set aside to handle print requests to a single printer. However, it is more commonly known as the fastest and brawniest PC around. It may be used as a repository and distributor of oodles of data. It may also be the gatekeeper controlling access to voice mail, e-mail, and fax services.

Simplex   Operating a channel in one direction only with no ability to operate in the other direction. For example, one side of a telephone conversation is all that could be carried by a *simplex* line.

SLA (Service Level Agreement)   An agreement between the user and service provider, defining the nature of the service provided and establishing a certain level of service to be maintained.

SLIP (Serial Line IP)   A protocol that allows a computer to use the Internet protocols (and become a full-fledged Internet member) with a standard telephone line and a high-speed modem. *SLIP* is being superseded by PPP.

SMDS (Switched Multimegabit Services)   A 1.544Mbps public data service with an IEEE 802.6 standard user interface. It can support Ethernet, Token Ring, and FDDI (OC-3c) LAN-to-LAN connections.

SNA (System Network Architecture)   Networking protocols and techniques defined for connecting IBM equipment, including mainframes and terminals.

SNMP (Simple Network Management Protocol)   A network management protocol originally designed for TCP/IP networks but now used in a wide variety of networking environments, including many frame relay networks. SNMP uses a query to retrieve information from SNMP agents (such as a router or probe) to perform network management.

Source routing   A method used by a bridge for moving data between two networks. Originally developed by IBM's Token Ring network, it relies on information contained within the token to route the packet between the two networks. Because the information in the token is supplied by the computer that sent the data packet, that computer must know on which network the destination computer is located.

Spoofing   *Spoofing* is a method by which the client or router filters network traffic to keep unnecessary traffic from going over a WAN link. It is the ability of a device to determine what is not 'meaningful' traffic; rather than forwarding the traffic over the connection, the device responds to the source of the traffic with the response that would have been generated by the intended destination device. Often used for SNA traffic to prevent polls from needing significant network bandwidth.

Statistical multiplexing   A multiplexing technique that differs from simple multiplexing in that the share of the available transmission bandwidth allocated to a given user varies dynamically. In other words, in *statistical multiplexing*, a channel is only assigned to communicating devices (voice, modem, etc.) when they actually have data to send or receive.

SVC (Switched Virtual Circuit)   A connection across a network. It is established on an as-needed basis and can provide a connection to any other user in the network. The connection lasts only for the duration of the transfer. It is the datacom equivalent of a dialed phone call.

Switch   A mechanical, electrical, or electronic device, which opens or closes circuits, completes or breaks an electrical path, or selects paths or circuits. Frame relay switches perform these duties on frame relay packets.

Tandem architectures   A physical network topology where connectivity between locations is achieved by linking several locations together in a chain using private-line circuits. In a *tandem architecture*, a packet may have to pass through several intermediate locations before reaching its final destination. A single network failure can affect connectivity between several locations, a primary weakness of the topology.

T-1   The standard North American carrier for transmission at 1.544Mbps. A *T-1* consists of 24DS0 channels.

Tandem points   An intermediate location in a tandem architecture.

Tandeming   The connection of networks or circuits in series; that is, the connection of the output of one circuit to the input of another.

TDM (Time Division Multiplexing)   A network transmission method assigning transmission facility bandwidth among users through time slots. *TDM* is the traditional method of sharing physical bandwidth resources.

Telnet   A part of the TCP/IP protocol suite governing the exchange of character-oriented terminal data. It is also the process by which a person using one computer can sign on to a computer in another city, state, or country. Terminal-remote host protocol developed for ARPAnet. Using *Telnet*, you can work from your PC as if it were a terminal attached to another machine by a hard-wired line.

Terminal   The point at which a telephone line ends or is connected to other circuits of a network.

Throughput   The actual amount of useful and nonredundant information that is transmitted or processed. *Throughput* is the end result of a data call. It may only be a small part of what was pumped in at the other end. The relationship of what went in one end and what came out the other is a measure of the efficiency of that communications link—a function of cleanliness, speed, etc.

Token Ring   A ring type of local-area network (LAN) in which a supervisory frame, or *token,* must be received by an attached terminal or workstation before that terminal or workstation can start transmitting. The workstation with the token then transmits and uses the entire bandwidth of whatever communications media the Token Ring network is using.

Topology   The Network *topology,* or defined more fully, the geometric physical or electrical configuration describing a local communication network—the shape or arrangement of the system. The most common distribution system topologies are the bus, ring, and star.

Transparent routing   A method used by a bridge for moving data between two networks. With this type of routing, the bridge learns which computers are operating on which network. It then uses this information to route packets between networks. It does not rely on the sending computers for its decision-making routine.

UBR (Unspecified Bit Rate)   Offers no traffic-related service guarantees.

UNI (User Network Interface)   The physical and electrical demarcation point between the user and the public network service provider.

VBR (Variable Bit Rate)   Supports predictable data streams within bounds of average and peak traffic constraints.

Virtual circuit   A communications link—voice or data—that appears to the user to be a dedicated point-to-point circuit. *Virtual circuits* are generally set up on a per-call basis and disconnected when the call is ended. The concept of a virtual circuit was first used in data communications with packet switching. See also *PVC* and *SVC.*

Virtual connections   A logical connection that is made to a virtual circuit.

Voice compression   *Voice compression* refers to the process of electronically modifying a 64Kbps PCM voice channel to obtain a channel of 32Kbps or less for the purpose of increased efficiency in transmission.

VPN (Virtual Private Network)   A *virtual private network* is a private data network that makes use of the public telecommunication infrastructure, maintaining privacy through the use of tunneling protocol and security procedures. A virtual private network can be contrasted with a system of owned or leased lines that can be used only by one company. The idea of the VPN is to give the company the same capabilities at much lower cost by using the shared public infrastructure rather than a private one. For more information, check out www.vpdn.com.

VTAM (Virtual Telecommunications Access Method)   Pronounced "Vee-Tam." A program component in an IBM computer that handles some of the communications processing tasks for an application program. *VTAM* also provides resource sharing, a technique for efficiently using a network to reduce transmission costs.

WAN (Wide-Area Network)   A network that covers more than a limited geographic area. Generally, a *WAN* covers more than a single building and can reach from a few blocks to thousands of miles. A WAN extends a LAN. See also *LAN*.

Windows   A flow-control mechanism in data communications, the size of which is equal to the number of frames, packets, or messages that can be sent from a transmitter to a receiver before any reverse acknowledgment is required. It's called a *pacing group* in IBM's SNA.

Window size   The minimum and maximum number of data packets that can be transmitted without additional authorization from the receiver.

X.25   Wide-area networking interface protocol that statistically shares bandwidth by transporting variable-length packets over virtual connections. *X.25* provides error recovery and other advanced features to safely transport traffic over unreliable physical links.

xDSL   A generic—*x* is the generic—name for Digital Subscriber Line equipment and services. For more information, check out www.xdsl.com.

Index

Note to the Reader: Throughout this index **boldfaced** page numbers indicate primary discussions of a topic. *Italicized* page numbers indicate illustrations.

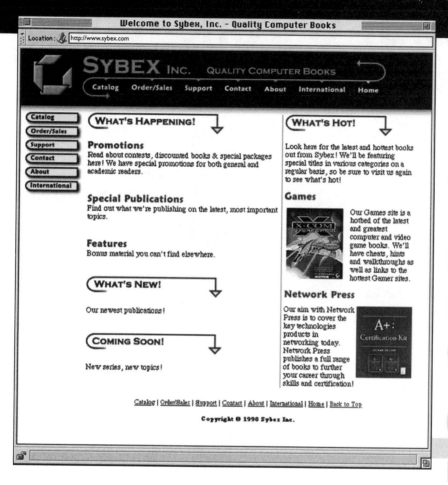

Boost Your Career with Certification

2nd Edition Completely revised and updated for 1999–2000!

Detailed information on all the key computer and network certification programs, including:

- Computer hardware
- Operating systems
- Software
- Networking hardware
- Network operating systems
- Internet
- Instructor and trainer certifications

COMPUTER AND NETWORK PROFESSIONAL'S CERTIFICATION GUIDE

SECOND EDITION

J. SCOTT CHRISTIANSON AND AVA FAJEN

FULLY UPDATED SECOND EDITION INCLUDES COVERAGE OF NETWARE 5 CNA/CNE, NETWORK+, AND MORE

SELECT THE RIGHT CERTIFICATION TO ADVANCE YOUR CAREER

COVERS THE FULL RANGE OF COMPUTER AND NETWORKING CERTIFICATIONS FROM MORE THAN 60 COMPANIES AND ORGANIZATIONS

UPDATED SECOND EDITION
COVERS MORE THAN 300 CERTIFICATIONS

ISBN: 0-7821-2545-X
640pp • 5 7/8 x 8 1/4 • Softcover
$19.99

Learn why to get certified, when to get certified, and how to get certified.

NETWORK+™ CERTIFICATION FROM NETWORK PRESS™

The Network+ certification from the Computing Technology Industry Association (CompTIA) is a vendor- and product-neutral exam intended to test and confirm the knowledge of networking technicians with 18–24 months experience.

Each Network+ book:
- *Provides full coverage of every CompTIA exam objective*
- *Written by experts who participated in the development of the Network+ certification program*

Study!

ISBN: 0-7821-2547-6
7.5"x 9" • 656pp • $49.99 U.S.

- Learn about networking technologies and network design concepts
- Includes hundreds of review questions
- CD includes exclusive Network Press Edge Test exam-preparation program

Practice!

ISBN: 0-7821-2548-4
7.5"x 9" • 480pp • $24.99 U.S.

- Reinforce your Network+ knowledge with detailed review questions
- Study summaries of all the information you need to know for the exam
- Gauge your test-readiness with tough practice questions

Review!

ISBN: 0-7821-2546-8
5.875"x 8.25" • 432pp • $19.99 U.S.

- Quickly learn essential information for each exam objective
- Contains detailed analysis of the key issues
- Preview the types of questions found on the exam

www.sybex.com

TAKE YOUR CAREER TO THE NEXT LEVEL

with 24seven books from Network Press

- This new series offers the advanced information you need to keep your systems and networks running 24 hours a day, seven days a week.
- On-the-job case studies provide solutions to real-world problems.
- Maximize your system's uptime—and go home at 5!
- $34.99; 7½" x 9"; 544–704 pages; softcover

Jim McBee
0-7821-2505-0
Available Now

Matthew Strebe
0-7821-2507-7
Available Now

Allen Jones
0-7821-2532-8
Available 2nd Quarter 1999

Rick Sawtell, Michael Lee
0-7821-2508-5
Available 3rd Quarter 1999

IIS 4 and Proxy Server 2

Shane Stigler, Mark Linsenbardt
0-7821-2530-1
Available 3rd Quarter 1999

Todd Carter
0-7821-2594-8
Available 4th Quarter 1999

THE ESSENTIAL RESOURCE FOR SYSTEMS ADMINISTRATORS

Visit the 24seven Web site at **www.24sevenbooks.com** for more information and sample chapters.

TAKE YOUR CAREER TO THE NEXT LEVEL

with 24seven books from Network Press

- This new series offers the advanced information you need to keep your systems and networks running 24 hours a day, seven days a week.
- On-the-job case studies provide solutions to real-world problems.
- Maximize your system's uptime—and go home at 5!
- $34.99; 7½" x 9"; 544–704 pages; softcover

Paul Robichaux
0-7821-2531-X
Available 3rd Quarter 1999

Craig Hunt
0-7821-2506-9
Available 3rd Quarter 1999

Gary Govanus
0-7821-2509-3
Available 3rd Quarter 1999

Matthew Strebe
0-7821-2529-8
Available 3rd Quarter 1999

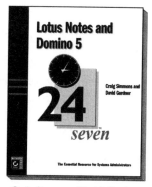

Craig Simmons, David Gardner
0-7821-2518-2
Available 3rd Quarter 1999

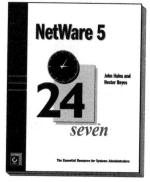

John Hales, Nestor Reyes
0-7821-2593-X
Available 4th Quarter 1999

THE ESSENTIAL RESOURCE FOR SYSTEMS ADMINISTRATORS

Visit the 24seven Web site at **www.24sevenbooks.com** for more information and sample chapters.

How do I?